Canadian artist Tom Thomson painted sixty-two landscapes on small wood panels during the last spring of his life—a daily record of the season's change from winter to spring in 1917. The panels and all of his personal property were missing upon his death. His body was hastily buried 36 hour later, exhumed late at night, and reburied in the family plot in Leith, Ontario. In 1956, his gravesite was dug up and a skeleton was discovered in what apparently was his coffin and burial box. Medical investigators stunned the nation when they reported the body found was not that of Thomson, but of a native Indian. Thomson's family refused to allow exhumation of the Leith plot. Thomson's story is full of interesting characters: the 18 year-old budding romance novelist Thomson fell in love with in Seattle; the park ranger still suffering wounds from service overseas in World War I, the woman some believe was pregnant with Thomson's child; the conniving owner of the Mowat Lodge on Canoe Lake in Algonquin Park, Ontario, where Thomson stayed; the beer-swilling, thuggish German-American private investigator staying at Canoe Lake with his family who despised Thomson; and the artist's highly accomplished but self-doubting older brother, George, who came to Algonquin Park following the drowning. Author Neil J. Lehto leads you through the evidence as it unfolds—blending fact and fiction—to arrive at his own conclusion about Thomson's drowning. Was it an accident, murder or suicide? You decide!

Algonquin Elegy

Algonquin Elegy

✦

Tom Thomson's Last Spring

Neil J. Lehto

iUniverse, Inc.

New York Lincoln Shanghai

Algonquin Elegy
Tom Thomson's Last Spring

iUniverse books may be ordered through booksellers or by contacting:

iUniverse
2021 Pine Lake Road, Suite 100
Lincoln, NE 68512
www.iuniverse.com
1-800-Authors (1-800-288-4677)

This story, of Canada's greatest landscape painter, Tom Thomson, and his life and death at Algonquin Park, Canoe Lake, Ontario, in 1917, is based on historical fact. The O'Gorman family and all characters involved in Jon Kristian's investigation are fictional and should not to be confused with actual persons, living or dead.

Cover painting, Spring Ice, Tom Thomson, 1916. National Gallery of Canada, Ottawa. Reproduced copies of various correspondence to Dr. James M. MacCallum, MD, courtesy of the National Gallery of Canada. 7.1T Thomson, Tom, Correspondence with/re.artists, National Gallery of Canada fonds, National Gallery of Canada Archives.

ISBN-13: 978-0-595-36132-8 (pbk)
ISBN-13: 978-0-595-80573-0 (ebk)
ISBN-10: 0-595-36132-3 (pbk)
ISBN-10: 0-595-80573-6 (ebk)

Printed in the United States of America

Not quite the same the Springtime seems to me,
Since that sad season when in separate ways
Our paths diverged.
There are no more such days
As dawned for us in that last time when we
Dwelt in the realm of dreams, illusive dreams.
Spring may be just as fair now, but it seems
Not quite the same.

—Ella Wheeler Wilcox, from a decorative
landscape painting by Tom Thomson in 1916

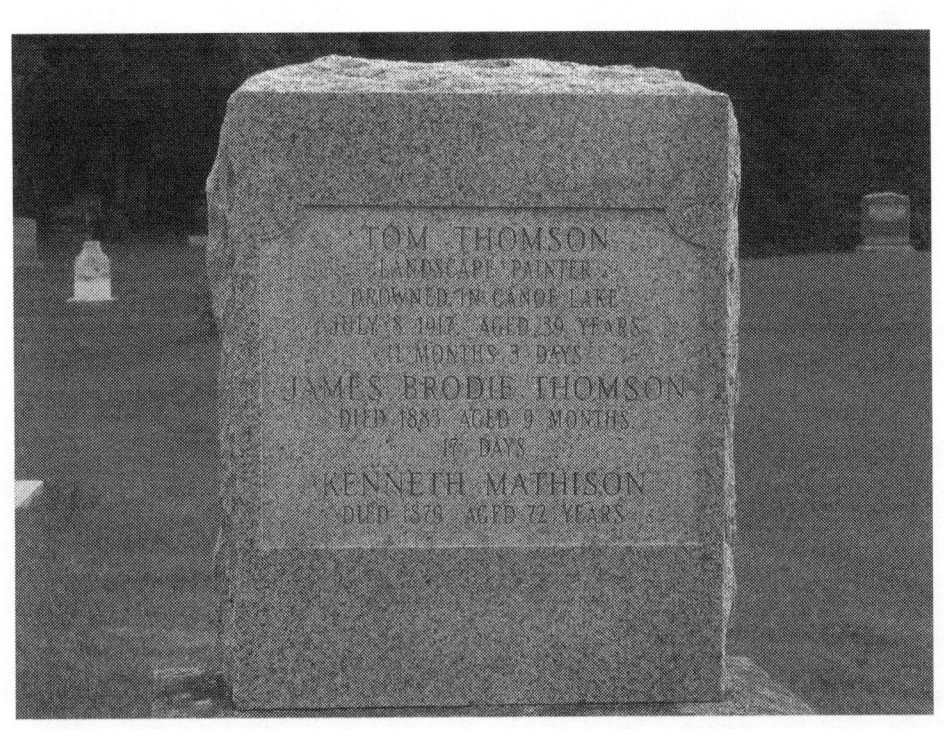

To Tess and the girls.

Contents

Historical Characters

George W. Bartlett [*]	Superintendent, Algonquin Park
John W. Beatty	Canadian artist, builder of a memorial cairn to Thomas J. Thomson at Algonquin Park, Canoe Lake, in 1917
Martin H. Blecher, Sr., and his wife, Louisa	Furniture manufacturer, Buffalo, New York, summer residents at Canoe Lake
Martin H. Blecher, Jr.	Private detective, son of Martin H. Blecher, Sr.
Miss Bessie Blecher	Daughter of Martin Blecher, Sr., elementary school assistant principal in Buffalo, New York
Frank Braught	Retired teacher and Canoe Lake resident in 1956
Franklin W. Churchill	Undertaker, Huntsville, Ontario
J. Edwin Colson and his wife, Molly	Owners, Hotel Algonquin, Joe Lake
Mrs. Daphne Crombie	Wife of Lt. Robert Crombie, who was recovering from consumption (tuberculosis) at Canoe Lake
Lawrie Dickson	Guide, Algonquin Park
Blodwen Davies	Wrote the first major biography of Thomas J. Thomson, privately published in 1935
Michael R. Dixon	Embalmer, Sprucedale, Ontario
Mrs. Irene Ewing	Canoe Lake visitor and friend of Winnifred Trainor
Jack Eastaugh	Retired school principal and friend of William T. Little, Canoe Lake visitor in 1956
Dr. Harry Ebbs, MD	Physician, Canoe Lake visitor in 1956
Mrs. Jessie Fisk	Daughter of Thomas Harkness, brother-in-law of Thomas J. Thomson

Robert H. Flavelle	Undertaker, Kearney, Ontario
J. Shannon Fraser and his wife, Annie	Owners, Mowat Lodge, Canoe Lake
Thomas Harkness	Brother-in-law of Thomas J. Thomson from Annan, Ontario, a lawyer and insurance agency manager
Dr. Goldwin W. Howland, MD, and his daughter, Margaret	Professor of Neurology, University of Toronto, vacationer on Little Wapomeo Island, Canoe Lake
Miss Alice Elinor Lambert	Eighteen-year-old girlfriend of Thomas J. Thomson in Seattle, Washington, in 1904, later a Dell romance novelist
Robert P. Little	Canoe Lake visitor and guide, from Columbus, Ohio
William T. Little	Reform school superintendent, Brampton, Ontario, Canoe Lake visitor in 1956
Dr. James M. MacCallum, MD, and his son, Arthur	Ophthalmologist, art patron, Toronto, Ontario
James E. H. MacDonald	Group of Seven artist, mentor and designer of memorial cairn to Thomas J. Thomson
Dr. Wilford T. Pocock, MD	Winnifred Trainor's physician following 1917
Dr. John McRuer, MD	Friend of Thomas J. Thomson, died in Colorado of consumption in June 1917
Charles F. Plewman	Canoe Lake visitor, pallbearer at the Canoe Lake burial of Thomas J. Thomson
Dr. Arthur E. Ranney, MD	Coroner, North Bay, Ontario
Mark Robinson	Ranger, Algonquin Park
George Rowe	Guide, Algonquin Park
Horace Rutherford	Friend of Thomas J. Thomson in Seattle, Washington, in 1904
Charlie Scrim	Canoe Lake visitor and florist, Ottawa, Ontario
Dr. Noble Sharpe, MD	Director, Ontario Provincial Crime Laboratory in 1956

Mrs. Mabel A. Shaw	Boardinghouse owner, Seattle, Washington, in 1904
Mr. and Mrs. Edwin Thomas and their daughter, Rose	Residents of Canoe Lake
John Thomson, his wife, Margaret, and their family	Parents of Thomas J. Thomson from Owen Sound, Ontario
Thomas J. Thomson	Canada's greatest landscape artist, born August 5, 1877, died July 8, 1917
George M. Thomson	Thomas J. Thomson's older brother, bookkeeper and artist, from New Haven, Connecticut
Ralph K. Thomson	One of Thomas J. Thomson's younger brothers
Hugh Trainor	Foreman, Huntsville Lumber Company, summer resident at Canoe Lake
Miss Winnifred Trainor	Daughter of Hugh Trainor

*   Correspondence and other early writing used only initials for the men's first and middle names. Verifying full names was challenging. In addition, earlier biographies use different names and spellings for many of the characters beginning with Thomson's mother, Margaret Mathison, frequently misspelled as Matheson or Mathewson. Her gravestone in Owen Sound's Greenwood Cemetery and Tom's own gravestone in the Leith cemetery spells the family name as Mathison as confirmed by U.S. Census records of her family, which trace their role in the U.S. Civil War. U.S. Census records also verify the Blecher family's name. Most biographers report it as Bletcher. Whether Dixon's surname was Lawrie or Lowrie eluded conclusion. Research could not confirm other first names, such as Michael R. Dixon, the embalmer. For example, William T. Little's error-filled text, *The Tom Thomson Mystery*, used "M. R. Dixon," while he footnoted the name twice as "William R. Dixon." Accordingly, future researchers may find other errors in this list.

Fictional Characters

Jon Kristian	Lawyer visiting Canoe Lake to research the tragic and mysterious death of Canadian artist Thomas J. Thomson in 1917
Howard J. Hancock	Retired heavy farm equipment repairman, age seventy-two, Canoe Lake resident
Tess Kristian	Jon Kristian's ex-wife
Bob and Beth Ann Francis	Friends of Jon Kristian and Tess Kristian
Dr. Ross H. Beckley, MD	Psychiatrist, Huntsville, Ontario, and friend of Howard J. Hancock
Margaret Rose O'Gorman and her family	Seventeen-year-old Canoe Lake summer resident in 1917
Mary Alice Gleason	Jewelry and souvenir shop owner in Dwight, Ontario
Dixie Waterford	Owner of a bar in Dwight, Ontario
Harold "Lucky" Haskins	Rental shop operator in Dwight, Ontario

Canoe Lake Map

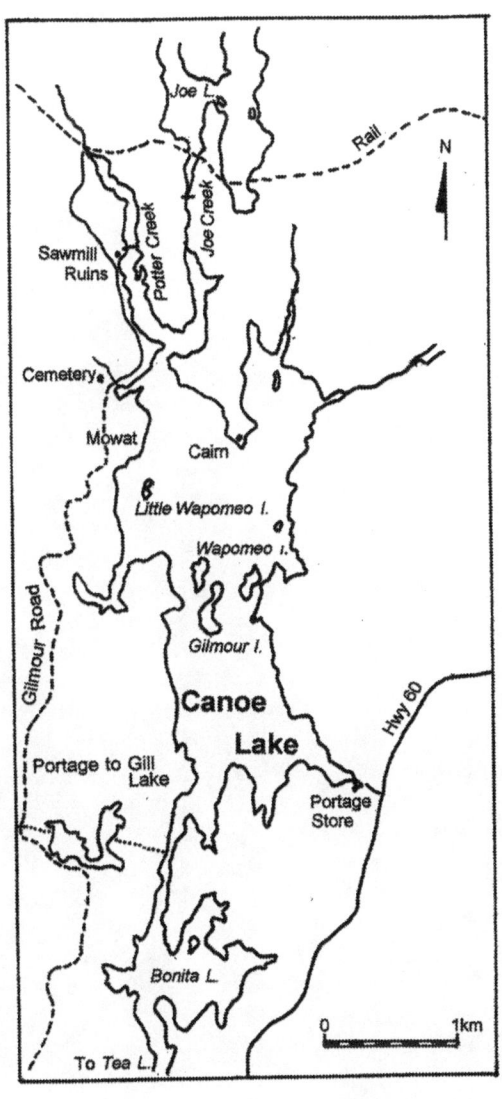

Kristian's Notebook: Final Entry

It is the night before my divorce. I will finish this notebook and sum up.

Maybe if I go to the park tomorrow, I will find new evidence or an eyewitness who saw what happened in 1917.

I don't think that will happen.

The enduring myth surrounding Tom Thomson's drowning in Canoe Lake is that what happened *should not* and *cannot* be cleared up. The chorus is unanimous.

Should not?

I believe that it should.

And I know that it can.

What makes his death even more tragic is that this Canadian landscape painter of Algonquin Park was unrecognized as a genius in his time.

Before I go on, look at what they said. Consider this their opening statement. I will make mine next.

The first biography—Blodwen Davies' *A Study of Tom Thomson: The Story of a Man Who Looked for Beauty and Truth in the Wilderness* (1935)—said, "And so mystery laid its imprint upon of the seal of Thomson's death—and the seal has not yet been broken."

In 1937, Albert H. Robson began his eight-page biographical sketch, *Tom Thomson*, writing, "Except to a very limited number of friends, Tom Thomson is a remote and mystical figure that broke into the art firmament with a sudden and dazzling brilliancy, and then disappeared as suddenly into the great unknown. During the last decade his career has been wrapped in mists of mystery and half-truths somewhat obscuring a clear vision of the man and his work."

Audrey Saunders's 1947 book, *Algonquin Story*, concluded, "No one is ever likely to know just what happened after he departed from the Mowat Lodge dock on the fatal Sunday afternoon."

One of the famous Group of Seven artists, A. Y. Jackson, footnoting the 1967 republication of Blodwen Davies's book, wrote

> The mystery surrounding Thomson's death will never be cleared up. Was he drowned in the quiet waters of a small lake? A man who had had paddled all

over the park, generally alone, in all kinds of weather, run rapids, and carried his canoe over rough portages and made his camp in the bush in wolf-ridden country? There were theories—suicide, heart attack, foul play—but the verdict was "accidental drowning"; not very convincing, but with no evidence of anything to the contrary, it stands, and must be accepted.

Then Ottelyn Addison and Elizabeth Harwood ended their 1969 book, *Tom Thomson: The Algonquin Years*, by writing

> Over the years, speculation has continued. The life of Thomson early took on a legendary quality, and his mysterious death contributed to the legend. It is idle to examine the various theories advanced to explain his death. Many of them are far-fetched and misleading: Facts to support any theory are almost impossible to obtain. It appears unlikely now that any completely satisfactory explanation of Thomson's death will be found.

Notwithstanding this opinion, in 1970, William T. Little, convinced he knew what happened, wrote in *The Tom Thomson Mystery*, "Seekers after truth usually have to settle for degrees of truth based upon what they personally will accept as sufficient proof or evidence…truths regarding Tom are not so plain or so easy to assess."

Charles F. Plewman's essay in the Winter 1972 issue of *Canadian Camping* said, "Actually, the truth regarding what happened to Tom may never be known with certainty."

In 1977, in *Tom Thomson: The Silence and the Storm*, David P. Silcox observed, "How he died has been a mystery veiled in surmise, yet there is no certain proof, and people will always prefer a mystery to facts. The hardest thing to accept, mostly because we don't want to, is that Thomson's death was an accident."

S. Bernard Shaw drew up short in 1996. His book on the subject, *Canoe Lake, Algonquin Park: Tom Thomson and Other Mysteries,* concluded, "So, let us not look here for a definitive answer, but consider the evidence which leads to a possible conclusion.…He was probably stunned by a fall…and drowned, although the possibility remains that he met his death as the result of a blow."

In 2002, Roy MacGregor, Thomson expert and national columnist of the *Globe and Mail,* added an author's note to his book *Canoe Lake,* "Exactly what happened will never be known, and in many ways this has become the true beauty of the Tom Thomson story."

In *Tom Thomson: The Life and Mysterious Death of the Famous Canadian Painter* (2003), Jim Poling, Sr., wrote

> Perhaps it is better that we can't know all the facts. One of the joys of the Tom Thomson story is just the telling and speculating about what really did happen. In some ways, it doesn't really matter that we don't know exactly what happened back in 1917.

In a summary of the Canadian literature, an academic review of these biographies, *Inventing Tom Thomson: From Biographical Fictions to Fictional Autobiographies and Reproductions,* (2004) Dr. Sherrill Grace, PhD, a professor of English at the University of British Columbia, concluded that none of these biographers discovered the real, original Tom Thomson. In the end, she said, all we have is their invention of him.

What happened to Thomson in 1917?

Accident, murder, or suicide?

You decide.

What time is it?

The clock says 11:34. I need to go to bed.

Consider this my opening statement.

An open-minded reader of this notebook *can* and *should* be able to decide beyond a reasonable doubt what happened to Tom Thomson at Canoe Lake in 1917 from all of the direct and circumstantial historical evidence. The English common law shared by the United States and Canada instructs us that a reasonable doubt is a doubt based upon reason and common sense. A reasonable doubt is a fair doubt, not vain, captious, or imaginary but growing out of the evidence or the lack of evidence. After a careful review of all the evidence, the reader *will* be able to decide that he or she has an abiding conviction, amounting to a moral certainty, of the true story of Thomson's death.

1

Kristian Meets Howard Hancock

Route 60, the main highway into Ontario's Algonquin Provincial Park, turns uphill outside the town of Huntsville, where a small, anxious black bear rose from a crouch on the roadside and dashed in front of Kristian's car. Kristian braked and watched as the bear disappeared into thick woods on the other side.

Over the two decades since his first trip to Algonquin, the provincial government had rebuilt this two-lane asphalt highway running across the southern end of the park between Dwight and Whitney, speeding vacationers carrying families and teamsters carrying goods to and from the Great Lakes.

Beginning outside Dwight, twenty miles west of the park entrance, construction crews blasted away thousands of tons of dark gray and pink-flecked Canadian Shield granite every five miles, putting in passing lanes a half-mile in length for passenger cars caught behind the freight-hauling semi-truck trailers that struggled along this gently twisting road.

It was as he passed his final truck that Kristian's car sputtered and quit. He steered the stark-red Mazda LX two-door sedan, leaning at a slight angle tight up against a sheer forty-three-foot-tall granite wall as the car came to a stop. Ever since his divorce a few days before, he had tried to be more cautious and thorough about everything he did. Despite the resolve, he had let his car ran out of gas.

"Damn," he said, pounding his left palm on the steering wheel, realizing that traffic would be sparse on this stretch of Route 60. Kristian pushed the emergency flasher button to the left of the radio, to ensure that any approaching motorists and truckers should be able to see him in the dusk on this hot Thursday in early July.

He leaned back into the seat and closed his eyes against images of the last few days, which flooded his mind. Kristian was traveling far north from his home in the village of Romeo, Michigan, a northern Detroit suburb, to a campsite he had reserved on Canoe Lake. He had planned to go there to work on a list of things to do that he jotted down on a yellow index card and slipped into in his left shirt pocket early this morning. Kristian fell asleep. When he awoke a few minutes later, he looked up over the steering wheel to see a yellow caution sign—with the black profile of a leaping buck—standing three car lengths ahead. He had passed such signs hundreds of times but had never before noticed the stark power and grace of the buck, which now, for Kristian, seemed to capture Algonquin Park's spirit of wilderness and to represent the potential dangers that lay on the road ahead. Kristian wondered why he had not noticed the sign before. But then looking ahead without seeing the obvious had been a recurring problem in his life.

Returning from an American Bar Association lawyer's convention in San Francisco fifteen years earlier, Kristian had made his first long list of things to do. At the top was "Make Law Firm Partnership," "Opera Season Tickets," "Write Tom Thomson Story," and "Help Tess Find Her Own Way." The first two he had succeeded in doing; the other two he had not.

That first written list of goals gave him a sense a purpose, helping him chart his successes and failures. Every year, during the lull between Christmas and New Year's Eve, he made a new list of things to do that he hoped would improve himself and his life with Tess and their daughters. One of his lists from two years ago began, "$100,000 Billings," "Get Speaking Engagements," "Finish Research on Tom Thomson Mystery," and "Spend More Time with Family." The first two he achieved; the latter two he did not. Last year, his list started, "Divorce Tess?" Kristian first thought of divorcing Tess during their final trip to Algonquin seventeen months ago.

The list in his shirt pocket today read, "Tom Thomson Mystery," "Owen Sound," "Canoe Lake," and "Suicide."

His trip to Owen Sound this morning to complete research on the mystery had failed. An angry Kristian learned that the Tom Thomson Gallery there had closed its reference library several years earlier.

He looked up into his rearview mirror and saw a vehicle coming eastbound with its headlights blazing. He wrestled with the idea of opening the trunk to check for a gasoline can. Kristian turned the key, the starter droned, and a white truck rumbled by. With a long sigh, Kristian looked again into the mirror. A tall blue truck appeared, its headlights shimmering in the heat rising off the highway.

"Help," he said to himself.

The truck sped up and went by with a whoosh. Kristian decided that he would have to get out and wave down a passing vehicle or leave his car and whitewater-equipped fourteen-foot canoe behind while he made the two-mile walk back to Dwight's two-pump gas station. The walk back would take him past an ageless souvenir store, The Trading Post, with its stuffed bear by the front door and Indian tepee next to the driveway. Ever since his first trip to the park with Tess twenty-five years earlier, and during every later summer trip with their daughters, he had never stopped to buy ice cream or souvenirs, or to use the advertised clean restrooms. Tess had always wanted to stop, preferring the shops to Algonquin's quiet wilderness.

Once each summer for the past twenty-five years, Kristian joined the hundreds of families driving north from Toronto to Georgian Bay's Wasaga Beach, farther on to Muskoka Cottage Country, and still farther on to Algonquin, following Route 11. Most drivers never stopped along the way, except at a roadside hamburger stand north of Orillia called Weber's.

The provincial government divided Route 11 with steel-barrier walls for miles after many left-turn accidents on the highway. The wall they built divided northbound tourist business in half, since the few turnarounds were miles apart. Weber's prospered, however, because the owner had bought land across Route 11, had installed a parking lot, and had constructed a brilliant-orange steel-, glass-, and concrete-covered walkway, enabling weekend visitors—who were northbound on Friday and southbound on Sunday—to stop for charcoal-broiled hamburgers.

A white late-model Chevy Malibu roared past. Kristian pushed the radio scan button and heard nothing but static all the way across the dial. He remembered that the Toronto AM rock stations his daughters used to tune in to would fade away by the time they got to Weber's, which was one hundred miles from the park. Kristian remembered that from there to the park, and whenever he was on the east side of the park in Whitney buying groceries, beer, and liquor, he could never tune in to any radio station except CBC Radio in Ottawa.

Howard J. Hancock drove red Ford pickup trucks all his life. This fifteen-year-old model F-100, with 174,000 miles on it, had a bullet hole in the rear window. Hancock was seventy-two years old. He wore his best clothes: a soft dark blue wool suit, a starched white shirt, and a conservative black tie. A brown Fedora rested on the passenger side. Stiff white hair poked up across the back of his head. He carried two white cotton handkerchiefs—one in his right front pants pocket and the other, damp, stuffed into the left pocket of his suit jacket, which Hancock pulled out and used to dab his eyes.

"Laura," he thought, "I miss you."

Hancock was going home, alone, to his cottage on Canoe Lake, when he came upon a red sedan carrying a bright green canoe parked by the side of the road, its well-dressed middle-aged driver waving broadly. Before retiring some years ear-lier, Hancock had worked for John Deere in Michigan, Ohio, and Indiana, repairing heavy farm machinery. Handy and resourceful, he had traveled country roads all of his working life, and most of the time he stopped to help strangers at the side of the road. He pulled over and stopped ten feet behind; he then turned off the ignition and pushed open the door, which reacted with a familiar rusty wheeze and a clank. Hancock noticed the red sedan's blue and white Michigan license plates. He stepped out and shouted, "What's the trouble, mister?"

"Ran out of gas."

Hancock, bent slightly at the waist, turned forward and back slowly, stretch-ing. He gestured to the rear of the pickup.

"Got some in the back."

The gas cans rested against the left and right sides of the truck bed behind the rear wheels, each secured in custom-made black steel racks with spring-loaded release handles. Hancock reached over the left side, pulled a handle, and hefted a five-gallon can over the side.

"Thanks for stopping," Kristian said. "Been here twenty minutes. A few semis and a couple of cars came by, but you're the only one to stop."

Hancock hauled the gasoline can over to the rear end of the sports car and set it down patiently. Kristian watched, hesitated a moment, and then darted back to the driver's door. "Sorry," he said. He bent over, reached in, and pulled the gas cap's release. The yellow index card fell from the left front pocket. Hancock saw it flutter up and away.

He twisted open the lid, pulled out the funnel, and lifted the heavy can care-fully into position. He emptied all the gasoline into Kristian's tank. The two men remained silent.

Hancock pushed the funnel back into place, tightened the lid, flipped the gas cap closed, and went back to his truck. There, on the bottom of the open rack, he saw the yellow card that had flown from Kristian's shirt pocket. He plucked it out. It was a short list. One of the entries caught his attention. He stuffed the card his right pants pocket.

Kristian stepped up, extending his left hand. "Here's ten dollars for the gas, mister."

"Okay," Hancock said, taking the U.S. bill, "but it's not necessary."

Wanting to get away, Kristian wondered if he needed to say any more.

Hancock persisted.

"You up from Michigan?"

"From Detroit. Headed over to Canoe Lake to be alone."

That last word struck Hancock.

"I'm going home alone myself."

The two strangers stood in awkward silence, feeling the emotional distance between them shorten.

"Buried my wife of forty-seven years back in Huntsville today," Howard said. "You worry sooner or later you'll have to drive home alone. I hoped it wasn't going to be me."

Kristian stared at the older man's bright blue eyes. Hancock blinked back a tear and looked at the sunset, the sky turning pink and orange. Kristian shuffled in the gravel, trying to find a response. He had none. He could not think of a thing to say to the old man about his wife's death. A white Corvette Stingray came up in the eastbound lane and roared past.

"Care to visit at my place on Canoe Lake?" Hancock asked.

Frustrated by his failure earlier that day, when he had visited Owen Sound to investigate Tom Thomson's death at Canoe Lake in 1917, Kristian was troubled over his plan for the next few days. He needed to squeeze in a visit to the Tom Thomson collection at the Huntsville Public Library. Yet, feeling indebted to this old man, he could not refuse.

"Well, sure," he said, reaching out his right hand. "My name is Jon Kristian."

"Howard Hancock," the older man responded, recognizing Kristian as left-handed. He brought up his right hand and made a good grip. "Friday night after dinner?"

The old man went back to his truck to scribble directions on a John Deere memo pad in the front seat. Hancock had a box full of them. He brought the note back, and Kristian took it from his outstretched hand.

"I'll be there," Kristian promised, pushing the scrap of paper into his shirt pocket. They walked back to their vehicles.

Hancock waved Kristian ahead and waited as the canoe-topped sedan sped away. He started his truck and pulled out. A few hundred feet later, a little yellow index card fluttered out the driver's side window.

2

Kristian's First Trip to Algonquin

Algonquin is a majestic 2,910-square-mile wilderness park on the highlands between Georgian Bay and the Ottawa River at the southern edge of the Canadian Shield. It was set aside for the public by Ontario in 1893. The park is about twice the size of Rhode Island, with high vistas of smooth granite outcroppings rising over innumerable streams, creeks, rivers, and clear, cold lakes. Algonquin's tallest and most important tree, the white pine, is characteristic of the park's east side.

The white pine's soft, clear wood and tremendous size brought thousands of pioneering loggers to the area in the 1830s. They stripped the tall trees and moved west by the early 1900s. Today, a few of the three-hundred-year-old giants survive—at Dividing Lake near the southwest boundary and at Big Crow Lake in the central part of the park. The western uplands cover the other two-thirds of the park. Spectacular in autumn are its abundant beech, maple, birch, and aspen forest trees, which hold their dancing orange, flaming red, and trembling, yellow leaves up against the deep green and dark blue boughs of the fewer spruce, balsam, and pine trees.

Kristian learned of Algonquin from a book called *The Canoer's Bible.* He studied the book late into the night for months while sprawled across his side of their king-size bed, as Tess, his bride of a few months, read romance and science fiction novels. He decided to take her on an interior canoe trip, along a route that park veterans call Main Street.

The route starts on Canoe Lake at the docks of a prosperous livery, The Portage Store, and goes north through Joe, Little Joe, Burnt Island, Otterslide, and Big Trout Lakes, returning through Trout, McIntosh, Ink, and Tom Thomson Lakes—a five-day circuit, the book said. He went over its checklists repeatedly before packing Tess, her father's old canvas tent, and two sleeping bags into their newly purchased burnt-orange Oldsmobile Omega sedan.

The early-July trip from their suburban Detroit townhouse in Rochester took about eleven hours. A few minutes before reaching the park's west gate, he stopped at the Algonquin Outfitters store on the west shore of Oxtongue Lake to pick up some camping equipment and food supplies. First, he headed for the restroom. Propped up on a display shelf on the right side of the hallway was a lithograph print. Bright cardboard framed an oil painting of a narrow between two lakes, painted from the viewpoint of an approaching canoeist. Tall black spruces framed the inlet. Hardwoods, flaming orange below a pleasant blue sky and billowing white clouds beckon the canoeist through the inlet and onto the lake beyond. The vibrant color and design of the painting gripped him as no landscape painting had ever done. From a note pasted on the back, he learned that the artist, Tom Thomson, had drowned in Canoe Lake on July 8, 1917. The note said the painting, *Black Spruce in Autumn,* was one of the artist's most famous.

Thomson, whose name alone evoked Canadian art, forever captured the emerging nation's independent spirit and love of the North Country. Thomson's three hundred surviving sketches on small wood panels and forty-five major paintings on stretched canvas are starkly realistic yet abstract in their use of vivid color and manipulation of texture. Adding to his artistic legend, he drowned in the waters of the northern wilderness. Museum curator and Thomson expert Joan Murray, writer of numerous coffee-table art books, described him as having all the attributes necessary of a mythic national figure. He lived a passionate life isolated in an unfriendly environment, made a genuine contribution to Canadian culture in a brief period, and suffered an early death in nature under mysterious circumstances.

Kristian pulled himself away from the print, looked around, and decided against buying anything else, as the prices seemed high compared to what he paid back home. He drove Tess into the park and found the left-hand turn off Route 60, which led onto a narrow asphalt driveway and up to The Portage Store at the southwest end of Canoe Lake. The Portage Store was a souvenir shop for tourists, an outfitter for hikers, and a restaurant for canoe campers starting and ending trips on Canoe Lake. In the upstairs shop, he found more Thomson books and prints. There, Kristian bought a reproduction of a Thomson painting that he found especially joyful, *Summer Clouds,* and two books about the artist's life and tragic death, *Tom Thomson: The Algonquin Years* and *The Tom Thomson Mystery.* He put them into the trunk of his car. Tess was looking over postcards when he returned. He yanked her downstairs to the rental store, where the sparse camping equipment and food selection persuaded him to take Tess back to the Algonquin Outfitters, another twenty-five-minute drive.

Once there, Kristian and Tess picked out three oversized canvas Duluth backpacks, a nested set of aluminum pots and plates, a fire grate, a plastic egg container, a collapsible water jug, two sets of utensils, fire starters, assorted fruit-drink mixes, dehydrated soups, crackers, oatmeal, two pounds of frozen bacon, two frozen steaks, and a selection of freeze-dried meals for six days and five nights.

He then drove back to The Portage Store, where he rented a seventeen-foot aluminum Grumman canoe, two life jackets, and three paddles. He and Tess spent an hour organizing their new camping gear, clothing, and food supplies among the three backpacks before setting out on Canoe Lake under a warm mid-afternoon sun. Standing at the dock while Tess sat in the bow steadying the canoe, he patted his left front pants pocket for car keys and right rear pocket for his wallet, where he carried his lucky silver nickel. His fingers reassured him that he had not forgotten them.

Algonquin attracts 65,000 interior paddlers every year. Since loggers pushed up the Ottawa River and discovered the region in the 1830s, Canoe Lake had changed from a pioneer lumbering center to the site from which canoe campers arrived, departed, and returned. Canoe Lake sprawled across the northern end of the Oxtongue River, which flowed southwest into a string of smaller lakes, winding and stretching to the Lake of Bays in Ontario's Muskoka Cottage Country, its waters eventually reaching Lake Huron.

Canoe Lake hosted The Portage Store, forty-three cottages, and two children's camps. Some cottages dated back to before 1917. Those predating 1954 are held under market-value leases from the provincial government that can be renewed only until 2017, when they are supposed to expire forever. Ever since the park's establishment in the late 1800s, the provincial government had slowly eliminated private land ownership in the park. The strongest resistance to the reclamation of the remaining private properties came from Canoe Lake residents.

The route Kristian planned to the park's interior goes north across Canoe Lake, winds among three islands—Gilmour, Big Wapomeo, and Little Wapomeo—and passes into a narrowing bay where a prominent point of land reaches out from the west and Hayhurst Point stretches down from the northeast.

In 1897, the western point of land (called Mowat) had six hundred residents, a lumberyard, a smoke belching sawmill, and many miles of railroad siding. To the south stood Mowat Lodge, consisting of two whitewashed-clapboard two-story buildings, each with twenty rooms and a covered front porch. The Gilmour Lumber Company used them as a mill-hand kitchen and boardinghouse before it went bankrupt and abandoned Mowat to mortgage foreclosure in 1901. J. Shannon Fraser, his gregarious wife, Annie, and his mother came to Mowat in 1907 to help remove the remaining sawmill machinery. When they finished, they stayed, taking up a lease on a smaller third hospital building behind the others, where they lived. They took up another lease on the kitchen and boardinghouse, which they reopened as Camp Mowat in 1913 as a summer vacation spot for park visitors coming to the nearby Canoe and Joe Lake train stations. In 1914, they added the adjoining storehouse and changed the name to Mowat Lodge, where Tom Thomson lived before he drowned a few hundred feet north of Big Wapomeo Island.

When Kristian and Tess passed, all evidence of these buildings was gone. A fire had destroyed them in 1920. What remained were a few cottages, a wide meadow littered with scrap wood, a few barely recognizable ruins of railroad tracks passing over marshy fields, and winding spring creeks trickling faintly through scattered moss-covered old logs and rotting, rough-hewn timbers.

Upon leaving, Kristian and Tess paddled across the bay to Hayhurst Point, where, in September 1917, friends of Thomson built him a memorial five-foot stone cairn with a decoratively inscribed brass plate. It stood one hundred feet uphill from a decayed wooden dock. Kristian took Tess up to see the memorial. Leaving Hayhurst Point, he suggested they paddle north along the shore to where the lake split into two bays, which narrowed into Potter Creek on the west and Joe Creek on the east. He looked across the water and pulled a route map out from underneath the flap of his backpack.

The map, published by the Friends of Algonquin Park in cooperation with Ontario Parks, was about three feet by three feet with a scale of one inch to two miles. It described in detail the park's hundreds of canoe routes. All critical landmarks, lakes, bays, rivers, creeks, and streams were clearly depicted, but the canoeist had to understand the park's majestic scale in order to follow it correctly. Kristian had not yet learned to match features on the map against what he saw from the canoe.

"Do you know where we're going?" she asked.

"Of course I do. I am following the map north to Joe Creek. We're right on course; we have plenty of time to find our campsite on Little Joe Lake."

He steered the canoe left with a stern draw stroke toward what he thought was Joe Creek. Instead, he took her up a bay that narrowed into Potter Creek a few minutes later. Kristian and Tess, knees braced against the bottom of the canoe, feet spread wide for stability in the gentle lake waves, paddled northwest against a southeast breeze and some infrequent gusts. The bay closed to thirty feet across, with the water shallowing to less than a foot as they progressed. As they paddled in the hot early-afternoon July sun, the canoe's keel scraped on the creek's many rocks. Father on, they passed under the remnants of a wooden railroad bridge, a signal Kristian missed that he was guiding them along the wrong route. With all of the railroad tracks long gone and wide sections fallen or missing, he wondered whose past they were paddling into. The air's moisture grew and the wetland's dank odor swept over them. The tamarack pine-lined shores pressed in as they came upon a portage sign on river right. (Paddlers always refer to the left and right sides of a river from the downstream perspective, whether they are traveling with or against the flow.) The sign was an eight-and-a-half-by-eleven-inch piece of yellow cardboard nailed seven feet up on a prominent shoreline tree. It featured a stark black silhouette of a paddler, canoe hoisted on his shoulders. Fallen limbs and rocks choked off the creek twenty-five yards ahead.

Portage signs marked Algonquin's many trails wherever there was a natural or unnatural obstruction in the water. Delighted by the ease with which he navigated across the wide lake to what he thought was their first portage, Kristian failed to check his map. It indicated that the route to Joe Lake went off the water on river left and extended 295 meters—not river right and 380 meters. At the other end of the portage, he expected to find a large clearing (the site of an early logging camp) and a narrow channel leading out into Joe Lake. There would be a hill on the left shore before a railway bridge at the end of the channel where the Algonquin Hotel had stood in 1917. Tom Thomson had eaten a late-morning breakfast there the day he drowned.

"Is this the portage to Joe Lake?" Tess asked.

"Yep."

They let the canoe float to shore. Two summers earlier, at a picnic site on the Au Sable River, a few miles east of Grayling, Michigan, Kristian and Tess had learned to respect the landing of a tandem canoe. His friends Bob and Beth Ann Francis safely landed their canoe at a dock on the left side of the river. Twenty to thirty people had gathered; some were busy with lunch at wooden tables, while others were preparing to depart. Bob yanked his canoe out of the water as Kristian and Tess floated up. Tess stepped out of the canoe onto the dock and turned to watch. Kristian stood, and the canoe responded by violently flipping to the right, away from the dock. He could feel himself standing upright and then falling into the cold greenish brown water. Bob, Tess, and the entire picnic site gathered, laughing and applauding.

"Never again," he had told himself, swimming back to the dock.

After they beached the canoe at the portage, Tess stepped out, turned, and crouched over the bow, steadying the canoe with her thighs and arms on each side, a maneuver they had practiced ever since the Au Sable River incident. Tess held the bow as Kristian carefully came forward and stepped out. He hastily unloaded, wanting to get to their campsite on Joe Lake well before dark. His internal clock was reawakened in the Algonquin wilderness, where the only clocks are those that visitors carry. Kristian never wore a watch. The lowering sun told him it was about six o'clock.

Tess waited as Kristian pulled their heavy packs out of the canoe, strapped one onto his back, and smartly hoisted the canoe over his shoulders. Kristian—age twenty-three, six feet tall, and 205 pounds—wore a red sweatband over his forehead, a long-sleeved flannel shirt to protect his fair-skinned arms against sunburn, tan khaki trousers (with cigarettes, a lighter, and a Swiss Army knife tucked into the left pocket), and dull black military boots for his trek up the portage trail.

The seventeen-foot canoe weighed seventy pounds. A single camper can carry even a large canoe across a portage—by hoisting the canoe up, over, and down onto his shoulders in clean-and-jerk fashion using its center thwart. All two-person canoes are equipped with seats across the front and rear, as well as a thwart across the center for structural support. In a well-made canoe, the center thwart is a carved piece of wood that fits comfortably on the shoulders of the portaging canoeist. The Grumman's thwart was a sturdy three-quarter-inch aluminum tube.

Many of Algonquin's portages have existed for thousands of years, first carved out and worn down by the Native American Indians, who moved birch bark canoes from one paddling point to another. They followed the shortest path across, not the easiest. This trail ascended 175 feet above the river, along a wide ledge that veered off into woods and back again. Kristian had stuffed his pack with seventy pounds' worth of stuff—his clothing, his sleeping bag, the tent, and other gear. Going up was grueling work. The thwart ground into his shoulders with each careful step he took over the trail's exposed roots and rocks, muddy puddles, and sharp turns. Exhausted at the top of the trail, he dropped the bow to the ground with a clunk and pushed the canoe off his aching shoulders. He shrugged off the pack and strolled over to the edge of a cliff twenty steps to his left, waiting for Tess to come along.

A few minutes later, wearing her backpack and carrying their paddles and life jackets, Tess came up red faced and puffing, sweat dripping down her forehead, upper lip, and neck. Her sweatshirt was soaked.

"Look at this," he called down from the granite ledge overlooking the river below. Miles and miles of woodland spread out across the horizon, as the sun shone brightly in the west in a blue summer sky dotted with a few lazy clouds.

A big woman at five-foot-six, two-hundred twenty pounds, she huffed and grunted, "You picked this trail?"

As became her habit on their Algonquin canoe trips, her weight growing every year, Tess never stopped during a portage. Off she went into the woods, following the downward trail marked by yellow signs far across the way, which he had not yet seen. Kristian stayed, admiring the magnificent vista while he chain-smoked a couple of cigarettes. Ten minutes later, he hoisted the pack onto his back, adjusted the straps, and lifted the canoe overhead.

At the portage's end, Tess sat by the creek waiting for him. Once he arrived, he dropped the canoe and his backpack and went back up the steep portage trail. He repeated the trip to fetch their cooking supplies. Thus, he made three treks across the 380-meter portage. It was a routine he came to dread—she went over once; he went over three times—which they followed on all of their subsequent trips every August with their daughters. They had four daughters, one every four years.

When he returned, they loaded the canoe, pushed off into the shallow creek, and headed downstream, looking for the railway bridge and channel into Joe Creek. They soon encountered the first of numerous rock gardens. The Grumman canoe was equipped with a one-inch-thick keel, which scrapped and caught on underwater rocks. They bumped and rocked the canoe over some, while others required one or both of them to jump out and wade with the canoe into deeper water.

In the early evening twilight, after his three portages, he realized, after studying his map and reconstructing their route at the end of the last portage, that they had been paddling in Potter Creek. Not wanting to confess a fundamental error the first day out and turn around, he instead set up camp before sundown on an unmarked campsite, a boggy mat of grass on a long, slow bend in the creek, where he prepared a good dinner of tomato soup and fresh steak cooked over an open fire. Tess flopped into their tent and fell fast asleep. Kristian stayed up with a flashlight and map, plotting a new route. He saw that they could paddle north into Potter Lake, cross a 180-meter portage to Pathfinder Lake, complete two more portages, and reach Tom Thomson Lake on the originally planned route.

The next day started out badly and got worse. For their wedding the previous June, she had picked out a unique gold ring for him at Marx Jewelers in downtown Royal Oak, Michigan. It was carved with the shapes of twenty tiny flowers. Tess always paddled on the right side of the canoe, while Kristian paddled left-handed. Only by paddling in unison were they able to keep the canoe on a straight course. Left-handed paddling, however, caused his palm to blister below the ring finger. Kristian shifted to the right side, and the canoe turned off course with every stroke. He had not yet learned that the serious paddler should use a stroke called the "Canadian" or "J" stroke. Correcting their course required her to shift over to the left side.

"Hey," she cried out. "Are you still back there?"

"Oh, yes. It's beautiful here, isn't it?"

"We're wandering all over. You paddle on the left side. I'll paddle on the right. That'll keep us straightened out."

The blister grew more painful. His finger had grown fat since the marriage, and the ring was tight. In between strokes, he struggled at it with his right hand.

"Paddle," she growled.

"Okay."

Finally, he took the ring off. He dipped his hand into the cooling water and stuffed the ring into the empty left rear pocket of his well-worn cut-off blue jeans. He should have tucked it into the thick leather wallet in the right rear pocket. Taking the wallet with him was a mistake, but it carried a lucky silver nickel his grandfather had given him many years earlier.

Kristian remembered his grandfather, John Palmer Jones, as a white-haired old man who had had his left eye surgically removed during a brain tumor operation. Kristian's mother dropped him off at Papa's—as Kristian called him—house every weekday on her way to classes at Wayne State University for two years before he started kindergarten. Kristian grew to adore Papa, who was different from the all the other older men and women in his life. Papa's zest for life grew out of his passionate faith in God, "from whom all blessings flow," he would say while sitting with Kristian on the front porch swing at his house. He lived near the Michigan State Fair Grounds, a few miles from Kristian's home.

Finding mother missing from the family home one day after school in early fall, a six-year-old Kristian fled on his bicycle to Papa's house. He pedaled two and a half miles down the alleys east of Woodward Avenue, seeking safety and reassurance. In the hastening darkness, he encountered barking dogs and cars with honking horns along the way. When he arrived, Papa reassured him that all was okay, and they shared a 7-Up on the front porch swing while awaiting his father's arrival. Papa reached out and put a small coin into Kristian's left hand.

"Kristian," he said. "This is a lucky nickel I got when I came here across the ocean from Wales to Canada in November 1917. Keep it with you."

Kristian promised to keep it with him always, and he had.

At the beginning of a short portage trail not much farther along Potter Creek, Kristian pushed back against the aluminum seat as they beached the canoe, and he sensed that his left pocket was empty. He reached back.

"Tess," he cried out, "I've lost my wedding ring!"

She turned around, scowling. "What do you mean?"

"I took it off. Put it in my pocket. It's gone."

"How could you let this happen?"

Her shoulders dropped, her head slumped, and tears filled her eyes. "You bastard!"

He left her weeping loudly in the bow of the canoe. Kristian turned and ran upstream in the middle of the creek, looking for a glint of gold. He went all the way back to where they had started out that morning, stumbling and falling as he ran in knee-deep water over slippery rocks. The creek was refreshingly cool and sparkling clear. The sun dried his T-shirt and warmed his shoulders on the long, empty walk downstream. He was away long enough that when he returned without his wedding band, she greeted him with little more than a sorrowful silence.

They reached Potter Lake late in the afternoon of that second day under an overcast sky threatening rainstorms. He could not find the 180-meter portage at what he thought was the halfway point up the long, dark green, and narrow Potter Lake. They beached the canoe, and he struggled over a narrow expanse of land through thick brush and tamarack pine trees, finding the mucky, weed-infested shoreline of what he thought was Pathfinder Lake. Here, he assured her that they would resume their planned trip after previous day's unfortunate detour. Carrying the canoe, backpacks, and all the other gear over would have been difficult, but not impossible. She balked at wading twenty yards through the thigh-deep muck to open water.

"Are you sure this is the right lake?"

"Yes, I am sure of it. Even if this is not the portage, this is the lake. What else could it be? Here, look at the map."

"Isn't that ironic?" she responded. "Pathfinder Lake?"

He relented, suggesting instead that they turn around and go back the way they came the next day. She readily agreed. Kristian paddled south and across to the west side of Potter Lake. Humiliated, he fell silent as they pulled up on shore under the humid afternoon sky, darkened by low-hanging gray storm clouds. Relieved to set up camp near the portage back to Potter Creek, he raised the tent. Tess went to work gathering wood.

Feeling alone against the Algonquin wilderness, he felt fear grow within him. She found none of the old, dead, dry wood he needed (as park regulations prohibited cutting live trees). She gathered a few damp twigs and small branches and piled them next to the fire grate. Kristian huddled over the stone fire ring with his three-box supply of waterproof matches. His sense of time filled him with an urgency to build a fire before rain or night fell. A whispering wind grew to a shout and then quieted, blowing away every flame. Slimy dampness darkened every spark.

Tess dug into the food pack and handed him a box of Triscuit crackers. They passed it back and forth, as he continued working in quiet desperation with matches, twigs, pieces of the box top, and its cellophane wrapper. The sounds of high rustling pine boughs and low mumbling lake waters filled the campsite as he tried and tried again to light a fire. He opened the last box, struck a match, and reached out gently.

In the silencing of the wind that comes with the setting sun, a wispy stream of blue smoke rose straight up from his little fire of twigs and scraps toward the coarse branches of the red pine high above. He hurried with another match and held his breath. He added larger and larger twigs, a twisted branch, and then another, as the flames grew. He positioned the heavy metal grate over the fire and warned an excited Tess to keep a close watch while he ran down to the lake for a kettle of fresh water. He came back, poured enough for a coffeepot full of freeze-dried vegetable soup, and set a kettle on the side to heat up for hot cleaning water later. He dropped in a dishrag and a bar of soup and waited. He added a large branch, and the fire grew. As twilight's violet duskiness faded into night's blackness, Kristian poured Tess a cup of soup, and she took a sip.

"Delicious," she said. Tess reached for the cracker box and removed a handful, which she crushed and stirred into her soup cup. "I was so hungry."

They nestled next to each other on their campsite of soot, dirt, and wide, smooth granite. He watched the flames and smoke rise into the tall pines with a sense of awe. The fire's warmth and the soup were soothing. As they sat, finishing the soup and all the crackers, the storm clouds passed. The sky opened up dramatically, revealing its brilliant stars. The divine stillness of night in the Algonquin scene etched itself into his memory, where it would remain forever.

Lying together under the stars, he asked whether she had understood the inscription on Tom Thomson's cairn, which they had stood in front of for a few minutes the day before. "He lived humbly but passionately with the wild. It made him brother to all untamed things of nature. It drew him apart and revealed itself wonderfully to him," Kristian read to her from a photograph on the back of the map.

"I guess it's not caring that we're miles and hours away from anywhere," she said, pulling his lips toward hers. They kissed gently. Lifting her head toward him with a delighted sigh, she whispered, "It's being loved away from everything else while being a part of everything too. It's knowing that, whatever happens, you will be there for me."

Moonlight crept through the treetops. She pointed out the constellations Cassiopeia, Big Dipper, Little Dipper, and the Northern Star. A pair of loons cried out to each to each other somewhere out on the lake far away to the north, their warbling tune echoing magnificently. Kristian pulled her down onto their sleeping bags, rolled out under the sky. She closed her eyes and held him tight in her arms as she fell asleep. He lifted his face and caressed her cheek lightly with his left hand, thinking that Tess had not understood.

3

Notebook: Tom's Drowning at Canoe Lake

Tom Thomson spent his last spring, in 1917, at the Mowat Lodge, painting around Canoe Lake. He produced sixty-two landscape sketches on small wood panels, a daily record of the season's change in Algonquin Park. It was an achievement, Tom declared, that no other artist had ever matched. At the time of his drowning, however, none of them remained among his belongings. He had given away many of them to friends and acquaintances, and destroyed and discarded the others. Apart from his paintings, the surviving traces of Thomson's life are abundant but thin. A few art books, biographies, and semi-fictional novels rehash and dispute the details.

On Saturday, July 7, 1917, one day before he drowned—having finished his last spring sketch six weeks earlier—Thomson wrote a letter on Mowat Lodge stationary to his art patron, dealer, and friend, Toronto ophthalmologist Dr. James M. MacCallum, MD. He described his plans for the following months.

Dear Dr. MacCallum,

I am still around the Frasers and have not done any sketching since the flies started. The weather has been wet and cold all spring and the flies and mosquitoes [are] much worse than I have seen them any year and fly dope doesn't have any affect on them. This, however, is the second warm day we have had this year and another day or so will finish them. Will send my winter sketches down in a day or two, and have every intention of making some more, but it has been almost impossible lately. Have done a great deal of paddling this spring and the fishing has been fine. Have done some guiding for fishing parties and will have some other trips this month and next with probably sketching in between. Received this slip of paper a day or so ago and don't know anything about it. Would you give it to Jim or someone around the building with permission to do anything about it they see fit? If they will, I will be greatly obliged. Hoping you are well, I am

Yours truly
Tom Thomson

Thomson often turned to steady family man James E. H. MacDonald—both mentor and practicing artist in his own right—to tidy up professional matters back in Toronto while Thomson was away at Algonquin Park. MacDonald occupied a suite in the Studio Building on Severn Street, behind which stood Thomson's winter studio and home, referred to as "The Shack," which was relocated to the grounds of the McMichael Canadian Art Collection in Kleinburg, Ontario. The slip of paper to which Thomson referred was one of many inquiries Thomson received about paintings he had promised, but not delivered, to Toronto's many art shows that year. Over the winter, Thomson had finished no canvases for the 1917 season.

Late Sunday morning, July 8, Thomson asked Fraser to bring two pounds of bacon down to the Mowat Lodge dock, as well as a dozen potatoes, pancake flour, and a fresh loaf of bread. Thomson put these food supplies into a kit bag and loaded his distinctive gray-green Chestnut canoe with some cooking and fishing gear. He told Fraser that he planned to catch a big lake trout for Park Ranger Mark Robinson at Gill Lake or at the Tea Lake Dam. At about 12:50 P.M., he paddled onto Canoe Lake. The shoreline channel west of Little Wapomeo Island was jammed with logs, so Thomson headed out around the east side of the island south of Hayhurst Point. Within minutes, he passed behind the island and out of sight from Mowat Lodge. The weather was in the low sixties and the lake calm with a depressing gray drizzle.[1] More than half an inch of rain fell that day.

Little more than two hours later, at 3:05 P.M., Martin H. Blecher, Jr., and his sister, Bessie, out for an afternoon fishing trip to Tea Lake in their family's motorboat, passed a distinctive gray-green canoe that was overturned off Kiowa Rocks at Big Wapomeo Island, between Stratton's Point and Bertram Island, southeast of Little Wapomeo Island. They investigated no further. Blecher later said he thought it was the canoe Edwin and Molly Colson had reported missing from its mooring below the Joe Lake Dam. Edwin and Molly were the new own-

---

1.   Several accounts described the afternoon as "hot and sultry" contrary to weather records kept at Cache Lake.

ers of the thirty-five room Hotel Algonquin. He said they had decided to tow it back when they returned, but it had drifted away.

The next morning, Blecher mentioned his sighting of a gray-green canoe to Fraser, who immediately recognized it as belonging to Tom. On Tuesday morning, an alarmed Fraser hurried over to Robinson's Ranger Station at Joe Lake. He burst in, exclaiming that Thomson was missing and that Blecher had spotted his overturned canoe a few hours after Thomson departed from the Mowat Lodge dock on Sunday.

Robinson reported by telephone to Park Superintendent George W. Bartlett, who ordered search parties and promised to send other rangers to help. Within hours, Charlie Scrim, one of Thomson's best friends, found the canoe floating upside down between Big Wapomeo Island and the mainland to the northwest. Scrim guided Robinson to the location, where they righted the canoe, finding two portage paddles lashed in place. Thomson's prized handmade black cherry canoeing paddle was missing and would never be recovered. It should have floated with the overturned canoe. In the canoe, Robinson found only a gallon can of maple syrup and a one-and-a-half-pound pail of jam wrapped in a rubber sheet and stuffed into the bow. Everything else was gone. Experienced paddlers secure all their gear in packs tied to the canoe's thwarts with short lengths of rope. The hopeful conclusion Fraser and Robinson drew was that Thomson safely landed, injured himself while unloading, and accidentally set the overturned canoe adrift.

Fraser, postmaster in 1917 for the 150 residents of Mowat, sent telegrams to both the Thomson family in Owen Sound and Dr. MacCallum in Toronto, dated Tuesday, July 10, each of which read, "Tom's canoe found upside down. No trace of Tom since Sunday."

Fraser followed up with a more detailed letter to Dr. MacCallum on Thursday, July 12. He wrote,

> Tom left here on Sunday about one o'clock for a fishing trip down the lake and at three o'clock his canoe was found floating a short distance from my place with both paddles tied tight in the canoe. Also, his provisions were found packed in the canoe. The canoe was upside down. We can find no trace of where he landed or what happened to him. Everything is being done that can be done. His brother arrived this morning.

Whether Fraser also sent a letter to the Thomson family remains unknown.

Mowat P.O., Ontario, July 12, 191 7

Dr. James MacCallum
Toronto

Dear Sir,

Tom left here on Sunday about ne
o'clock. For a fishing trip down the lake
and at three o'clock his Canoe was
found floating a short distance from
my place with both paddles tied
tight in the Canoe also his provisions
were found packed in the Canoe.
The Canoe was up side down.
Wee can find no trace of h when he
landed or what happend to him
Every thing is being done that can be done
his brother arrived this morning
will let you know at once if we
find him
           your truly
              J. S. Fraser

Shannon Fraser's July 12 letter to Dr. MacCallum.

Chief Constable Thomas O. Foster, of Owen Sound, received a letter from Dr. MacCallum on July 12 reporting Tom's disappearance. He wrote back, "I have placed your letter, which I received today re: Tom Thomson, in the Rev. Mr. Pilkey's hands. He has taken it to Mr. John Thomson, 528 4th Ave. E., of this town. Father of the late Tom Thomson."

Thomson's older brother, George, responding to Fraser's earlier telegram, arrived at Canoe Lake on Thursday morning, July 12. George stayed at Canoe Lake only two days, interviewing witnesses, meeting Thursday and Friday nights with the park rangers and others, who dragged the lake and patrolled its shores and portages looking for clues to Tom's disappearance. George found none of Tom's valuable belongings or any of his paintings from the previous spring at the Mowat Lodge or elsewhere. Stories he gathered suggested that a friend of Tom's, Winnifred Trainor, might know what happened to the paintings, but she was in Huntsville and her father refused to offer any cooperation.

On Friday, July 13, Robinson discovered the missing Colson canoe across the Gill Lake portage. "Found no traces of any person having been there for some time," Robinson recorded in his journal.

George asked Robinson to assist him searching Winnie Trainor's cottage. Robinson refused. Deciding he could do no more, George Thomson boarded a morning Grand Trunk train for Owen Sound on Saturday, July 14, taking none of Tom's few belongings with him.

On Monday, July 16, Tom's body surfaced in the same area where Blecher had spotted his canoe. Lake veterans said seven to eleven days is what it usually took. Late that morning, Dr. Goldwin W. Howland, MD, professor of neurology at the University of Toronto, who was staying at Taylor Statten's cottage on Little Wapomeo Island, [2] saw something out on the water in the shallow bay across from Hayhurst Point.[3] He shouted at two guides passing in a canoe to investigate. George Rowe and Lawrie Dickson, Thomson's friends, paddled over. They recognized Thomson's clothing. Rowe and Dickson towed the body the three hundred yards over to Big Wapomeo Island, where they secured it to weathered Jack pine roots in the shallow, rocky water, where it was partly shaded by overhanging branches. Leaving Dickson behind, Rowe paddled back to Mowat with

2.   Taylor Statten first visited Canoe Lake on a family canoe trip in 1913. He took a lease and built a summer home on the island in 1916. Tom Thomson hauled sand over from Sim's Pit for construction of the fireplace chimney. Later, Statten started two children's camps. Camp Ahmek for boys opened in 1921 on the northeast end of the lake. Camp Wapomeo for girls opened on the island in 1924. Fearing scandal over boys and girls sharing the same lake, his entire board of directors resigned.

news of their startling discovery. Scrim recounted the story to Robinson, who reported Thomson's death to Bartlett. In turn, Bartlett called the coroner and crown attorney in North Bay. Provincial law required a formal inquest. The coroner was a licensed physician appointed to investigate unattended deaths and report the medical findings to the crown attorney, who had the final responsibility of determining the cause of death and initiating criminal prosecution in appropriate cases. Dr. Howland sent over a flour sack, or a blanket, to protect Thomson's body against the hot noonday sun, awaiting, on Robinson's orders from Bartlett, the coroner's arrival. Bartlett ordered a search for Tom's belongings and authorized a search of Trainor's cottage. Robinson seized thirty-three of Tom's last spring paintings at the Trainor cottage. There, Robinson also found a stack of letters to Thomson from Trainor's daughter, Winnifred, one of which was unopened. "Your daughter's letter to Tom," he said to Hugh Trainor. "Keep them. Give them to her."

Meanwhile, late Monday morning, Fraser sent a perversely terse four-word telegram to Dr. MacCallum and Thomson's family: "Found Tom this morning." The *Owen Sound Sun* reported that the family received a similarly ambiguous telephone message secondhand the next morning, Tuesday, July 17, probably from Bartlett to the Ontario Provincial Police in North Bay. Subsequent telegrams from Fraser arrived on Wednesday, July 18, confirming Thomson's death.

---

3.   Blodwen Davies wrote in her book that Dr. Howland was out trolling on the lake with his small daughter at nine o'clock in the morning when the child felt something heavy on the end of her line. He took the troll and hauled up what he soon recognized as the body of a man. "I think we'll just let it go," Blodwen Davies quoted him as saying quietly as he let the line slip back over the edge of the boat. To the contrary, in her book, Audrey Saunders said Dr. Howland was sitting on the porch of the cabin when he saw an object come to the surface of the lake.

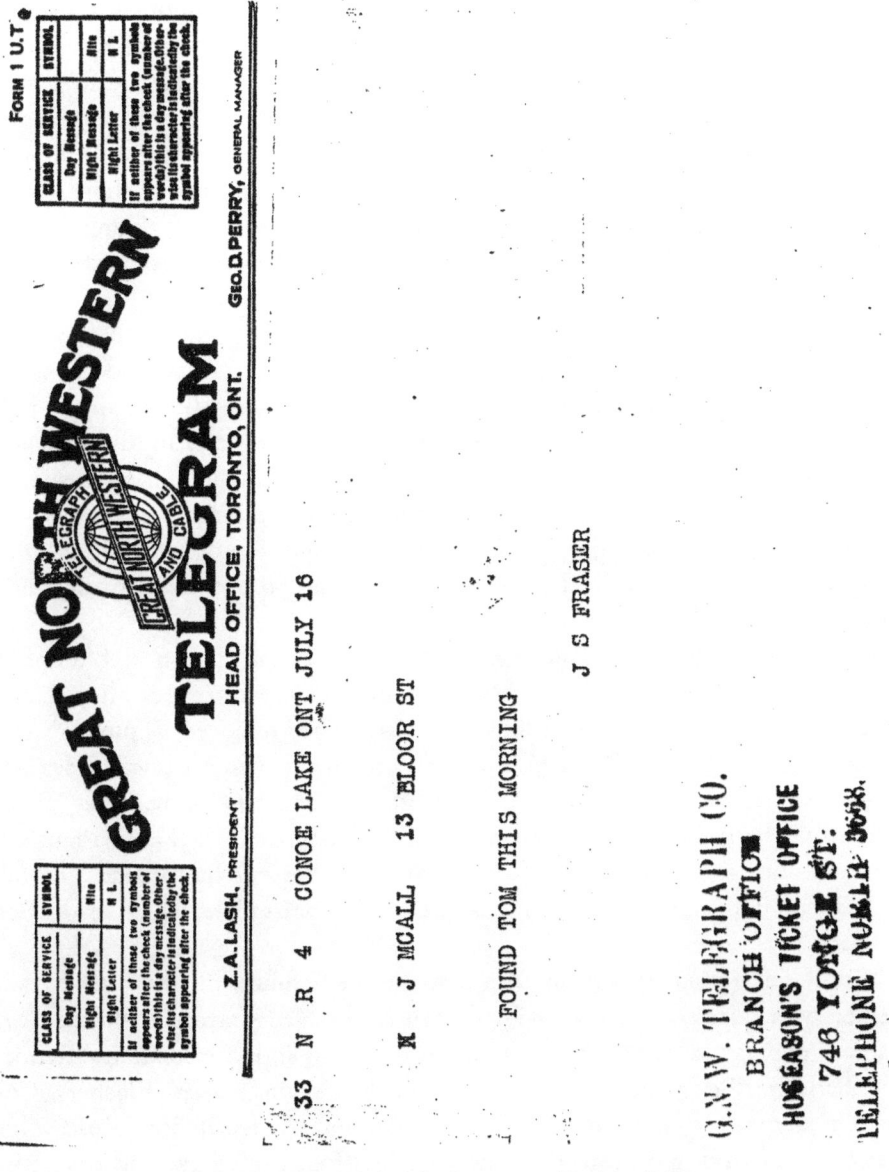

Shannon Fraser's July 16 telegram to Dr. MacCallum.

Alarmed at the condition of Tom's body, Fraser also summoned undertaker Robert H. Flavelle of Kearney and embalmer Michael R. Dixon of Sprucedale, both a few miles west of the park. They arrived on the Monday evening train. Bartlett refused to give Flavelle and Dixon permission to do their work, because the coroner was delayed. Dickson and Rowe agreed to stay at Big Wapomeo Island and watch over the body, which they had strung up to the shore. When the coroner failed to come in on the morning train, at Robinson's urging, Bartlett ordered the rapidly decomposing body removed from the water, examined by Dr. Howland, and buried in the tiny Mowat Cemetery.

According to a statement given by Dr. Howland at the inquest that evening, the body was in an advanced stage of decomposition, with its face, abdomen, and limbs swollen and blistered. Thomson had a four-inch-long bruise on his right temple and some bleeding from the right ear. He had no water in his lungs, and air was issuing from his mouth. Dr. Howland found fishing line that appeared to have been carefully wrapped around his left ankle seventeen times.[4] Nobody who was there mentioned anything unusual about the condition of his clothing or his heavy khaki trousers. (A great majority of men who go overboard from canoes and drown die with their flies open.)

In view of the body's advanced state of decomposition, Dixon used a double dose of embalming fluid, which the Thomson family disputed when Dixon sought payment from the estate for his services. They removed Thomson's gray woolen lumberjack shirt,[5] khaki trousers, and grimy white canvas shoes and pulled a burial shroud that Flavelle had brought onto the body. They placed Thomson's body into a fine oak casket and cedar box, which Flavelle had also brought, and transported it across to Mowat on Fraser's motorboat. Nobody took the time to engrave his name onto the casket's brass plate, which read, "Rest in Peace."

Canoe Lake residents organized a late-afternoon funeral at the little Mowat Cemetery, a quarter-mile northwest of Mowat Lodge. Martin H. Blecher, Sr., read an Anglican service at the graveside. It was a sad and forlorn affair, attended by Charles F. Plewman, Robinson, Dickson, Rowe, the Frasers, Blechers, Colsons, Trainors, Mr. and Mrs. Edwin Thomas, and their daughter, Rose. They lowered the casket and protective box into a six-foot-deep grave and covered it

---

4.   Accounts differ on whether this was copper trolling wire or fabric line.

5.   In stories told at Camp Ahmek, in a few books, and in a stage play, a ghostly paddler wearing a tan-yellow shirt has haunted Canoe Lake ever since Thomson's death. These stories played a major role in propelling his myth.

over. Robinson's official report of these events, submitted to Bartlett on September 7, 1917, no longer exists, according to the Algonquin Park archives.

The coroner, Dr. Arthur E. Ranney, MD, arrived on the eight o'clock train from North Bay a few hours after the burial. Dr. Ranney first took evidence from the Colsons at the Hotel Algonquin before visiting the Trainor cottage. From there, he proceeded to the dining room of Mr. and Mrs. Martin H. Blecher, Sr., and took testimony beginning at about 10 P.M., following a fine dinner of lake trout, potatoes, and hot coffee. He rendered his final verdict at about 1:30 A.M.: "Death by accidental drowning." Dr. Ranney left on the morning train. Two days later, he mailed a handwritten death certificate and burial warrant to Robinson confirming what had occurred at Mowat.

On Wednesday afternoon, July 18, Shannon Fraser received a telegram announcing that George Thomson was shipping a steel casket and sending an undertaker to bring Thomson's body back for burial in Owen Sound. The exhumation, conducted late into the night by a Huntsville undertaker, Franklin W. Churchill, had no witnesses except Fraser. His horse and wagon, formerly used as a hearse, delivered the steel casket, which had been soldered shut, to the Canoe Lake Station around midnight, where it awaited loading on a train bound for Owen Sound.[6] Dr. Howland signed a second death certificate listing the cause of death as drowning.

The family hurriedly arranged an early-Friday evening sitting of the casket in the parlor, and a private funeral service took place on Saturday, July 21, at the Knox United Church in Owen Sound. Final burial was in the family plot at Auld Kirk in Leith, a few miles west of Owen Sound, Ontario. Many years later, family friends said only that Thomson's father and a neighbor, John H. McKeen, viewed the body, verifying the identity of the corpse.

---

6.   Robinson's journal entry for July 19 noted that "[t]he body went out on evening train to Owen Sound to be buried in the family plot." William T. Little commented in his book, *The Tom Thomson Mystery*, that "in all probability it was the morning train—westbound—as the evening train was eastbound." However, because the casket arrived in Owen Sound on Friday afternoon—an eighteen to twenty-four-hour trip—timing indicates that the casket, indeed, departed on the Thursday evening train. Furthermore, Little, who proves to be not only unreliable but a minor fabricator of what happened, was wrong about train schedules. Robinson's journal noted his own arrival at Canoe Lake on April 11, 1917, on an eastbound morning train. In addition, a Thomson letter to Dr. MacCallum dated May 8, 1917, mentioned that a westbound afternoon passenger train passed Canoe Lake at 2:50 PM.

It was not until 1956 that Thomson's drowning in Canoe Lake, burial in the Mowat Cemetery, exhumation, and reburial in the Auld Kirk Cemetery became an inextricable part of his legend as Canada's greatest landscape artist. Algonquin Park's Canoe Lake, David Silcox, wrote, "has ever since been muddied by the clubfooted wading of art ghouls and plain fools, who turned Thomson's creative adventure into the pedestrian plot of a bad drugstore paperback novel."

4

Camping on Big Wapomeo Island

Kristian paddled away from The Portage Store dock on Thursday evening, a few hours after his encounter with Howard Hancock. He headed for the same camp-site on the northwest end of Big Wapomeo Island where Dickson and Rowe had towed Thomson's body and then sat up all night awaiting the coroner's arrival. As he canoed across the quiet lake in the bright moonlight, Algonquin engulfed his imagination.

After pulling ashore where he had planned, he unloaded, raised a pup tent, and tossed in his sleeping bag and backpack. He slung a line between two yellow birch trees thirty-four yards away, attached his food sack, and pulled it eleven feet up to protect it against Algonquin's many mammal marauders, which frequent campsites in the early-morning hours, when all is quiet and the occupants sleep. Out of the backpack, he retrieved a one-burner dinner of beef stew, which he ate sitting by the water. Kristian cleaned and secured his cooking equipment. He washed up naked in the lake and dragged his thirty-nine-year-old, six-foot-one-inch, 205-pound body into the tent to dig out from his backpack a strip map, a book about the Oxtongue River, and his three-ring Thomson binder from his backpack to read again, by flashlight. He turned back to the opening of the tent and spread himself out on top of the sleeping bag, as a deepening sense of repose and peace in the pervading calm and silence of the island filled him.

After going over the Oxtongue River strip map, Kristian skimmed through his well-thumbed copy of *Algonquin Adventure*, by James Dickson, who had jour-neyed up the river in 1885. Kristian read slowly, absorbing details about the waterfalls, rapids, and swifts he would encounter during his two-day trip. Early Saturday morning, he would load all of his gear into the canoe and paddle about sixteen miles down the Oxtongue River to Gravel Falls, where he would stop for the night. Sunday morning, he would paddle ten more miles into Oxtongue Lake and across to Dixie Waterford's Bar. A porter from The Portage Store would deliver his car at noon. From there, he would drive into Huntsville to do research at the local library on Tom Thomson's last spring series of paintings.

Kristian had collected prints of many of the paintings, all on trips to Algonquin. Thomson was the subject of remarkably few books and media articles, available only in Canada. He had found nothing about Thomson in Michigan libraries. When he had come to Algonquin Park each August with Tess and their daughters, they visited Ontario museums—the National Gallery of Canada in Ottawa, the Tom Thomson Gallery in Owen Sound, the McMichael Canadian Art Collection in Kleinburg, and the Art Gallery of Ontario in Toronto—looking for Thomson paintings. There, and in the art books he bought, Kristian studied Thomson's three hundred wood panel and forty-five stretched canvas paintings, a magnificent body of work Thomson completed during the last five years of his life. Kristian thought he knew all about Thomson's life and death from the biographies and art books.

Kristian opened his notebook and turned to a copy of the coroner's handwritten death certificate. He did not accept the verdict of accidental death by drowning. An experienced canoeist, Thomson would not have drowned in the calm waters of Canoe Lake on a cool and misty July afternoon because of an awkward fall over the side of the canoe when he stood to urinate or suddenly snagged a lake trout, and he would not have died lifting his canoe overheard at a portage. Moreover, such mistakes are seldom fatal, and none explains what he was doing for upwards of two hours before the Blechers spotted his overturned canoe. The location of their sighting—midway between Little Wapomeo and Big Wapomeo Islands, in the same location where his body surfaced nine days later—is hardly half a mile from Mowat Lodge, a distance easily traversed in less than thirty minutes. If he drowned, the overturned canoe would have drifted southwest in the remaining ninety minutes. Otherwise, he must have drowned moments before the Blechers arrived.

Previous biographers doubt that poachers killed him. There are two prevalent murder theories, one of which emerged many years later, from one of the last surviving Mowat residents of July 1917. The source of the story offered no personal knowledge but suggested that another woman, an old friend, long since dead, told her an eyewitness account of violence or, more improbably, a confession of manslaughter and silent complicity in Tom's death. The possibility that someone at Canoe Lake had committed his murder and escaped prosecution troubled Kristian, as it did others familiar with his story.

Unthinkable to Canadian biographers is the possibility that Thomson committed suicide. They passionately argue that no man who created such joyful, life-affirming landscape paintings in that last spring series would have killed himself even though we know now that overtly manic episodes often precede suicides. [1] The mysteries of love and art, life and death, had come together for Kristian during his divorce from Tess, throwing him into a deep, soulful crisis he believed he could resolve by completing his investigation of Thomson's drowning at Algonquin Park.

His plan began to take shape during the last spring before his divorce concluded. Kristian absorbed himself in researching the mystery of Thomson's death in exacting detail, building his cross-referenced and footnoted three-ring notebook. He organized copies of all the available documents and handwritten notes from them well into the late-evening hours in his silent apartment, night after night, waiting for the final divorce court date, which had been at nine o'clock in the morning last Tuesday, July 8. Kristian exhausted all the materials he had gathered over the years and decided to add to his trip a visit back to the library collection he had perused seven years earlier, at the Thomson Gallery in Owen Sound.

As the court date neared, he wondered whether experiencing Algonquin again would inspire in him some new understanding of what had happened. He also thought that the season's change from spring to summer would bring him to a new beginning. He knew of no other place that might provide solace from the despair of his divorce. From the pastel green of trembling aspen leaves to the pink wash of distant red maples to the white of cherry blossoms and the silvery puffs of the largetooth aspen trees, the colors of Algonquin in late spring were glorious. Kristian decided that when his divorce concluded, he would visit the library and take a trip alone through Algonquin on fast-running water, which would test the limit of his canoe skills. He picked out the Oxtongue River, a difficult route that few canoeists take, where he could find himself away from the bars, strip joints, and liquor stores back home, which distracted him without satisfying him. Frustrated with Tess's delay and deliberate indifference, Kristian focused all of his days on the business of the law firm and his nights on studying Thomson's daily series, completed during his last spring in 1917.

---

1.   A 1962 biography by R.H. Hubbard, *Tom Thomson*, said, "There is something tantalizing about the life of an artist who dies comparatively young, and in such cases there sometimes appears a feverish activity that almost compensates for a short career."

Thomson painted mostly on eight-by-ten-inch birch wood roofing shingles. Some were five-by-seven-inch end plates from fruit, vegetable, and flour crates rescued from the Mowat Lodge kitchen. Thirty-eight of his paintings that season were reproduced in a 1994 book, called, *Tom Thomson: The Last Spring*, by Joan Murray. She observed,

> They have crispness, brevity, and, most of all, a firmly resolved focus; their quality suggests that through them, Thomson was gearing up to say more, to attempt more....He was in his element, painting at his best....Even the use of a series...shows us that Thomson had begun to think more of the future—his future.

If so, struggling with his own future, Kristian puzzled why Thomson gave away, destroyed, and discarded all of these extraordinarily vivid images of spring's awakening on Canoe Lake in Algonquin Park. Whatever Thomson had thought about his future as an artist and the last spring series had been forever obscured and dispersed.

Whatever Kristian thought about love and art, life and death, crashed in upon him in the hours following his divorce. Big Wapomeo Island's quiet under the Algonquin sky persuaded Kristian to put away his thoughts, close the notebook, and put it carefully away into two extra-large freezer bags, where it would be safe against water damage in the event he dumped the canoe on the Oxtongue River. He pushed it against the bottom of his backpack.

Kristian nestled into the sleeping bag with his head sticking out of the pup tent. He looked up. The night sky over Canoe Lake was clear, and the stars were bright. A southeastern breeze was coming across the lake, rustling the tender white birches and scraggly green Jack pines around his campsite. A pair of loons out on the water cried to one another.

Campers never forget the sound. The cry of a loon at night heard from an island in the middle of an Algonquin lake while one is surrounded by a dense wall of trees is strikingly beautiful, filled with longing and loneliness, joy and sadness. He crossed his arms over his chest and fell deeply, peacefully asleep in the calm breeze still blowing southeast down Canoe Lake. An hour before dawn, a noise in the woods awoke him from a dreamless sleep. Kristian sat up and looked around. "A raccoon snuffling around, looking for the food sack," he said to himself, turning and pulling the sleeping bag around his shoulders.

5

An Evening with Howard Hancock

Dr. Ross Beckley, MD, was an obsessively neat and trim man with a well-groomed gray and white beard and piercing blue eyes. His psychiatric office in downtown Huntsville was open Tuesdays and Thursdays for evening appointments. At these sessions, he received preadolescent girls referred by the staff of St. Mary's Catholic School, teenage boys sent over by the juvenile court, drunk drivers ordered by the magistrate's court to undergo alcohol therapy, and, lately, four to seven men per month convicted under Ontario's domestic-violence law. Dr. Beckley ran a group therapy session for assaultive men from 7:30 to 8:30 P.M., every Thursday. He oversaw the hospital's suicide-prevention line. His patients included eleven suicide attempts over the previous seven years. This Friday evening, he was visiting Howard Hancock, a former drunk-driving client whose wife had died a few days earlier.

Hancock's cabin sat in a hemlock grove on the northwest shore of Canoe Lake near the Mowat Lodge site. In July 1917, this cabin was the summer home of Joseph and Eleanor O'Gorman and their sixteen-year-old daughter, Margaret Rose. Joseph O'Gorman's father was the supervisor of an early lumber camp at the park border near the railroad line running into Scotia Junction, a two-and-a-half-hour train ride away in those days. A lake south of the lumber camp was said to be named after him, although another O'Gorman served on the park staff in the early years.

Margaret Rose married into a prominent Toronto family. She and her husband, a Toronto manufacturer of building products, spent their summers here, hosting legendary picnics on the broad, well-tended grass lawn spreading across the Canoe Lake shore. Margaret Rose was mother of a boy who died at age four of tuberculosis, and a daughter, Millie, who grew into a fine, tall woman, educated overseas. Millie married a Canadian diplomat, who took assignments all over the world. They had one child, Laura Kettelman. Millie and her husband died in an airplane crash in the Belgian Congo. Margaret Rose was widowed in her early sixties. As sole surviving heir, Mrs. Laura Hancock inherited the Canoe Lake lease rights when Margaret Rose died of breast cancer at age seventy-eight. Laura and Howard Hancock used the cabin every summer, until they moved up permanently after his retirement six years ago.

Kristian knocked on the cottage door at precisely 7:56 P.M., according to the clock he saw through the doorway hanging over the fireplace. Since he refused to wear a watch, Kristian instinctively looked for clocks wherever he went. Hancock looked up from a chair by the right side of the fireplace and gestured for him to come in.

"Hello, Jon Kristian," he called loudly.

Kristian pulled open the screen door and walked into the living room. It was much larger than it looked from the outside. A great, wide fieldstone fireplace across the room rose sixteen feet to the ceiling. The room was furnished with oak chairs, side tables, and a tall desk, its slots stuffed with papers. Three windflower-print easy chairs circled the fireplace in front of an ornate Oriental rug. He turned to take in the view of the lake through a row of three unadorned windows across the front of the cabin to the left of the door. The unvarnished floor was laid with expertly fitted pine wood planks. Mr. Hancock stood and greeted Kristian with a warm handshake. Kristian, not knowing what to say, fell back on the obvious.

"Thanks again for stopping yesterday, Mr. Hancock. I was, well…it was…it was a dumb thing. I appreciate your help."

Hancock's smile and firm hand told Kristian to relax, to be at ease.

"I been stopping for folks by the side of the road for years. Don't give it a mind."

Dr. Beckley stood, and Kristian shook his hand. He was still taking in the room. On the left end of the mantle over the fireplace was a brilliantly colored five-by-ten-inch painting of a lake scene, which drew Kristian across the room. Stepping forward, he saw that it depicted a gray-green canoe, its bow rising over a small wave in quiet lake water on a misty late-spring day under a bright blue, cloudless sky. Newly burst leaves, a pale shade of green, topped the trees in the background, reflected off the lake in a noontime pose.

Kristian recognized it as a work by Tom Thomson: maybe it was one of the last of the spring series, completed in 1917. Over the last two years, for ten dollars each plus shipping on eBay, he had purchased seven reproductions of Thomson panels from the last spring series. The prints, framed, numbered, and signed in printed block letters, "Tom Thomson," he knew were semi-frauds. Thomson had never signed any of his last spring panels. They were not finished works, but frail sketches he would take back to Toronto the following winter to inspire much larger, finished works on stretched canvas. Thomson never made any lithograph prints of his panels, but Canadian art dealers sell them by the hundreds, fooling more than a few ill-informed buyers.

Original Thomson panels are valuable. In 2005, one of his small sketches sold for $370,000. In May 2003, a panel given by Dr. MacCallum to his daughter in 1914 sold for $194,500 in Vancouver. In December 2004, a New Yorker offered two Thomson panels on eBay for a minimum $5,000 bid. Following inquires from Kristian and others, the seller abruptly withdrew them from the market. Thomson prints and posters plaster the walls of the souvenir shop in The Portage Store and elsewhere east of the park, but not in shops to the west, north, or south, for what reason he never understood. Kristian had purchased several more prints at The Portage Store on the way in the previous evening.

"Is this a Tom Thomson?"

"An original. Her mother left it to Laura when she died. Actually, it's in exactly the same place it was when we first visited up here. Laura never mentioned it to me. Her mother told me the whole story one afternoon, and now I'll tell you. I suppose it's worth a few bucks these days."

Hancock's response stunned Kristian, who had always wanted to put one into his own hands.

"May I?" he said, moving to pick it up.

"Sure, why not?"

Thomson grasped the unframed panel carefully with the palms of his hands at each side and twisted his arms around to see the back. He made out the words "old Meda" in faint black letters running off the sides of the panel. Painted in neat black lettering in the lower right corner was a name Kristian recognized: "Winnie."

Kristian puzzled over the inscription. Winnie Trainor was a woman intimately linked to Thomson in the few years before his death. He placed it back on the mantle. Hancock gestured for Kristian to take the plush armchair on the far left, with the rustic oak side table and brass floor lamp behind it. Dr. Beckley had the armchair across from him. Hancock told the story of the night in May of 1917 that Margaret Rose O'Gorman acquired the sketch. Dr. Beckley, puffing on his pipe, had never heard the tale before, and thus he listened with interest.

Hancock explained that Laura Hancock's grandparents, Edwin O'Gorman, his wife, Emily, and their sixteen-year-old daughter, Margaret Rose, often dined at the Mowat Lodge in 1917. The family especially enjoyed the lodge's well-cooked roast beef, browned potatoes, rich gravy, sweet carrots, and warm bread and butter. One evening, the family joined Mr. Jack R. Riddle of London, Ontario, Mr. and Mrs. Edwin Thomas, ten-year-old Rose Thomas, and her cousin, Jack Wilkinson. While the others sat finishing applesauce cake and coffee, Margaret Rose, who would celebrate her seventeenth birthday on July 8, 1917, wandered around the room looking at paintings Thomson had propped up against the walls all around the room and offered to anyone interested. She looked at each painting, illuminated by the fireplace, lanterns, and candles. Margaret Rose had picked the panel Kristian held in his hands. Mrs. Thomas, her daughter, Rose, and Jack took home Thomson sketches too.

"Your story does not mention Winnie Trainor, whose name is written on the back," Kristian said, handing the sketch to Howard and pointing out the block lettering. "She was rumored to be his girlfriend, maybe even pregnant by him."

"I never saw that before," Hancock responded, scratching his left ear. "I don't think that Margaret Rose ever mentioned that name."

Hancock put the sketch back up on the right end of the fireplace mantle and turned to Dr. Beckley.

"I got to know this screwball doctor seven years ago, when I was arrested for drunk driving out on Route 60. Retiring and moving up here was more boring than I figured. Anyway, I ain't had more than a drop since," Hancock told Kristian, winking; then, thinking about the yellow index card, he added, "You'll like him. He's a good listener. He asks a lot of questions. Give him straight answers. Tell him what you think."

Kristian was not listening, distracted by the ceiling fan's blades. They turned so slowly; his eyes followed the brass-tipped blades going around. On one of the circling blades, a short piece of red string tied to the end flung itself away from the center. The string stood straight back, fluttering, barely perceptible as the blade moved around.

"Party balloon?" he said.

"What?"

"That string tied to the ceiling fan," Kristian said, pointing. "Right there. Must have been a balloon. What else would you tie to a ceiling fan?"

Hancock looked up but did not see the string. He closed his eyes for a moment and shook his head.

"Laura held a birthday party for her friend's seven-year-old grandchild, Andrew Dixon, five days before her death—when I was away at a plowing competition over in Pembroke," he said. "Balloons tied to the fan were a big hit with the kids. She told me over breakfast Sunday about the party."

Kristian's face screwed up for a moment.

"I wonder how she got them up there."

The blades of the fan were twelve feet up.

"Want some coffee? Water? Pop?" Hancock asked, moving away from the fireplace toward the kitchen on the right.

"Nice to meet you," Dr. Beckley said.

"Same here," Kristian said and, turning his head. "Nothing for me, thanks."

Neither yet knew the other's name. Kristian did that often—failed to introduce himself to strangers, thinking that's what men did to each other. Hancock disappeared through a small archway and turned on a light beyond. A few moments later, he returned with a coffee cup for Dr. Beckley and an ice-filled glass of water for himself. He took the armchair in the center of the room.

"What brings you up here?" Dr. Beckley asked Kristian, who hesitated, choosing to let Hancock break the silence.

Howard told Dr. Beckley of their encounter out on Route 60 and the yellow index card. Dr. Beckley perked up at the note's mention of suicide. Kristian flushed; his right hand moved into his left shirt pocket and found it empty but for a piece of white John Deere notepaper with directions to the cottage.

"I buried my wife of forty-seven years yesterday. Until then, I thought I knew about living and dying. The preacher at the service in Huntsville said something I had been thinking about when I saw you by the side of the road. He said that you learn to live from the people who die. That didn't make any sense to me until I saw that yellow card."

Kristian stared at the ceiling fan, barely listening. His mind was filled with dull images of his ex-wife, Tess, graduating from Detroit's Wayne State University in a white nursing cap and uniform and first camping with her in Algonquin and every summer since, and with their daughters, too. He remembered them best laughing and bouncing in their chairs around a weekend dinner table. How much he missed tucking them into bed late at night, one by one, kissing each on the cheek as he passed. His wrists and shoulders, too, remembered hot, sweaty hours spent digging eleven forty-seven-inch-deep postholes for the new landscaping and front porch deck he had added to their home in Rochester Hills and the seven-pound sledgehammer he had bought to break up the old concrete walkway. Kristian had left that behind too when he moved out.

"All for nothing," he blurted out.

"Pardon me," said Dr. Beckley.

"I was thinking how I lost everything in the divorce."

"Everything?" Hancock asked. "What did you lose?"

Dr. Beckley listened as Mr. Hancock continued.

"I lost my wife yesterday. You didn't lose anything that you really wanted, did you, except that yellow card? I lost it, too. Wind picked it off the dashboard and sent it out the side window."

Kristian turned to look at Hancock and noticed his frayed shirt collar. The knot in his black tie was lopsided. The handkerchief in his left front suit pocket had a hole in the corner. His eyes were brilliant blue. These things he ordinarily missed.

"You probably did the right thing getting away from her."

Hancock leaned forward, putting hands on his knees to emphasize his next statement. He looked at Dr. Beckley for a moment and turned to speak to Kristian.

"Laura's dying leaves me all alone up here. We did not have children. All of my family is gone. When we moved from Defiance, Ohio, after I retired, I left behind all my friends. I don't know anybody up here but Dr. Beckley, Art...I forget his last name. He's over at the Portage Store. And Lucky Haskins in Dwight. He's sure enough a strange character. I talk to the neighbors, but they only come up on summer weekends with their friends from Toronto."

Hancock paused, taking a long sip of ice water. He cleared his throat. His eyes glistened.

"Sad but true, you see. Laura died peeling potatoes in the kitchen over there. She was humming a tune we used to ask for when we was dancing over at the Veteran Hall in Dwight. You know the song, 'Misty'? It was a great old Errol Garner piano piece. She turned to me and smiled wide and turned away."

Dr. Beckley scratched his elbow and raised his eyebrows. Kristian remembered a line sung by Johnny Mathias, "On my own..."

Mr. Hancock continued, "Laura dropped to the floor. One minute she was humming, smiling, and the next—complete and final silence. Death took her in one furious stroke."

Kristian listened, numbing himself. He looked over at Dr. Beckley for sympathy, but he was emotionless.

"You know something? You know what?"

Kristian was ready to weep.

"When she dropped," he said, his voice falling to a clear, crisp whisper, "I thought I saw her turn toward me and smiled. I jumped up from my coffee and newspaper and stopped all of a sudden because I felt something else."

His voice rose.

"When I think about it now, the room filled up with a loving feeling that she left behind even as she was going. In her smile, I saw all the good times we'd had, Laura and me, the blazing trees in autumn, winter snows, spring thunderstorms, and summer sunsets on the lake. Everything was okay, because I knew once and for all time that she knew I loved her and that I knew she loved me."

Kristian shook his head and wondered if he understood what the old man was saying.

"Your wife is dead," Kristian said. "What else is there?"

Dr. Beckley interrupted. "What else is there, Kristian?"

The older man nodded. Kristian thought about the yellow index card, imagining it fluttering away in the early evening sky. He reached out, grabbed it back with his left hand, and crumbled it up in a tightly clenched fist. Tears welled up in his eyes as he turned to look directly at Mr. Hancock.

"My ex-wife, Tess, committed suicide the afternoon of our divorce."

6

Kristian Meets Mary Alice Gleason

Following a pleasant night on Big Wapomeo Island, Kristian loaded his canoe, pushed off south across Canoe Lake, and crossed into Bonita and Tea Lakes and the Oxtongue River. He portaged around the Tea Lake Dam, Whisky Rapids, Upper and Lower Twin Falls, and Split Rock Rapids. A few hours later, the Oxtongue River began picking up speed. Hearing the roar of Cedar Rapids ahead, Kristian angled his bright green fourteen-foot whitewater-equipped Kevlar solo canoe toward river right. The late-morning sun sparkled over the fast-moving current in the middle of the river. One hundred yards ahead, he saw a woman fly-casting, standing amidst a field of boulders jutting out from the left shore. She was singing. He brushed the dull green leaves of an overhanging branch.

"Hey, ho, there," she called out, reeling in her line sharply, out of his way.

He did not answer, but looked her over as the canoe rapidly picked up speed, drawn directly toward her. She was a slender, dark-haired woman wearing a forest-green wool pullover cap. A circle of lace topped her long-sleeved white blouse. A blue plaid skirt reached below her knees, underneath which she wore a pair of blue jeans and brown hiking boots. Kristian guessed she was in her mid-forties.

"Pretty big water ahead," she warned, pointing to the opposite side of the big rocks where she stood. "Pull up over there."

A boulder stood on river right. Through churning current, he paddled toward the left side of the boulder. As the bow swept past the boulder, he planted his paddle in the eddy current behind him, leaned hard upstream, and the canoe crisply pivoted 180 degrees, coming to an unsteady stop facing the boulder. The ease, power, and grace of the simple maneuver still fascinated Kristian.

The woman watched admiringly as the canoe bobbed in current rushing by both sides of the boulder. Kristian held the bow steady, with his paddle firmly planted in the eddy. He looked across and decided on a course. A single, long stroke pulled the boat; it leaned downstream, rocked forward and back, and bucked side-to-side, moving back into fast-moving current. Pointing upstream, he ferried across to river left, his paddle holding the canoe's angle at forty-five degrees despite heavy waves. With two strong strokes, he pulled the canoe out of the current and up into the calmer water behind the big rocks, fifteen feet from where she stood.

"Nice paddling," she called out.

He saw her dancing dark-brown eyes. Kristian smiled to himself. He could not ordinarily distinguish a woman's eye color.

"Thanks," he called back. "I'm still learning solo maneuvers."

Kristian put his paddle up, leaning it against the bow, and carefully stepped out of the right side of the canoe into the shallows. He came ashore, grabbed the canoe's bowline, and pulled it halfway out of the water. He then jumped across the boulders to come up closer and turned to look downstream. Ten yards ahead, the current roared, churning up a line of impressive, angry rollers and rising haystacks. Kristian tried to remember the name of the song she had been singing.

"Was that Pat Metheny you were singing?" he said.

"Yep. 'Secret Story.'"

"'Facing West'?"

"I think so," she responded, recognizing the other Metheny song reference. She paused and then said, "You seem to be heading south."

"I guess you could say that," he laughed. "Here I am a week after my divorce taking a canoe trip on the Oxtongue River."

He always talked more easily to women.

"You don't look divorced."

"I feel divorced."

"You get what you deserved?"

"I got nothing."

"You got everything you deserved."

"Yeah," he admitted, "divorced."

He put his hand out.

"Northway Jon Kristian," he said, adding a nickname he had given himself seventeen months earlier, on his last trip to Algonquin Park with Tess.

"I'm Mary Alice Gleason. Call me Mary Alice." She reached out and shook his hand firmly.

"Is there a portage around that big stuff?"

"Here, let me show you," she said, expertly bounding across the rock field to the left shore, where she propped her fishing pole against a black spruce tree and darted up a narrow path into the trees. He followed. The path turned sharply to the right and divided about twenty yards from the river. Up one path, about a hundred yards away, he made out the outline of an old two-story clap wood house with a screened-in back porch. Two large brown shorthaired dogs barked in the yard. Mary Alice stopped, turned back toward him, and gestured.

"Up there's my jewelry shop."

She pointed down the other path.

"That way is the portage around what they call Cedar Rapids. It's about fifty meters long."

Kristian hesitated, looked up at the sun's position in the sky, decided it was noon, and looked back. She stood with one hand on her left hip, the other hand across her midsection, grasping her side. Her right forearm lifted her breasts and tightened the blouse around them.

"Maybe I should break for lunch."

She stared at him. He waited. The rapids rumbling beyond punctuated the silence between them.

"I've got two brownies up there," she said, pointing up toward the house. "Cleaned and filleted. Ready for the pan. What do you say?"

Kristian smiled, nodded, and they headed up together. Mary Alice was a perky and compact—five-foot-two, 137 pounds, with brown, ill-kempt hair curled at the shoulders, bouncing below her cap as she went ahead. She walked with the strength and grace of a dancer. She was self-possessed—able to land a speckled trout, dress it for the freezer, cook it in the pan, and offer it up for lunch.

"I like this woman," he said to himself.

As they emerged from the woods, the dogs yelped, jumped at him happily, and greeted Mary Alice with open-mouthed snuffles and low mutterings.

"Rocky and Horowitz," she said, rubbing their snouts. The dogs sniffed and lifted their heads for Kristian's hand. He scratched them behind the ears.

"Collie and shepherd mix. They're okay with you."

She continued on to the back porch and he followed. Working in the kitchen, Mary Alice explained that she had inherited the house from her father, a salvage boat captain on the Great Lakes. Robert Barrett Gleason, as listed on the deed of conveyance she got from him later, had played Texas Hold'em poker with the crew and two wealthy Canadian investment bankers he had picked up in Owen Sound for a voyage across the Trent-Severn waterway, from Georgian Bay to Lake Ontario.

"The long, slow trip moved through two of the world's highest hydraulic lift locks, went abroad a marine railway, and passed through two sets of flight locks and thirty-six conventional locks," Mary Alice said. "The seven-day trip across Ontario was a financial bonanza for Captain Bob, my Dad. On the last day, I was dealing what turned out to be the final hand of poker. Captain Bob landed the deed to this cabin with a heart flush, beating the Toronto tech-sector specialist, who went all in holding two queens."

She flushed with excitement.

"This guy went all in for thirty-four thousand dollars."

She paused and dealt an imaginary card.

"The queen of hearts turned on the river."

Kristian laughed.

"That took a lot of nerve."

"Captain Bob was a Navy Seal and deep-sea diver, one of the best in the United States," Mary Alice whispered. "He helped position the super-secret sensors that sent signals back from the Soviet submarine base at Sevastopol to the U.S. Navy throughout the Cold War. He was pretty good at poker, too."

Mary Alice said she moved up seven years ago, the spring after her father passed away from colon cancer at age seventy-four. Luckily, the investment banker had winterized the plumbing, which survived a particularly cruel season.

"I had to replace a leaky front porch roof and the flooring underneath. Otherwise, the cabin came furnished, with items dating back to 1917, when visitors up from Toronto and across Ontario used it as a fishing base or romantic vacation spot. It's been a good home. The jewelry business keeps me pretty busy."

Mary Alice offered him a cold beer, Molson Canadian.

"Don't mind if I do," he said. He let it sit.

"What makes a woman like you happy and healthy alone out in the woods, away from TV, radio, and newspapers?"

Mary Alice smiled broadly. Then she demurred. She checked the fillets, turned down the propane, and reset the lid.

"They'll be a couple more minutes."

Northway decided to ask a direct question.

"What do you do with your spare time?"

"I do whatever I want to," she said.

Kristian did not know what to say next.

She served lunch, and the conversation eventually came back to her story.

"I grew up in Alpena, Michigan. Got beat up at home and at Alpena High School and escaped to the University of Michigan. All of my roommates moved out before the semester ended. Don't ask why. I graduated when they kicked me out, went back to Ann Arbor for the Science Fiction Society meetings once a month, and got a job as a pharmacy technician at the Detroit Medical Center Building and Receiving Hospital in Detroit. I remember listening over and over to Tangerine Dream on the car's cassette player there and back. I quit when I met a goldsmith apprentice named Peter Crowe at a jewelry store in Fairlane Mall. He taught me what he knew and loaned me his tools, and I got to be good—even better than him. He had no gusto."

Kristian pushed his empty plate away.

"Did you love Peter?"

She stared at him.

"We were friends who looked after each other. It happens. He was sick, a diabetic. Could never get a hard-on. Not that I didn't try."

Mary Alice stacked her plate on his, gathered up the silverware in her fist, and stood.

"You want to know anything else?"

Kristian pushed away from the table, staring at the still-unopened Molson for a moment, and stood.

"I'm sorry," he replied. "I want to know more about you, Mary Alice."

He walked over to the stove and moved the two pans she had used for the fish and potatoes over to the sink, where she scrubbed them all clean. After he dried them with a U of M kitchen towel, she put them away.

"Let me show you the place."

She took his right arm and led him into the front of the house. It was a cluttered showroom of knickknacks—Canadian woodwork, pottery of all kinds and shapes, string hangings with feathers, painted plates, teacups and saucers, Tom Thomson prints, and a small, neat jewelry counter. Mary Alice positioned herself at the cash register as he wandered around.

"What did you expect?"

"Do you get a lot of tourists?"

"Yeah, I should be open. It's Saturday, you know."

"You were out fishing."

"I make my own hours."

"Spend the afternoon with me?" Kristian asked.

She took his arm and led him back into the kitchen, where they sat.

"Okay, tell me: How come you're paddling down my river?"

Kristian told Mary Alice about his first trip to Algonquin Park, canoeing and camping in morning mist, afternoon clouds, and evening stars, the Tom Thomson mystery, his divorce from Tess, and her suicide.

"Why did she kill herself?" she asked finally.

"I don't know."

"You feel guilty?"

"Yes."

"You're not."

"I know."

It was 4:30 P.M., according to the kitchen clock. Mary Alice burst out of her chair.

"I should get some steaks for dinner. That suit you fine?"

Kristian nodded.

"How about you get the grill going, and I'll get some good Scotch?"

"Okay by me."

Mary Alice pulled on her boots and was out the door before either of the dogs resting on the porch roused to go with her. Attractive, shapely, direct, and honest. Kristian was definitely attracted to this woman. She was as fresh as the air over Big Wapomeo Island campsite at Canoe Lake. She made him feel like his nickname again, renewed. He reminded himself to tell her he had quit drinking, remember the night he had lapsed after his ex-wife's funeral, ripping the Thomson poster from the wall, shattering the glass, and cracking the frame into pieces. Before she returned, he cleaned the grill and started a fire.

The sky turned pink across the horizon, and he watched as it faded during the many minutes she fussed over two New York strip steaks. First, she brushed them with olive oil, and then she meticulously peeled and crushed a dozen garlic cloves with the blade of a wide butcher's knife—a process that took eleven minutes according to the clock on the stove. She generously spread the garlic paste over both sides, added salt and pepper, and then covered each with fresh, fragrant basil leaves from a well-manicured herb garden by the back door. Mary Alice set the steaks on a plate and pushed it aside.

"They'll marinate for a few minutes."

Next, she dabbed butter over two baking potatoes and wrapped them in aluminum foil. She trimmed two handfuls of asparagus and set a pot of lightly salted water on the stove to boil. Gesturing for him to follow, she took the potatoes out to the grill, where she pushed them into the hot coals.

"We'll let them cook for thirty minutes."

Mary Alice pulled him out of the yard, through the porch, and back into the kitchen, where she invited him to sit.

"Why did the marriage fail?"

Kristian abruptly confessed that he was a recovering alcoholic.

"God grant me the serenity to accept the things I cannot change," he told her, reciting the prayer that begins all meetings of Alcoholics Anonymous, "courage to change the things I can, and wisdom to know the difference."

She put away the Scotch and the twelve-pack of Molson.

"My dad was a stone drunk. It didn't hurt his poker sense, but it lulled other players into underestimating him."

She and Kristian left no scraps for the two eagerly awaiting dogs of the steak, potatoes, or Caesar salad she had made tableside in a spinning bowl, egg yolks and all. He spent a long evening with her after dinner, sitting on the second-story sun porch under the Algonquin sky, telling stories about Tom Thomson. She left for her bed, alone, at 2:45 A.M. He awoke from the sofa at 4:30 A.M. to have a couple of cigarettes and a cup of coffee. Kristian then fell back asleep, dreaming of wrapping himself around Mary Alice, cupping each of her soft, full breasts, his thighs pressed against hers, his lips softly caressing her ears and neck.

7

Paddling the Oxtongue River

While she cooked breakfast, Kristian and Mary Alice shared their experiences on the Oxtongue River. He told her how he had paddled the river's upper section with his two elder daughters, Shelley and Sheila, when they were eleven and seven years old. The river is named after the lake into which it flows a few miles southwest of the park. Exploring upstream, surveyor Alexander Murray named the lake during a geological expedition in 1853. "Because of the shape," he explained.

The Oxtongue River twists and turns, stretching the ten miles from Canoe Lake to Oxtongue Lake into twenty-two miles or more, with numerous portages. Most of the upper section is easy. Below Park Lake, outside Algonquin, it offers challenging but runnable whitewater. Even though it is never more than a few thousand yards from Route 60, it is remarkably quiet. This is because few paddlers take this route, even in July, since it flows out of the park. Still farther along, it passes into Muskoka Cottage Country at the Lake of Bays on the east side of Huntsville, a trip of twenty miles through isolated, dangerous rapids. Kristian arranged to pick up his car at Dixie Waterford's Bar on Oxtongue Lake.

He had stayed inside the park with Shelley and Sheila. At Upper Twin Falls, near the park's west gate on Route 60, they landed bow first at one of the more harrowing portages many miles upstream from Mary Alice's cabin. They went off river left in deep, slow-moving water above a narrow, three-foot waterfall, dropped two feet, turned sharply to the left, and dropped another foot or more, rushing over a jagged field of rocks.

"I watched helpless as the canoe slowly spun 180 degrees in the light current, carrying the stern, where he sat, out over the brink."

"I dropped the paddle across my lap. Then I reached out, grabbed onto a tree root, and pulled tight to shore, steadying the canoe," he told Mary Alice. "I don't think they knew what danger we were in. It's not that we would have been badly injured, but we sure could have wrecked the canoe and lost our camping gear and food. It all happened so gently."

"'Everybody, please keep still,' I urged my daughters. I told Sheila, first, and then Shelley, to turn around carefully, come back toward me, and climb out while I held the gunwale fast to the root. I was shaking as they crawled over the packs and tents and stepped out. Once we were safely on shore, I hugged each of them and sighed to myself at how near we'd come to disaster."

Over bacon, scrambled eggs, and toast, Mary Alice went through the strip map with Kristian. She said the lower section of the Oxtongue River he planned to paddle that morning was eight miles of constant twists and turns—a canoeist's nightmare. There were also frequent deadheads—logs jammed against underwater obstruction. He would encounter a few ledges, souse holes, and maybe a sweeper. Personal experience over the years had taught him about the dangers lurking over even small river-wide ledges. Fast-moving water falling over a rock in the middle of a river creates an up-and-down circulating current, creating an air-filled hole that river runners call a souse hole, into which a canoe and its occupant literally fall. Ordinarily, the current sweeps them out but some souse holes are "keepers," because the circulating downstream wave pushes the swamped canoe and swimmer back into the hole repeatedly. A paddler might try to swim out sideways, back into the current, or shed his or her life jacket and dive deep into a bottom current to escape. Nevertheless, it is difficult for anyone to escape a souse hole that stretches fully across a river, because there is no edge to it in that case. Experienced canoeists pull up and carry around all river-wide ledges and dams.

Mary Alice told him of a young woman who drowned under a fallen tree a half a mile south of Gravel Rapids. The Oxtongue River is narrow and winding, with many trees sprawling precariously along its banks. In spring flood, the current undercuts some of those trees and they drop over into the river, creating an extremely dangerous condition river runners call a "sweeper," which novice paddlers are likely not to recognize. Lean the wrong way against a fallen tree's branches, even in low water, and the current pushing against the upstream side of the canoe will quickly pull it over, dumps its paddlers, and push them underwater and into the branches. That was how the girl died.

Mary Alice pointed out the dangers awaiting him on his eight-mile downstream trip, suggesting where to take the eddy out and where to ferry across for a safer run through the ten rapids and swifts. She pointed to one particular portage well above the dangerous Ragged Falls, which plunges down a ragged 120-foot slope and curves to the left about a mile before the river passes under Route 60, two miles before his trip's end on the west Shore of Oxtongue Lake.

"Continue, Northway, but only if you're nuts," she warned, smiling.

He objected.

"Look, the Oxtongue turns sharply north past his marked portage well above Ragged Falls, making a hairpin right and another left to a last second—but safe—take-out on the left side of the river, guarded by a one-foot-tall wall of boulders above the brink of the main chute," Kristian said. "I've been up there on a trip to the park with Tess and the girls. We watched a group of Boy Scouts pass the marked portage and, one by one, hugging river left in low water, run two short swifts and eddy into the unmarked takeout."

"The scoutmaster was taking a huge risk," she warned. "If you dump in the two swifts downstream from the portage, you could go over the falls. In high water, that river exit is extremely dangerous. A flooded current washes out the eddy reaching up, over, and around the boulder wall. A canoeist who didn't know what he was doing could end up going right over Ragged Falls."

8

Running Whitewater

Kristian was still learning to paddle solo, but he was enjoying it, kneeling in the center of his responsive canoe. The canoe leaned to the left, on which side he held his paddle. A year earlier, Kristian had learned to balance a leaning solo canoe by using the Canadian stroke, an elegant and efficient way to move through the water in a straight line. It is a practiced art, unmentioned at Michigan canoe-rental stations. The stroke requires an odd, full twist of the wrists at the end of each stroke. The path of the paddle's power stroke traces a *J* in the water, and the canoeist knifes the paddle forward under water with the working face flat and facing up. The Canadian stroke both powers and steers the canoe.

Running fast and true, he reached the Hardwood Rapids in a few minutes. It appeared around a left bend. He pulled ashore to decide whether it was runnable and, if so, to survey a course. Paddling with light gear in low water, Kristian decided to make the run. Canoeing whitewater is like riding a galloping horse through rough terrain—you have to stay with the bumps and grinds, bracing the canoe with a paddle in the water. It is not intuitive. Whitewater paddling demands confidence in one's mental and physical precision, and that comes only with practice. It requires the use of a wide variety of forward and backward strokes: bow cut, draw, pry, cross draw, sideslip, low, and high brace. Once into whitewater, a paddler is committed to making the full downstream run to either make the full run in the canoe or in the water swimming—feet forward—down to the next take-out. The relentlessness of a whitewater rapid took him by surprise the first few times he dumped, while taking lessons from experts.

When Shelley was seventeen, Kristian signed up for a five-day novice whitewater course at the Madawaska Canoe School, forty-five miles east of the park. Then, last summer, when Sheila turned seventeen, he signed them up for a three-day-weekend course. Both courses were designed for parent and child teams. Twice he dumped Shelley in the warm water of the Madawaska River. Testing their bracing skills near shore below the Bark Lake Dam, an instructor pushed hard on the left side of the bow. Kristian and Shelley lurched in response, paddles flaying as the canoe dumped over. The current grabbed and carried them thirty yards away in seconds. The both of them found the helplessness frightening but exhilarating. Later, in the lower section of Siberian Ripples, they made a perfect run into the entrance to the rapid, but he inexplicably dumped the canoe over on the left side of an innocent-looking wave in mid-river, which the instructors had warned against running. Kristian held onto his paddle and his daughter as the rough river carried them to calmer water at the bottom. Terrified at seeing the confidence in her father rattled, Shelley insisted on walking around Gravel Pit Rapids on the last day, but she let him put in below for a gloriously long paddle down in very fast water.

He never did dump Sheila at Palmer Rapids, a world-famous stretch of whitewater ideal for training novice canoeists. It was a misty day in July. That afternoon, refreshed by lunch, they ran the lower section, taking the final sharp-left bend then over a five-foot drop with all the skill of a veteran tandem.

"Let's do it again!" Sheila pleaded. Shaky with excitement, Kristian begged off, filled with fear and respect for whitewater paddling. Perfection is not required to run a whitewater river, but even small mistakes can be unforgiving, dumping a paddler over.

Leaving Hardwood Rapids, Kristian paddled strong and steady for six hundred yards downstream. Past another swift, the Oxtongue took Kristian to a portage right, close to the brink of Gravel Falls. He heard the awesome roar of the waterfall, but all he saw was the line across the top. Walking the portage trail down and back up, he saw that the falls took three drops totaling thirteen feet and turned sharply left at the bottom, where it tumbled into Gravel Rapids. Only an expert canoeist could safely negotiate the drops and make the turn without spilling. Two kayakers were playing in the currents below Gravel Falls as he passed left on the short portage trail. After looking it over carefully, he plunged back into the river below the falls and ran Gravel Rapids. It was such fun that he walked back up the steep three-hundred-yard trail to take a second ride down.

The next section of the river meandered for two miles or more beside tree-covered cliffs before reaching awesome Ragged Falls. Kristian took the safer marked portage on river left. It was an awkward take-out for Kristian, the water rocking and bopping the canoe at the muddy exit site. He hauled his backpack and canoe up onto his shoulders and headed off into the woods on the portage trail. Along the way, he took a detour, going to the top of the falls. The portage Mary Alice warned against trying to reach from that approach looked safe enough in low water.

Ragged Falls is well named. A huge gray log, two-feet thick, juts out from the middle of the main chute, which pours thunderously into a violently foaming pool eight feet below, dumping steeply into another, and another, and another, as its curves twenty-five degrees to the left. There it sweeps right, over sturdy boulders and underwater remnants of a century-old logging chute. The cascading water, boulders, and debris would tear apart canoe and canoeist on the 128-foot drop.

The 380-yard trail down to the bottom of Ragged Falls first goes steeply uphill through a rock cut and then steeply downhill to the put-in. The weather had allowed the trail to dry these last few days, but any rain would render it treacherously slick. Today, the portage was easy enough that Kristian could carry his canoe and gear down in one trip. The subsequent paddle to and under Route 60 on to Oxtongue Lake was serene. A great blue heron flew over the water ahead of him six times during the final sixty-five-minute section. He paddled north over to the Algonquin Outfitters Store, where he stopped on the east shore to look over its book and map collection. Then he paddled south down Oxtongue Lake to his take-out.

9

Kristian and Tess Visit the Barron Canyon

Kristian took Tess to see Algonquin's Barron Canyon the last weekend of September, a few months before he filed for divorce. She quit partway up, and he went on without her. They had traveled all the way across the park. He wanted to see from above what they had missed seeing from below on the Barron River the summer before. It was a trip they made with all four girls crammed into one over-loaded ninety pound, eighteen-foot aluminum canoe.

The family paddled across Grand Lake and camped on the eastern shore of Stratton Lake, in a white pine forest. The next day, they made the paddle and trek down the Barron River. Doing triple-duty at each portage wore him out by the end of his first walk down to the bottom of Brigham Chute. There, he saw nothing but a still-longer paddle. He looked at the sky and over at his daughters playing in the splashing water. He looked back to Tess, relaxing on a boulder, for some signal that she would help. She sat firm, her eyes communicating refusal.

Kristian reluctantly announced that they should turn back for their campsite on Stratton Lake. It was too late to keep going, he explained. She shook her head and turned back up the portage trail. They made a slow trek, taking the well-named Ooze Lake route. Before leaving that morning, their ice supply having melted away, he had left a package of chicken fryer parts in a mesh bag offshore in seven-foot-deep water. Upon their late-twilight return, he retrieved the chicken for dinner, but the odor was terrible. Instead, he fixed what his four daughters would later refer to as the "dark dinner," consisting of chipped beef on toast, cooked in darkness. Relaxed and clean in their pajamas after yet another romp in the lake, the four girls spread out in two tents aligned to the left and right of Tess, who slept alone in her tent in the center. He had a pup tent across the campfire.

Finally, Kristian ate his dinner alone by firelight, engulfed by Algonquin's grandeur while Tess and his daughters slept in the quiet pine forest. Afterwards, he carried the chicken fryer parts up into the woods and tossed them away. Algonquin's night sky spread out across the shore, where he went to sit against a white pine with his map and flashlight. After close examination, he saw how near he had come to Barron Canyon, which was only a few minutes' paddle from Brigham Chute. He deeply regretted turning around and forfeiting this long trip's goal. Going back tomorrow meant having to do it all over again. Disappointment filled him as the mournful sound of a train grew. That year, the Canadian National Railroad still traversed the eastern side of the park. Stratton Lake campers would always remember its nightly passing. The powerful, resonating drone of the diesel engines, the clomp and wail of the rail cars echoing off the east and west sides of the lake, noise slowly growing and spreading as it approached and rumbled past, dimming and dying to a whisper as the train sped away. He struggled into his pup tent and sleeping bag and fell into a fitful sleep.

At three o'clock in the morning, a wail and a screech pierced the silence, waking Kristian and his family. A fierce battle ensued one hundred yards away. Kristian's flashlight focused on a large hawk and a larger fisher, one of Algonquin's many mammalian predators, struggling over the discarded chicken parts. The fight lasted only seconds. The loser flew away, taking a hard-won piece or two. The winner stayed, dining quietly. The next morning, Kristian found no chicken, no bones, no plastic container, no cellophane wrapper, and no evidence of the night's event.

He took Tess back alone to Barron Canyon, trying to recapture for her the excitement and anticipation she had felt at Brigham Chute before turning around. Part-time volunteers from the Friends of Algonquin Park, whose work season ended September 1, maintained the rocky trail up from the parking lot. Kristian was a proudly contributing member of the Friends of Algonquin Park, and a listing of donors he had discovered in the park visitor center earlier that day noted him prominently.

"What did that cost us?" Tess had asked.

He explained that the donation of four hundred dollars was not only a tax deduction for him but also an act of reverence toward a place he considered sacred.

"That's no excuse."

She looked away from the contributor's book in the lobby toward the visitor center's bookstore, where she picked out gifts for her sisters and brothers.

The autumn colors of Algonquin were spectacular this late September. They arrived at exactly the right time. The scarlet and gold forest tapestry of the season was both brilliant and brief, lasting only a few days. The drive from the visitor center through the park's highland hardwood forest was stunning—the sugar maples set blazing red and orange against the stern softwood black spruce, standing tall and sturdy against the lakeshores. About halfway between Barrie's Bay and Pembroke, he stopped near an exquisite old Polish Catholic Church. He had never experienced anything as beautiful and as overwhelmingly large as the sweep of color across the horizon from church's hilltop vantage. The trip from there to Algonquin's unguarded Sand Lake gate took another two hours. Kristian marveled, again, at the scope and grandeur of the park.

The trail out of the empty parking lot sloped gently downhill for a few hundred yards before turning upward. It crossed through a craggy, rocky, pristine white pine forest. It was an arduous trail up to the vista. At two-hundred eighty-one pounds, Tess was struggling.

Kristian let her go ahead, her trail guide in hand. He followed. Tess huffed along for a while and stopped, her hands on wide hips. She turned to him.

"Do you really want to do this?" she asked, anguish filling her eyes.

"Of course," he said with a chuckle. "I'm Northway Jon Kristian!"

She turned away and continued up the trail. When she stopped to rest again a short while later, Kristian stopped too. It was a much more strenuous walk than he had expected. As he looked up, the end was nowhere in sight. "I don't think I want to do this!" she wailed, heading off again. The Barron Canyon trail led upwards still. He followed. She stopped again and bent over at the waist, grimacing.

"You're doing fine! What a beautiful walk! Look around!" he shouted, realizing that his enthusiasm for Algonquin Park, which had inspired Tess on earlier trips, left her feeling ridiculed today.

"We'll rest a minute," he reassured her. "Wait and rest."

He waited as she rested. Both remained standing. She refused a drink or sandwich from the pack Kristian carried.

"It took so long to get here," he pleaded.

"Take me home."

"Northway will take you up."

"If I cannot go on myself, I do not want to go."

"It's not that far. Come on. Please come up with me." Tess refused his hand and turned away. The tall white pines shrouded them in shadow and trapped still, stale air. He looked up ahead. She looked down below. To go on into sunlight at the top of the ridge would have put them face to face with its brilliance, something they wanted to avoid.

She turned and said, "I can't go on."

She started down.

"I can and will go on," he said, continuing up. It was a remarkably painful moment for them both, a married couple with four children—she going down, he going up, the distance between them growing with each step.

Tess waited for him in the car, still struggling for breath when he returned from the top of Barron Canyon. He tossed his daypack into the trunk and slid into the driver's seat.

"Did you get any photographs?" she asked plaintively.

He had forgotten about the camera tucked into the daypack. He wished he could describe it for her. The vista south from the cliffs above Barron Canyon looked along and across the Barron River into the dark-green white pine forest, generously sprinkled throughout with many brilliantly colored orange, red, and gold hardwoods. The river sparkled four hundred feet below sheer black cliffs. Yellowing and reddish bushes clung to the canyon walls.

"Cameras capture a moment of time," he tried to explain. "The Barron Canyon's beauty is timeless."

Seven months later, after Kristian filed for divorce, on a pleasantly warm evening in early April, she told him about the breast cancer. Tess called his apartment and said she had to talk. She had never called before that and never called after. When he arrived and parked in the driveway, she burst out the front door and across the wooden porch onto the lawn. Kristian stepped out of the car warily. He hardly recognized her. The woman's brow was deeply furrowed, her eyes darted about, her lips stiffened, and her voice quavered. She paced a wide circle. He stood bewildered on the brick walkway he had installed the previous summer. She widened the distance, still pacing a large circle, speaking rapidly.

"I need you to take care of the girls."

She circled.

"I will be in the hospital for three days."

Tess moved counterclockwise. He saw the time on her stove through the kitchen window: 7:38 P.M.

"I have a tumor in my left breast."

Her words came out in a staccato rhythm, like gunshots. "It has to be removed," she spat. "You...I...you..." she struggled. "I...you...I..."

The silence was long; she was deep into herself, circling around him.

"You...you have to come and be with my girls."

"Mine—my daughters!" he thought.

Kristian stood quietly as she continued pacing, knowing nothing he could say would change anything. Breast cancer comes or not upon the best and brightest as he thought, they were

She paced around the front lawn across the dry, unmowed grass.

Of course Kristian would come back to watch over his four daughters. Underlying the obvious demand to the father of her children was the woman he had married. He moved toward her. She moved away, continuing to move in counter-clockwise circles. She stopped. He waited for her to speak.

"I've been thinking about this for a long time," Tess began. "You're going to have to make a lot of changes before I ever let you come back here. Everything that is wrong in this marriage is your fault."

She did not wait for his response and started pacing again.

"Everything?" he said, searching for her eyes.

Tess slowed and came to a stop. She looked back at him. He saw nothing in her steady gaze. He waited. She said nothing. Kristian felt liberated at that moment to be himself with her. Kristian had learned long ago that Tess replied to personal questions only if she had a prepared answer. She had none to what he decided to ask. It was a brilliant stroke in the conversation, which Kristian made in a moment of high realization and profound sadness.

"How are you feeling?"

She replied by striding straight back into the house, where two girls ducked from under kitchen curtains at the windowsill. Kristian wanted to wave, but the remaining Kristian wanted to duck down away from his daughters' gaze.

"Of course I'll take care of the girls!" Kristian cried out as the screen door slammed shut.

As Tom Thomson traipsed about Algonquin Park in 1915, Albert Einstein proved that each of us has his or her own personal measure of time, depending on where one is and how fast one is moving. That spring, after learning of her breast cancer, the divorce lawyers adjourned their case. Time stopped as they stopped moving, awaiting her surgery, weeks of recovery, chemotherapy, and rounds of tests. Kristian sent a bouquet of yellow wildflowers to her hospital room after the operation. Tess put them first among the others on a bedside table, and he noticed. Neither said anything, the pending divorce having armored over their hearts. During the next few days, the wildflowers withered and fluttered to the floor. Nurses scraped up petals each morning. Time did not stop long enough for them to find each other again.

Kristian awoke every morning, got the girls off to school, and went to work, as he had when he lived there with Tess. When she came home, he moved out again. Tess never told him one way or the other about the outcome of the cancer surgery, but she did have expensive plastic surgery to restore the breast, the cost of which he accepted in the divorce negotiations. Living alone and getting on with his law practice, which was booming with new clients and opportunities, Kristian decided that she could have whatever she wanted in their houseful of furniture and furnishings, collected over seventeen years. He had already taken what little he wanted: a few CDs, his books, remembrances from the girls, some Thomson art prints, photographs of the girls, a clock, a radio, a dresser, a few pots and pans, plates, utensils, knifes, and some towels and bedding.

Tess was square jawed and her speech was crisp as she stood in front of the judge on Monday, July 8, answering her lawyer's self-serving questions about the divorce settlement. Kristian did not hear anything in her words or voice that indicated what she would do in a few hours.

"Well, you got what you wanted," she said finally, by the courthouse elevator.

Kristian asked a passing lawyer, "What time is it?"

10

Dixie Waterford's Bar

Kristian pulled his canoe on shore and leaned it vertically against a weathered black cherry tree. Dixie Waterford's Bar was a ten-minute walk from Oxtongue Lake. The dusty path up to Oxtongue Lake Road sucked all the moisture out of Kristian's wet boots. At the road, a shorthaired tan-colored dog trotted by on the shoulder, wagging its tongue. Heat radiated off the asphalt roadway. He passed eleven old houses, all dingy white and tightly closed up, with curtains drawn, doors closed, and windows tightened down. He saw nobody in the yards mowing the dry, brown lawns or hanging laundry. A half-filled plastic baby bottle stood on one of the porch banisters of a clapboard house seven blocks from the lake. He thought he heard a baby crying. A badly rusted red gasoline can was overturned at the far corner of the porch, a pair of gray-blue leather work gloves carelessly draped over the railing.

These houses filled Kristian's mind with the same sadly ominous feeling he got visiting the mean streets of Detroit on Saturday mornings when he went to mow the lawn of his grandmother's abandoned house. His mother and Aunt Alice had moved ailing Grandma Jones into a seniors' residence when Kristian was seventeen years old. Her family struggled over what to do with the house. Kristian remembered an old black man sitting on the front porch next door swatting flies with a rolled-up newspaper as he paced back and forth with Grandma's electric lawn mower. The man's eyes smoldered with hatred.

Sweat dripped off Kristian's forehead and upper lip. He passed a post office and a liquor store south of Route 60, both closed this Sunday at noon. The next building was Dixie Waterford's Bar, which was a white cinderblock building with eye-level windows of dirty frosted glass, pulled shut. His car was not among the seven he counted in the parking lot. In the window on the left side of the door-way, a tube of red-orange neon that always seemed to be on bent into a single word in cursive: *Bar*. Dixie Waterford tried to find the sign's switch but never had, and she had forgotten about it. The outer door was a rusted metal screen with wood trim painted dark green. The inner door was heavy varnished oak with three glass panels angled from the upper left to the lower right. The inner window displayed stickers from VISA, MasterCard, and Tourism Canada.

The bar was singularly uninviting. It scared off tourists visiting the area during the spring fishing and summer canoeing seasons. Despite the stickers, Dixie did not accept credit cards. She hated paperwork and did not understand it anyway. The only drinkers that she welcomed paid in cash, which every evening after closing she deposited in the Scotiabank where Dixie was setting up retirement accounts. Dixie Waterford promised herself she was not going to fall, drunk and homeless, on the streets of Toronto in her old age, like her mother had.

Kristian pulled the door open and stood still a few moments, letting his eyes adjust to the darkness as it closed up against his rump with a slap. A woman in her late thirties sat at the far right end of a well-worn red Formica bar across from a yellowed refrigerator and a dark orange metallic cash register illuminated by a small brass lamp, both of which were in need of a polish. The woman was Dixie Waterford, dressed in a red silk blouse and blue jeans, her hair trimmed by her neighbor, old Louise Addelson, who used a dinner-sized soup bowl as a guide every Sunday evening after closing. Dixie wore no makeup other than bold red lipstick. Her dark-brown eyebrows were thick and broad. She wore pants because she'd given up shaving after the death of her late husband, the former owner, Bradford Gettings. Wearing anything else was too much trouble, and she had no reason to be worried what the men in her life thought, because there were none she cared about except the seven in baseball hats, overalls, and flannel who were sitting evenly spaced across the thirty-four-foot-long bar, eleven feet from the door. The heads of all seven turned to see Kristian and turned back to four beer bottles and three mixed-drink glasses. Uneasy, Kristian detoured into the men's room on the far right side of the bar.

Her bar had no jukebox, no shuffleboard, no pinball, and no dartboard. Dixie stocked several kinds of whiskey, rum, peppermint schnapps, brandy of various flavors, bottled beer, and mixers. She had nothing on tap. Nobody ever ordered a martini or a Manhattan. You couldn't get a cigar, but there were cigarette machines in both the men's and the women's restrooms, each equipped with a musical condom dispenser that played the James Bond theme song with every one-dollar purchase, Kristian had learned. Dixie got a twenty-five-cent cut and made twenty-five dollars per week from each machine. To the left of the ancient cash register was an unused grill with a dull stainless-steel hood. Her bar sold no popcorn, chips, or beer nuts. Long ago, snack food salesmen had dropped Dixie's bar from their routes. She never bought anything except liquor, beer, and a few varieties of soda pop. This was a bar where tired men and desperate women came to drink alcohol. The same men were here every workday, every weekend. The same women were here each weeknight, and some weekends. They knew each other's preferences in whiskey and beer, but not each other's wives, husbands, or children.

They told stories of bar fights. A favorite involved a housewife from Huntsville who followed her husband and girlfriend up here three years earlier, charging through the front door with a baseball bat. She shattered her husband's left elbow and the girlfriend's right ankle before two truckers from Thunder Bay grabbed the bat and held her down until a highway patrolman arrived to take her away.

A woman named Rita who told one regular that she lived in Burk Falls had been coming in by herself every Thursday night this past year. She and a trucker spent twenty-five minutes in the cab of his truck in the parking lot one night. Two regulars caused an uproar when one of them asked what was going on in the truck out front and announced that the cab had a bumper sticker that read, "If the Cab is rocking, don't come knocking." Some of the regulars considered buying one of those James Bond condoms and taking up the stool next to her, but none had yet made a move. Rejection would end the loser's career as a regular here. Failing, he would have to find a new bar. The nearest was many miles away, in the village of Whitney or, worse, in the town of Huntsville, where bar regulars had more money, time, and experience with lonely women from Burk Falls. Kristian did not know he was walking into the middle of a new bar story that would be told for years to come.

Dixie Waterford turned from her stool to see who had come in and watched Kristian head for the restroom. The seven men sitting at her bar were the only ones she usually saw until seven o'clock, when the lumber mill closed. Dixie had been a tired and desperate woman when she had come here eleven years earlier, a newly divorced twenty-five-year-old girl with two babies in the backseat of her pale blue 1983 Dodge Colt. The three-and four-year-old girls were sleeping, wedged in between plastic garbage bags filled with blankets, clothing, and pillows. Pots, pans, plates, and other housewares filled the trunk. It was eleven o'clock at night when she pulled into the parking lot, removed the last two fives and a one-dollar bill from her purse, brushed her hair, applied some lip gloss, and walked into the bar she would end up owning.

The former owner, fifty-six-year-old Bradford Gettings, was sitting on the right, at the far end of the bar across from the cash register and refrigerator, when Dixie let the screen door slap behind her. Dixie was a hard five foot six and 133 pounds. Her complexion was pale, her arms and legs bruised from years of domestic abuse, her blue eyes red from years of worry and tears. Dixie surveyed the bar from right to left and back to Bradford Gettings, who she identified as the bartender and owner. She took the stool next to him. The nine men watched her every move. The two women pretended to ignore her.

"A shot of whiskey and a Blue," she said.

"Sure, honey," he responded, getting up and moving around the bar. "You want water back?"

"No thanks. Is this your place?"

"Yep. Since my brother died last month."

"Oh. Too bad. Need a bartender?"

Seven weeks later, Dixie Waterford and Bradford Gettings got married in the gazebo in Oxtongue Park put up by the Dwight Chamber of Commerce. Eleven months later, Dixie buried him at the municipal cemetery next to his brother, Fred. Death, they say, was by heart attack in the back storeroom one early afternoon on July 11. Emergency Medical Service crewmembers from Dwight told the highway patrol that Bradford Gettings' pants were down around his ankles when they found him slumped over in a chrome and orange vinyl chair. Dixie said it was nobody's business why her husband died with his pants down. A female officer of the highway patrol took Dixie aside to the women's restroom and, following a brief, angry shouting match, got the whole story, which Mr. Hancock had told Kristian Friday night.

"Nice-looking man," Dixie said to herself as Kristian emerged from the restroom and took the stool next to her at the end of the bar.

"Can I get some lunch?"

Dixie coughed, turned, and moved around the bar.

"Nope. Not here."

He frowned.

"You want a drink?"

He winced. "No. How about a Diet Pepsi?"

"No Pepsi. Just Coke. You in recovery or what?"

"What?"

She knew, and she was not letting this go easily.

"Just make it a Diet Coke," he said.

"Don't carry the stuff."

She held up an icy can of Coke.

He nodded, and she popped the top and handed it to him. Nobody ever took cola straight here.

"AA," he said finally.

"Been there, done that," she replied. "Ain't any meetings in here. You're at the wrong place. You gotta' go over to Whitney on Tuesdays at noon in the basement of the VFW Hall, or in Huntsville at the hospital—Wednesday at 7:00 and Saturday at 11:00. Great bunch of guys from Whitney. I get a few of them in here every weekend."

"I'm not into meetings. I prefer Diet Pepsi."

"Where you from?"

He told her about his trip down Canoe Lake on the Oxtongue River, where he met Mary Alice fly-casting. Dixie exclaimed, "I know her. Tell me more."

He told of landing the canoe, the trail up to the cabin, and the jewelry counter.

"I came in off the river ahead of Cedar Rapids, where I was planning to take the portage. She happened to be there and kindly invited me up to her shop."

Kristian was flush with good thoughts of Mary Alice. Dixie sucked out every detail of his visit, learning that he had stayed the night.

"She is a good woman, Mary Alice. Know her well. Hope it works out."

"I didn't come up here to find a woman," he said, and Dixie saw another opening. She had done it before, and she would do it again. She had spent too many days with the same old drunks. A new one comes along a few times a year, and she needed to brush up her skills.

"Look it, honey, I sell booze, and lots of it. You got a story to tell, tell it. You don't want to drink, okay, but you're not gonna' take up my space or get another Coke unless you talk. I did AA myself. You're in denial if that's all you got to tell."

Kristian sized her up as an expert in the art of bar storytelling. He thought the shuttle driver should have been here by now and decided to buy some time by asking for a glass of water.

"I sell booze, big fella'," she sneered. "Tell me the story."

Kristian hesitated, reminding himself that he had told his story many times before at AA meetings, where he had explained how he had drank every night before he left Tess and the four girls. He told Dixie Waterford how he sat by the computer in the living room, a glass on the shelf above pushed to the back, filled with melting ice cubes and vodka. One late autumn evening, it struck him: "I can't stay. She hates herself, and she hates me, too."

"Who was the other woman?" Dixie asked, rolling her eyes.

He hesitated, because there hadn't been one when he decided.

"Later, a brief affair. Didn't mean a thing."

"Honey, she took you hook, line, and sinker, didn't she?"

Kristian tried to think. The divorce was not about going for another woman. That relationship fizzled faster than it had fuzzed up his thinking. No, it was all about Tess having sunk away, him feeling lined out of her life and hooked into caring for their home and four daughters.

"I don't want to," Tess responded to anything he suggested—painting, wallpapering, landscaping, laundry, cooking, visiting friends, going to the movies, shopping at the mall, taking a walk—during those many months before he plunged over the side, out and away.

"I am not happy," he told Tess a few days after a final drunken epiphany that the marriage was over and he had to tell her how he felt.

"I'll call a counselor," he said. "You find out about that marriage-encounter weekend you told me about a few weeks ago."

He did. She did not.

"You left her?"

"I was drunk."

The door sprung open and a teenager shouted. "Kristian?"

"Got to go."

He flung ten dollars on the bar and followed the teenager out the door, leaving Dixie Waterford and her seven regulars looking at his reflection in the mirror over the bar.

11

Notebook: Tom's Life Before 1917

Thomas John Thomson was born August 5, 1877, the sixth of ten children to John Thomson and Margaret Mathison in Claremont, Ontario, on Rural Route 5 east of today's metropolitan Toronto. His parents named him after his grandfather, a well-educated and well-married man who came to Canada from the village of St. Fergus, Aberdeenshire, Scotland. The elder Thomson died in 1875, leaving an inheritance consisting of his late wife's money, which enabled John to pay six thousand dollars cash for the hundred-acre Rose Hill Farm on Georgian Bay. The will also established a sophisticated trust account, awarding his grandchildren two thousand dollars each when they reached age twenty-one. The care he put toward his estate planning suggests why the family knew how to react as it did to Tom's death.

Rose Hill Farm is in the rural colony of Leith, seven miles east of downtown Owen Sound, a busy Great Lakes fishing and shipping port. Leith sits on the Nipissing Bluff, a pre-glacial shoreline of Georgian Bay from which young Tom could see the water, choppy and white capped in summer, covered with ice and sparkling pale blue in winter. The farm lacked electricity and telephone service as he grew up with his five brothers and four sisters. Also living with the family was Margaret's sister, Henrietta, and the daughter of another of his mother's sisters, Lottie Trip. In later years, his mother's father lived there as well.

All of the Thomson youngsters had intellectual, artistic, and musical talent. The first son, George, nine years older than Tom, moved to Seattle with a college friend in 1892, where they operated a storefront business school. While growing the Acme Business College, which was the eleventh largest in the United States by 1904, George joined the first class and graduated from the University of Washington Law School in 1901. He sold his share of the business and moved to New York City in 1906 to study painting at the prestigious Art Students League before joining the impressionistic art colony of Old Lyme, Connecticut, and finally settling in New Haven, where he went to work for the Republican Union League Club as a bookkeeper, continuing to paint on weekends. In 1926, he abruptly returned to Owen Sound, where he came to be revered, teaching and painting landscapes, which he did for the remaining thirty-nine years of his life. Today his works occasionally can be found at summer flea markets throughout Canada's Muskoka Cottage Country south of Algonquin Park. The incongruity of his obvious talents with his actual achievements in life plagued him.

In 1833, Tom's grandmother, Elizabeth Brodie, and other members of the Brodie clan, also voyaged from Scotland. Tom's cousin, Dr. William Brodie, born in 1831, was one of Canada's finest naturalists. He is known in the United States for the 20,000 entomological specimens that the Smithsonian purchased from him and the 92,500 specimens of Ontario's flora and fauna he left to what is today known as the Royal Ontario Museum, of which he was biological department director from 1903 until his death in 1909. Dr. Brodie, who earned the title as a wealthy Toronto dentist in the mid-1850s, took an oft-visiting young Tom with him on hiking trips to High Park and the Scarborough Bluffs, collecting specimens and taking summer photographs at seven o'clock in the morning.

Tom grew up fishing in Leith's famous trout stream, Tefler Creek, and he fished for lake trout from the family's sixteen-foot rowboat on Georgian Bay. He learned to play the cornet, mandolin, and violin and had a good tenor voice, talents he used in the community band and primary school performances. His family regularly went to Leith's Presbyterian Church. Although he never exhibited much early interest in art, his sisters and brothers later told stories that Tom made sketches in the hymnbooks during services and drew caricatures with which to tease them. He had a great love of poetry.

Tom missed Tom many years of away from primary and secondary schooling in Leith. Later, his highly protective family members explained that Tom suffered "inflammatory rheumatism" and frequent attacks of "lung congestion." [1] Nonetheless, his father did not leave him idle those many days and months. Until 1898, when he came into his inheritance, the youngster worked Rose Hill Farm alone, doing the solitary chores of rural family life, learning skills of mind, body, and hand that he later put to use exploring and painting in Algonquin from 1912 until his death in 1917.

---

1.   In later years, no co-workers, friends, acquaintances, or biographers ever suggested that Tom exhibited any of these physical symptoms or the faulty arches and broken toe the family said he suffered as a youth.

By age twenty-one, he had grown into a handsome, six-foot-one-inch, lean, muscular man with dark hair parted in the middle, falling and curling over his right brow. With brooding eyes, a sharp nose, and tight lips, Tom was quiet, introverted, often difficult, erratic, and indolent. All of his friends agreed that he suffered fits of unreasonable despondency. Many described him as a creature of depression and ecstatic moments, his melancholy giving way to outbursts of great passion and energy during his travels, paintings, and bouts of heavy drinking. Today, they would say he suffered from bipolar disorder or manic depression, a chronic and progressive mental illness that often ends in suicide if left untreated. [2] Few biographers have dealt with this critical part of his story. It is irrefutable from what he did and what happened at Canoe Lake on July 8, 1917, that Tom was suffering from severe depression in the days before his drowning. All of the events preceding his death point to this sad conclusion.

Tom's inheritance of two thousand dollars was a considerable sum compared to the five to eleven dollars per week he later earned as a commercial artist in Seattle and Toronto or the two hundred and fifty dollars he would collect from the provincial government, which in 1913 bought his first exhibited canvas, *A Northern Lake*. Some biographers stress that Tom had a fierce sense of duty to make the best of himself, pointing out that in 1916 he illustrated the words of Dick Heldar, painter hero of Rudyard Kipling's *The Light that Failed*: "I must do my own work and live my own life, because I'm responsible for both." Nonetheless, personal resolve is not borne out by the facts of his life. Habitual tardiness, borne of depression, cost him his first job. In 1899, Tom entered a machine shop apprenticeship with a foundry owned by a close friend of his father, William Kennedy, who manufactured ship propellers, provided parts for machines, and trained machinists to use them in the booming factories and shipbuilding yards of bustling Owen Sound. The town had a population of more than 10,000, a Canadian Pacific Railway yard, freight sheds, and an impressive new grain eleva-

---

2.   Not everyone who knew him reached this conclusion. Albert H. Robson, director of the engraving department at Toronto's Grip Limited, who hired him in 1908 and worked with him there at later at Rous Mann Limited, published a thirty-two page book about Thomson in 1937. "Shortly after hiring him I received a gratuitous and unsolicited telephone call from his previous employer belittling Thomson as an erratic and difficult man in a department," Robson said. "That was as absurd as it was untrue. Thomson was a most diligent, reliable and capable craftsman. Nothing seemed to disturb the even tenor of his way." The biographical part of the book was only eight pages long.

tor. Tom lasted eight months before a foreman fired him, saying he never showed up for work on time.

Late in the summer of 1900, and the next, instead of staying on the farm, Tom's manic side took him away on a Canadian Pacific Railway train to Midland, where he boarded a steam ship across Lakes Huron and Superior to a connecting train to Winnipeg. There, he put his boyhood experience to use, working the farms to bring in the harvest. He returned home to his family each winter.

Wintering at Leith those two years was a mixed blessing for a young man whose inward personality and genuine artistic drives stripped the pleasures of family, friends, and female company from him. Following the Winnipeg harvest of 1901, his father encouraged Tom to enroll in the Canada Business College. Tom boarded with the family of William Baxter, a printer with a shop on King Street in Chatham, Ontario. He learned the basics of the emerging advertising design industry from Baxter and the college. Older brothers George and Henry had graduated there earlier. Tom enrolled in at the college's highly regarded department, which offered courses in the technical craft of fine penmanship. These were the early days of commercial advertising. Well-trained artisans in lettering were growing in demand across North America, and Tom excelled in the florid style taught there.

While attending, instead of focusing on his academic study, he spent many hours sketching and painting in watercolor. As become a frequent habit during his life, he gave away two exquisite watercolors to a young woman in Chatham before dropping out of college in 1902, only eight months after enrolling. Tom's disappointed father sent him away to older brother George in Seattle. There he found work as an elevator operator at the Diller Hotel, while living with his brother and attending classes for six months at the Acme Business College.

George oversaw his Acme Business College with college classmate and brother-in-law Franklin R. McLaren. Their friend, Charles C. Maring, owned the first photoengraving shop west of the Mississippi. At Acme, Tom exhibited great talent at design work. George persuaded Maring to hire him and to put Tom up at his boardinghouse. A short time later, contrary to family advice but true to character, Tom left to work for a competitor, the Seattle Engraving Company, while still living with Maring, who must have respected the impetuous talent he kept under his roof.

The few years Thomson spent in Seattle working at the solitary and creative art of lettering shaped in him a unique sense of design, composition, and style, and he learned to produce artistically attractive pieces with great precision and speed. While in Seattle, he also learned his first hard lesson about women and romance.

12

Howard Hancock Returns a Rented Garden Tiller

Haskin's Motors occupied a corrugated metal pole barn at the eastern edge of Dwight on Route 60. Chrome and black skimobiles, shiny green Kevlar and dull aluminum canoes, and new and used lawn equipment covered the yard next to its gravel parking lot. Cardboard cartons of summer jet skis were piled an impressive six high, ten across, and three deep along the south side of the building—an impressive sight.

At precisely 7:47 P.M. Monday, in the dusky, muggy heat of July, stormy weather threatening for the next day or two, Howard Hancock pulled into the parking lot to return a garden tiller he had rented that morning. Hancock awkwardly pushed the orange machine on its two rear wheels over the gravel into the garage and eased it down. Never in a hurry, he eventually found his way up to the front counter. A blue and white Ontario license plate hung on the wall. It read, "Lucky."

Hancock looked around again at the calendars of semi-nude women from the 1950s, when they were plumper and smiled more genuinely than those who posed today. He never understood why men were attracted to such photos, and he tried to look away.

"You hoo!" He called. He paused and called again, "You there, Lucky?"

A tall, gaunt man in his forties with pale gray eyes the shade of wet cement and thin brown hair tucked under a blue baseball cap emerged from the rear office, which doubled as living quarters. He wore fingerless leather work gloves and carried a torque wrench in his right hand. Hancock had met Harold "Lucky" Haskins years earlier at Dixie Waterford's bar, when he had first retired to Canoe Lake. Lucky had then spent several months in group therapy meetings with Harold at Dr. Beckley's office following drunken driving arrests. Lucky was a loudmouth and a drunk. Tonight, again, he was red faced and walked with a stagger.

"Need my deposit back?"

Hancock worried that the court-ordered therapy sessions had done little for Lucky; he reminded himself again that God grants serenity only to those who accept that which they cannot change. Lucky was a loose alcoholic again, his court-ordered probation having ended a few months earlier, when both were released by the court from having to report to meetings at AA and with Dr. Beckley. Lucky sat at Mr. Hancock's AA table for a few weeks, and what he spewed was so terrible that Hancock moved elsewhere. He still saw Lucky at the rental store several times each year and felt obliged to consider him a friend.

Hancock nudged his pink receipt across the counter. Lucky nodded at him, opened a brown accordion folder labeled alphabetically, and pulled out a stack of pale green receipts from the space marked *H* without saying a word. Lucky quickly fingered through, looking for Hancock's name.

"Stubborn son of a bitch," Lucky said.

Using his left hand, Lucky started over. Then he stopped abruptly, pulled one out, placed it over the pink copy, reached underneath the counter, and brought up a stapler attached to a small chain.

"I saw Mary Alice Saturday about five o'clock," Hancock said. "She was coming out of the LCBO with a bottle of Johnny Walker Black and a twelve-pack of Molson's. She's a good-looker, better than that snapshot on the wall over there you been showing off all these months."

Lucky's eyes narrowed as Hancock spoke. He held the two receipts steady with the butt of the torque wrench, positioned the stapler over the upper edge, and pounded with his left hand, making two loud thumps. Lucky tossed them and the stapler under the counter. He punched the cash register, a loud bell rang twice, and the drawer sprang open. He grabbed two twenties and shoved them at Hancock, who pocketed the money as he turned to leave without saying a word. Lucky turned away too, bringing his right hand up high and smashing the torque wrench down hard onto the back counter. It splintered, sending a large display of plastic motor oil bottles, a Gideon Bible, a *Hustler* magazine, and a container of aftershave lotion flying. Startled and mystified at the boom and crash, Hancock swiveled around and exclaimed, "Holy cow!"

Lucky turned and stumbled into the back room toward a ringing telephone, as Hancock hurried back to his car and drove away.

13

Tom Meets Alice Elinor Lambert

When Tom Thomson got off the train from Owen Sound more than three years earlier, Seattle was a city of eighty-three thousand, the largest center of commerce and trade in the northwest. Prospectors made this open and lively town a regular stop on their way to and from the north's reputed gold fields. Almost twenty-five percent of the population had arrived in the preceding few years from foreign countries, some of whom had traveled across Canada on the Great Northern Railway, which first reached the city in 1893, carrying the older Thomson brothers and many of their friends.

On June 3, 1904, a Friday night, the Owen Sound boys gathered at their favorite downtown Seattle pub, Fogerty's, five blocks west of the towering totem pole in Pioneer Square, to celebrate Ralph Thomson's twenty-fourth birthday. He was three years younger than Tom and worked at Maring's shop as a photo-engraving salesman. He too attended the Chatham Business College. A bright, affable young man, Ralph regaled them with news of a girl he had met at Mrs. Mabel A. Shaw's boardinghouse at 1011 Thirty-fifth Avenue, where he was staying.

"She's Mrs. Shaw's daughter," he announced and, seeing Tom's surprise, added, "Her older daughter. Miss Ruth Shaw is her name. She was away at the Portland Teacher's College until today. She came home on the train."

Ralph shivered with excitement.

"I went with Mrs. Shaw this afternoon on the James Street line over to the station to meet the 3:08 from Portland," he continued, excitement mounting in his voice. "Mrs. Shaw wanted help with baggage. Did I say her name is Ruth?"

He went on and on, describing the train's rumbling arrival in a cloud of steam, grease, and oil, rolling to a stop at the platform, brakes hissing and wheezing.

"Three passenger car doors opened and station hands sprang forward out of the darkness. In unison, they swung identically grimy wooden step stools into place under each door."

"One, two, and three," is how he described it, as each conductor emerged, stepped out, and jumped down, all wearing smart dark blue uniforms, bow ties, and caps with shiny black brims.

"Then she—she had to be Ruth—looked out the door of the middle car. She was tall and lovely, with reddish-blonde hair falling in gentle waves to her shoulders. I was dumbstruck, boys!" he exclaimed, his voice rising with excitement.

"'Ruth,' her mother cried, 'Ruth!'"

"The girl waved gaily, stepped down gently, and took the uplifted conductor's hand as Mrs. Shaw ran over. I stood spellbound by the luggage cart as they greeted and embraced.

"Mrs. Shaw promptly took her arm and marched her over to where I was waiting, straight across the platform. 'Mr. Thomson,' she said, 'I want you to meet my fine daughter, Ruth Susan. I am very proud of her.' Mrs. Shaw was beaming. I didn't know what to say.

"Then Mrs. Shaw chimed in, 'Mr. Thomson is a commercial art salesman, Ruth, and has the front bedroom on the main floor.'"

Several other people lived in the warm and gracious boardinghouse of Mrs. Shaw. Her husband, Pitt Pill Shaw, was a solicitor on senior staff at the Seattle Electric Company. The other inhabitants included their son John, age ten, daughter Laura, age twelve, and Tom's friend, Horace Rutherford; Clarence Jones, a retired ice wagon operator, Clara, his wife of forty-three years; and two forestry students attending the Seattle College, both of whom were away for the summer. A recent weekend-only addition was Alice Elinor Lambert, an eighteen-year-old woman,[1] as she described herself to Mrs. Shaw the weekend before she first came to stay. Alice had Ruth's vacant third-floor bedroom. She was put to work as a saleslady at her uncle's millinery store while waiting for her last year of high school in the fall. Ralph went on and on about Miss Shaw and would not stop until the Owen Sound boys nominated Tom to visit and report back.

"What a day!" George Thomson pronounced, congratulating Ralph with a proper clap on his back. "She walks into your life just like that, and on your

---

1. Some biographers say that she was fifteen, perhaps due to a desire to exaggerate certain details of Thomson's life. Records from the U.S. Census give her birth as January 8, 1886.

birthday. Well now, everyone! Drink a toast to Ralph and the girl of his dreams. And raise high your mugs—I've got an early finance staff meeting tomorrow."

Tom arrived at the boardinghouse on foot thirty-eight minutes late the next evening. Three street-side buttonwood trees basked in yellow twilight. Ralph was waiting, pacing back and forth on the wide porch that wrapped around the three-story brick home, built during the residential boom following the great Seattle fire of 1889. The fire started in the Pontius Building, at Madison and Front Street, and went on to destroy the business district and all of the city's railroad terminals, leaving four of the city's wharves. Although no one was killed, a million rats were said to have died in the flames.

Tom wore his finest black bow tie, a white shirt with a high, stiff collar, a gray jacket, and vest, and a hat characteristically cocked back on his head. As was his habit when visiting, he carried a sketchbook and a mandolin.

"Please, Tom, let me introduce you to Ruth," said Ralph, taking his brother by the right arm.

"Who else is here?"

Tom hesitated as Ralph drew him in through the screened double doorway. The foyer stretched twenty-five feet to a hallway leading out back and to an open door on the left. A handsome stairway eight feet from the door went up on the right. Tom hung his hat on the rack to the left of the doorway and dropped the sketchbook and mandolin on a narrow side table. On the right side of the foyer, in front the stairway, was the closed doorway to Ralph's room, which he shared with Horace. On the left side of the foyer, a broad archway announced the parlor. Stepping forward, brushing hair out of his right eye, Tom heard the laughter of girls and Mrs. Shaw's piano. He followed Ralph into the room.

"Hi, Tom," chirped Laura, jumping up from the stool by the upright piano, where her mother was studying her sheet music. To the right of the fireplace, beyond the piano, Mr. and Mrs. Jones shared a loveseat, teacups in hand. Horace rose from a straight-backed chair next to Laura and greeted his friend.

"Hello, Tom."

They shook hands warmly. Horace clapped him on the shoulder. Two young women standing together in front of the wide couch to the left of the fireplace attracted Tom's attention. He recognized one of them from Ralph's rapt description. The other tall but slight girl wore a green sweater revealing flat, boyishly square shoulders and high, round breasts. Her luminous, widely spaced blue-green eyes looked out under dark lashes, with eyebrows that were long and thick. Her fine chestnut-brown hair, neatly tied up at the back, framed a highbred Irish face, less round than long, with a soft mouth, full lips, and a cute, pointed chin. Mrs. Shaw stepped up to greet Ralph and Tom.

"Tom, I want you to meet my daughter, home from teacher's college."

Ruth nodded. Ralph and Tom stepped across the room to the four-cushioned chair in front of the fireplace where Ruth and the other girl stood. Tom noticed nothing else except the other girl's gaze. His tucked his right hand defensively into his pants pocket. His left arm dropped to his side.

"Ruth, this is Tom Thomson, Ralph's older brother," Mrs. Shaw said, turning from her place on the piano stool.

He smiled, bowed slightly, nodded again, and closed his eyes instinctively. He looked up, but at the other girl.

"Tom, this is Miss Alice Lambert," Mrs. Shaw continued. "She is going to be staying here on weekends until fall, when she will be a senior in the high school."

Alice's parents had been Episcopalian home missionaries. Her father, the Rev. Charles Edward Lambert, born in 1843, immigrated to the United States from Ireland, enlisted in the Union Army, and fought in the Civil War. He studied Latin, history, and theology at Yale in Connecticut before becoming a home missionary. He met a brilliant Irish woman, Ella Amelia "Nellie" Carey Lathrop, in the course of his travels across the country. She became his wife in Chicago before they headed west. Eventually, they had seven children, all home educated in Orvallis, Oregon, a wilderness settlement eleven miles from any railroad and eighty-three miles south of Portland. Nellie taught all her children English literature, French, German, music, woodcarving, and Bible stories. Later, the family moved to Tacoma and then to Portland, Oregon, where her father taught university classes and completed a doctoral degree in history at Northwestern University. He later became president of the Willamette University of Washington.

Alice left Portland to finish high school in Seattle, living with her mother's wealthy sister on Beacon Hill, south of downtown. Her aunt's family spent weekends at Puget Sound. Alice stayed behind, earning her keep, working as a clerk in a millinery shop in the Occidental Building at First Avenue between James Street and Yesler Way. The family owned the shop and several others around town, as well as many other commercial buildings.

Tom nervously coughed into his left hand.

"Good evening, Miss Lambert," he blurted out.

"And to you, Tom!" she tossed back, striding forward with strong, graceful steps to offer her left hand, her long silk skirt swishing around her. He admired her long, thin neck and delicate ears. Her green sweater clung to her waist, crossed by a wide white ribbon. Tom reached out with his right hand, but Alice instead took a hold of his upper right arm firmly, swung around gaily, and pressed her body against him.

"Mrs. Shaw tells me you are quite a tenor, Tom," she said, focusing her blue eyes directly into his. He stared back, mesmerized.

"Won't you sing for me?" she cooed, letting her voice out with a faint lilt and girlish sigh.

Mrs. Shaw looked up from the piano and saw the opportunity to play a new song she had been working on all day.

"I've a new song here, Tom," said Mrs. Shaw. "It's from *The Wizard of Oz* that played at the opera house last April. Do you know it?"

Tom stared at the sheet music as Mrs. Shaw struck the opening cords a few times and adjusted herself on the bench. Alice clung to Tom's arm. Mrs. Shaw played through the opening verse twice and then played the sweet refrain that had charmed Seattle audiences, including Tom Thomson, the previous spring.

Halfway through the first act, Sir Dashemoff Daily, the Poet Laureate of Oz, sings a love song to heroine Dorothy Gale. Paul Tietjens and L. Frank Baum wrote a tender piece for the spot called "Love is Love," which some considered drab and tedious. Occasionally, actresses playing Sir Dashemoff wanted something new and lighter. Women always played the role. "I Love You All the Time," by Will R. Anderson, was the first song tried out as the production moved around the country.

The nightly Shaw parlor gathering heard him sing many times and buzzed with anticipation as Alice positioned herself next to him, behind Mrs. Shaw at the piano. Mr. and Mrs. Oliver inched up on the two-seater. Mr. Shaw, who arrived home from an executive committee meeting at the Seattle Electric Company, leaned into the room still wearing his hat and cloak. Ralph and Horace stood over Laura's shoulders. Mrs. Shaw let herself relax for a moment, playing scales faster and faster, then slower and slower. Tom was accustomed to her routines. She straightened herself, tensed, let the quiet settle, and let her fingers down onto the keys to begin the six-bar intro, while Tom readied himself and, at last, joined in, following a two-bar pause:

> One summer's day when the skies were blue,
> Two little sweethearts like me and you,
> Strolled and told the story old, just as we all have tried.
> "If it is true," said the boy impressed,
> "That you love me more than all the rest,

Tell me when you love me best?"
Softly the maid replied,

Alice squeezed Tom's arm. He took the cue, and she lifted her light, soprano voice into the refrain:

"I love you when it's sunshine,
I love you when it's gray,
And I love you through the night, love,
And I love you all the day.
No heart could ever carry
More precious trust than mine,
But I don't know when I love you best,
For I love you all the time."

Mr. and Mrs. Oliver rose to their feet. Ralph and Horace looked at each other in awe. Ruth pushed in beside Laura's stool. Mr. Shaw stood dumbfounded. Mrs. Shaw took a deep, satisfying breath, letting the delighted gathering wait in admiring anticipation. She reprised the intro and began the second verse for Tom:

But said the boy in a playful jest,
"There must be times when you love me best,
Times when you are truer, too, that you will not deny.
Then if it's so, that this all must be."

Alice turned to Tom, lifted her eyes to his, and took the next key line of the verse:

"'When,' said the maid, 'do you best love me?'"

Tom gazed back at Alice's dazzling eyes and let his tenor tones fill the brightly lit parlor on that warm Saturday evening in July. He took the next lines:

Laddie thought, but quick to see,
He made the same reply.

Alice came into the final refrain in perfect descant harmony, leaving the simple melody to Tom. It was a stunning moment for everyone there, except her, who knew what she was doing, as they sang together:

"I love you when it's sunshine,
I love you when it's gray,
And I love you through the night, love,
And I love you all the day.
No heart could ever carry
More precious trust than mine,
But I don't know when I love you best
For I love you all the time."

Alice dropped his arm. The others, including Tom, clapped loudly as the song ended. Alice stepped away from Tom and clasped her hands together against her chest. Her face glowed and she curtsied for all gathered in the parlor to see, as if she were on stage alone, playing the part herself in Portland. The applause died off as Alice rushed over to Ruth and whispered in her ear. They giggled, squealed, and, with girlish delight, ran off together up the stairs and away.

"Those girls!" Mrs. Shaw sighed.

In days following, Tom often returned to Mrs. Shaw's boardinghouse to visit Ralph and Horace, hoping to see Alice. Their budding romance in the parlor suffered under the attention of Mrs. Shaw, Laura, and even Ruth, so she persuaded Tom to meet her elsewhere.

"Join me at noontime tomorrow, downtown."

He eagerly agreed.

She made the trip from her shop, taking the St. James Street cable car to the powerhouse on Broadway at the end of the run. Meeting there on weekdays, they walked hand in hand, seldom speaking, his heart bursting with love. Later she said, "We had ESP, hardly needing words."

On a humid Friday evening, August 27, 1904, she asked him to take her out to dinner at Fogerty's. Later, she pulled him aboard a passing cable car for the ride out to Alki Point. There, sitting by a campfire on the beach, Alice stroked the hair falling across his right brow with tender fingers. Earlier that day, Ralph told him that Alice had accepted Horace Rutherford's Saturday-night theater invitation.

"Tom, Tom, this is my last weekend at Mrs. Shaw's," she began. "I have to stay up on Beacon Hill now, because I have schooling and work on Saturday. I don't think there is any chance I can get away. Oh, maybe Sundays in the afternoon, if they aren't having people over after church. I just don't know."

She pushed herself into his arms sorrowfully, took his head in her warm hands, and brushed her lips across his neck.

"What do you want?" she whispered into his left ear.

Tense with excitement, Tom's mind swirled between yearning desire and a growing sense of disgrace. He tightened his arms around her, moving his hands up across her back. Boldly, the fingers of his left hand caressed the nape of her neck. She gently pushed him away, holding her hands against his chest. He looked into the girl's glistening blue eyes. Tom was enthralled with wonder at her budding beauty.

"I want to be an artist."

Thomson held out his hands between her forearms, palms facing each other a foot apart, his fingers spread wide.

"I want to paint," he said, staring at the panel he imagined between his hands. "Look out across the Puget Sound and see the sky against that tall pine there, with the sun setting. I want to paint that glow of color across sky and water. It's different every night."

She pushed him hard enough that he fell back.

"No, what brought you here?" she shouted.

Startled, Tom sat up quickly, wiping sand from his hair. He breathed deeply, steeling his desire and resolve against the humiliation that swelled in his chest. He tried to smile. His jaw muscles refused.

"The work I could get in the photoengraving business—*like Horace.*" He spat out the words. "You know Horace Rutherford, don't you?"

She shook her head and took his left hand in hers.

Thomson shrugged.

"Tom," she said. "Maybe we'll see each other again. Sure, we will."

She stood and brushed her flowing skirt. Clutching her bag to her waist, she turned away.

"Well, I suppose," Tom replied.

He walked her back to the cable car station and they rode quietly to Tom's stop. He rose and turned toward her. She looked up and leaned forward. He put his left hand on her shoulder, squeezed gently, and walked away. Alice cheerfully waved good-bye as he departed. Strolling the early-evening streets back to Maring's boardinghouse, Thomson felt a refreshing chilly wind coming off Puget Sound, reminding him of youthful late-summer nights back home and the breeze up from Georgian Bay.

14

Lucky Haskins Gets Drunk

Lucky ordered a beer and whisky, neat. Dixie Waterford already had the bottle and shot glass ready, because every night after closing his shop, Lucky ordered double shots of Johnny Walker Red and longneck Molson Canadians, usually several of each. Haskins took a ten-dollar bill from his front shirt pocket and slapped it down on the bar with a loud crack.

After closing up Saturday night, he was here ordering the same for himself and Mary Alice, who never showed up. "Can't let it go to waste," he said, pulling them over at ten o'clock, and three rounds later, at eleven o'clock, he staggered out, stammering, "It was date night, goddamn it."

Dixie poured the whisky and opened the beer bottle.

"What's that for?" she asked, glaring at the ten-dollar bill.

"Paying up!" he growled.

"You ain't never paid up till quittin' time in all the years I been here."

"Well, I'm paying up for two rounds. Got some business with Mary Alice."

"What'll that be?"

"Where she was Saturday night? We had a date."

"What date?"

"You know we got a date here every Saturday night."

"That your idea of a date? What a dumb SOB you are."

Lucky Haskins spent well and often, but Dixie Waterford would rather do without him. More than a few times, Lucky had thrown some quick punches at new drinkers who took too many glances at him or Mary Alice. Once, two months ago, a lightning-fast left cross from a North Bay biker knocked Lucky off his stool. Making a quick exit, the biker turned to Dixie and tossed a twenty-dollar bill onto the bar.

"Sorry," he growled. "I got tired of that guy's ugly face."

Nobody told their side of the story, certainly not Lucky, splayed on the floor, or the biker, who sped away east on Route 60. Mary Alice got a couple of the regulars to haul Lucky out to her pick-up truck and drive him to his room at the shop.

Deciding she wanted to get rid of Lucky early that hot, moist Monday night, Dixie knew what she needed to say.

"Had a man in here earlier today," she confided in a low voice, barely more than a whisper.

"Seems Mary Alice took this guy up to her shop from off the river Saturday afternoon. Nice-looking man, he was. Told me about her old man's winning poker hand that got that cabin and stretch of land on Highway 60."

Lucky stiffened, pouring the double-shot of Scotch whisky down his throat and chasing it with a long, slow gulp of beer. Every word Dixie spoke cracked like summer lightning in his ears. Lucky considered Mary Alice his exclusive girl-friend. Sometimes he went home with her and slept in her bed on Saturday nights after closing. She always drove and he always slept. Lucky had never asked Mary Alice to marry him.

"Damn," he told her whenever the subject came up, "I can't get married until I get divorced from Suzy."

This had long been a convenient excuse, as Suzy had escaped to somewhere in Vancouver with the unrecorded deed for the land under Haskin's Motors, which her father had given them as a wedding present. Without a recorded deed, Lucky would be out of luck; he would lose everything, he explained week in and week out, until Mary Alice bored of hearing the story. Dixie's story continued.

"This fellow said he was a lawyer from Detroit spending time in the park, doing research on a painter. Said he was heading over to the Huntsville Library after he loaded up a canoe on his car shuttled up from Canoe Lake. Dumb bastard tried to buy lunch here."

Dixie poured another double Scotch, cracked open another dripping wet Molson from the bin below the bar, and deftly swept up the ten-dollar bill. She pushed the drinks across to Lucky Haskins, took a deep breath, and lowered her voice still further. Only Lucky heard what she said next. Four regulars at the bar quieted, crocked their necks, and leaned in. Haskins put the whisky to his lips as she continued.

What she did not know was that Lucky's wife had called the shop tonight at closing time. Suzy's voice was what he heard as he felt Scotch whisky warm his lower lip, its sweet, earthy aroma filling his nostrils.

"I burned the deed, you son of a bitch," Sue Ellen told him. Sue Ellen was what she called herself now. "My lawyer told me if the deed cannot be found and recorded, I inherit Haskin's Motors outright. Well, it can't be found now, so I asked the lawyer to open Dad's estate, and he already has an order evicting you from the property. I get everything. Go ahead and file the divorce. Good-bye and good riddance."

She hung up.

He hated Monday nights, and this was the worst he had ever experienced. As he dialed and redialed Suzy, Lucky decided he had to move the business. The only place he knew was Mary Alice's property. If he got the inventory out soon enough, he could keep going. He slurped the beer and decided that he needed to begin moving tonight, before Suzy's solicitor had the entire place padlocked and tied up in estate proceedings.

"This lawyer from Michigan sat right there where you are. We talked, and he drank nothing but Coke," Dixie whispered. "He said Mary Alice and him talked and talked and talked."

She paused.

"They talked."

She paused again.

"All night long."

She heard herself say it too fast and decided to say it again, slowly.

"All…night…long."

Dixie stood, waiting for Lucky's reaction. She looked for a familiar scowl to grow across his face, but Lucky's head drooped.

"She's gonna' to need persuading!" Lucky slurred.

Dixie did not understand. She turned back to her bar, reached for a familiar bottle and a shot glass, and poured.

"Here," she said, turning back and nudging his shoulder. She pushed the drink in front of him. "Have one more on the house. You look like you need it."

Haskins looked up, grabbed the glass, tossed his head back, and the whisky disappeared. He grabbed the longneck with his right hand, covered in a filthy black fingerless glove. Lucky held it out and brought it toward his face. Beer foamed at the corners of his mouth as he sucked it up and drank it down. Lucky coughed, burped, turned away from the bar, and headed for the restroom. All of the bottles and shot glasses were empty.

Startled by his reflection in the mirror, Lucky Haskins shook himself but forgot to zip up. Behind his left shoulder on in the mirror was the chrome James Bond condom dispenser, its mirror reflecting his eyes, nose, and mouth in ever-receding images. He grinned, and the broken left side of his mouth gapped darkly from years of neglect. Lucky violently turned away and pushed the restroom door with his right hand. At that moment, Joe Granger yanked the other side open.

Lucky fell forward through the doorway and tumbled into the narrow passage-way, landing at the young's man boots. Granger gasped and jumped back.

"Son of a bitch!" Lucky moaned, rolling over against the wall. His eyes opened and squinted desperately into space. His mind tried to understand what had happened. He looked up. Granger offered a hand. Haskins focused, grimaced, and slapped it away. Dixie Waterford appeared at the far end of the hallway.

"What the hell is going on here?"

Granger, still catching his breath, said nothing. Haskins slowly pushed himself up to his feet, leaning back against the wall. His face red with rage, he shoved a right hand into his leather bomber jacket and pulled out a dull silver revolver. Granger's eyes widened. His arms fell limp. Haskins put the barrel up against Granger's nose and pushed him back against the wall, resting his left hand on Granger's right shoulder, taking easy command of the twenty-five-year-old electrician's apprentice, who had rewired Lucky's shop sump pump the previous Friday. Granger shook with fear. Holding the gun firmly against Granger's nose, Haskins turned to Dixie, refocused his eyes, and scowled.

"Get outta' the way," he said, spitting out each word.

Dixie Waterford decided against moving, but the gun was persuasive. She had had one drawn against her before. Lucky was not a person she knew to be capable of pulling the trigger against anyone.

Haskins slid his left hand down to Granger's collarbone and pushed hard, pressing Granger against the wall. He brought the gun around, leveling it at Dixie Waterford's forehead.

"Get outta' the way!"

She did not move. Dixie would not move. Her eyes saw that his zipper was open, and she mumbled, "Oh, you dumb shit."

Haskins turned his eyes back to Granger and grinned. The skinny young man, who was wearing a blue T-shirt that read "DORK" in bright red letters across the chest, squirmed sideways against the wall. Granger's face grew redder by the moment.

Dixie, who chafed under any man's demand, looked for a chance to move.

Haskins's right hand stretched back, and he swung the revolver back sharply against Granger's left ear. Granger fell over, crumbling to the floor.

Dixie lunged toward Lucky and fell, sprawling into the hallway. Lucky stepped back and watched as she rolled over, and he caught her eyes.

"God damn you, Dixie," he growled. "I said to get outta' the way!"

Haskins darted forward and started to step over her, putting the revolver back into his jacket.

Dixie was looking up as he came forward. She had a sudden thought: "Kick the son of a bitch in the balls."

She tensed her leg and readied.

Granger's moan grabbed her attention as she drew her leg back and kicked. She missed.

Haskins was past her, out the door and gone.

15

Notebook: Mark Robinson's Journal of Spring 1917

First reported by his daughter, Ottelyn Addison, Mark Robinson's daily journal, which he kept at the ranger station up by the dam at Joe Creek, is the primary and most reliable source of information about what happened at Canoe Lake from July 8 to July 19, 1917. The entries are uniformly short—two to ten lines. He recorded with obvious enjoyment the park's natural beauty and wildlife, the dates upon which he first heard the calls of robins, redwings, black birds, phoebes, song sparrows, tree swallows, hooded mergansers, loons, and many other creatures. He noted the appearance of foxes, woodchucks, wolves, deer, the holes of wood thrush and yellow legs flying north. The ever-changing weather is mentioned frequently but always briefly, as are as his regular visits with good friends, such Harry Watkins and Mr. and Mrs. Edwin Thomas, whose farm supplied residents of Mowat. Together they played euchre.

The journal is a cheap, paperboard-bound twelve-by-eight-inch notebook, which is now housed in the archives of Trent University in Peterborough, Ontario. Its front cover is broken loose, and the paper is gray with age. While the pages reek of authenticity, nevertheless, relying on the account of events Robinson recorded has led Thomson biographers into all sorts of misinterpretations, even his own daughter.

For example, regarding the four-inch bruise on Thomson's temple, there is remarkable inconsistency between his journal's report (which mentions a bruise to the *left* temple and does not mention bleeding from any ear) and the reported observations, official report, and testimony at the inquest of Dr. Howland. (Dr. Howland noted a four-inch bruise on Thomson's *right* temple, with bleeding from the *right* ear.) In May 1931, the coroner, Dr. Ranney, responding to an inquiry from Blodwen Davies, wrote,

Received your letter asking for information....This occurred in 1917, fourteen years ago, and naturally you must admit the circumstances are not fresh in my memory, but upon looking up my notes, I am able to give you the information you require. The body was in such a state of decomposition when found that it had to be buried as quickly as possible. The body was thoroughly examined by Dr. Howland...who gave me a full description of the condition of the body. There was only one bruise on the *right* side of the head, temple region, about four inches long, this no doubt caused by striking some object, like a stone *when* the body was drowned.[1] Dr. Howland swore that the death was caused by drowning. In addition, the evidence from the other six witnesses points that the cause of death was drowning. Those who were present at the inquest were as follows: Dr. G. W. Howland; Miss Bessie Blecher; Mr. J. E. Colson, Prop. Algonquin Hotel; Mr. J. S. Fraser, Prop. Mowat Lodge, Canoe Lake; Mr. Mark Robinson, park ranger; Mr. Martyn (sic) Blecher, tourist; and Mr. G. Rowe, resident guide. [Emphasis added.]

Robinson was one of those seven witnesses. Dr. Howland attended the inquest personally and was questioned by Dr. Ranney. His inquest testimony should have cleared up such a major discrepancy. After all, if the contradiction arose solely due to the differing perspectives of Robinson, a lay observer, and Dr. Howland, a trained physician, one would tend to trust the observations of the doctor. Nonetheless, following the day's events, Robinson made an entry in his journal on Tuesday, July 17, 1917, relied upon by Mrs. Addison and Little. He wrote, "We found a bruise on *left* temple about four inches long. Evidently caused by falling on a rock. Otherwise, no marks of violence on body. Dr. Howland and undertakers advised having body buried." [Emphasis added]

Even if Robinson reported the site of Thomson's wound from his own perspective, he did not record that he saw a left temple wound until after Dr. Howland had examined the body and testified at the inquest to a right temple wound, as Dr. Ranney noted and Dr. Howland confirmed in his now-lost written statement delivered to the crown attorney in North Bay.[2] Under these circumstances, Robinson's description of the wound should have matched Dr. Howland's. His journal is replete with inconsistencies, missing details, and ambiguities, leading Thomson's daughter to several erroneous conclusions in her 1969 book, *Tom Thomson: The Algonquin Years*.

Even more critical from a law-enforcement perspective, Robinson failed to record any other medical or background evidence, which one would need to con-

---

1. Dr. Ranney's statement about how the wound occurred is overlooked in Thomson biographies. The wording suggests that Thomson suffered the wound during or after his drowning, not before.

firm drowning as the cause of death. By today's standards, the following evidence would be needed to prove intentional or accidental drowning: 1) whether there was bleeding from the left or right ear, and 2) why string was wrapped seventeen times around Thomson's left ankle (even if it was simply the means by which Rowe and Dickson's secured the body to shore at Big Wapomeo Island).[3] Robinson and the search teams he directed failed to find Thomson's handmade cherry wood paddle and failed to secure the canoe and portage paddles, all possible murder weapons, all of which disappeared in the following weeks.

Establishing a cause of death from drowning in the modern era requires a thorough examination of personal background evidence. Most importantly, thorough investigators would need to know that all of Thomson's paintings, and almost all of his personal belongings, were missing from Mowat Lodge. This information would lead them back to the events of May 24, when Thomson gave away his last spring panels, as well as Robinson's startling recovery of thirty-three of them before the inquest at the Trainor cabin. Along with these, he found letters addressed to Thomson from Winnie Trainor, one of which was unopened.

Finally, and most troubling, the journal does not mention Robinson's later oft-repeated suspicions about Blecher and Fraser, or his doubts about the exhumation of the body. All he wrote on July 18 was, "There is considerable adverse comment regarding the taking of evidence among the residents." The journal entries made by Robinson from July 8 to 19, 1917, in retrospect, are incomplete if not unreliable.

---

2.   In her 1931 book, Blodwen Davies wrote, "The chief piece of evidence [at the inquest] was Dr. Howland's signed statement on the condition of the body, now on file at the office of the crown attorney at North Bay." Little quotes the statement in his book, in full, as follows: "I saw the body of a man floating in Canoe Lake Monday, July 16, at about 10:00 A.M., and notified Mr. George Rowe, a resident, who removed the body to shore. On Tuesday 17, I examined the body and found it to be that of a man aged about forty years in advanced stages of decomposition, face, abdomen and limbs swollen, blisters on the limbs, was a bruise on the right temple size of four inches long, no other signs of external marks visible on body, air rising from mouth, some bleeding from right ear, cause of death drowning." Some may question whether Little did, indeed, have a copy of the statement, because he reports that it was signed by "Gordon W. Howland, MR, NACP." Dr. Howland's name was Goldwin. He signed other documents using initials for his first and middle name, he was a MB (bachelor of medicine) and member of the NRCP (Royal College of Physicians of the United Kingdom). Therefore, it appears doubtful that Little was looking at a copy of the statement as he wrote his book.

For example, in 1931, Thomson's coroner, Dr. Ranney, omitted Hugh Trainor from the list of inquest attendees in Robinson's journal, adding Shannon Fraser instead. Ranney may have been working from partial notes. He probably did question Hugh Trainor at his cabin earlier that evening, but Dr. Ranney's handwritten notes, as reported by Ms. Blodwen Davies, cast further doubt on the details of Robinson's journal entries, even if Dr. Ranney also took the testimony of Shannon Fraser at Trainor's cottage.

When interviewed in 1979, Audrey Saunders remarked that Robinson was, indeed, "a storyteller, and a good one."

"Yes, Mark was a great guy, but if you listened to his stories as often as I did, you could see variations in them. He had certain fixed ideas, which have gone into the history of the Tom Thomson story, [and] which I don't think are necessarily so. And you see them repeated over and over again."

---

3.   Ralph Bice—a legendary Algonquin trapper and guide who received the prestigious Order of Canada, the nation's highest civilian honor—wrote an account of his knowledge of Thomson's death that was serialized in the *Huntsville Forester Weekender* from December 1995 to January 1996. Bice said Shannon Fraser told him, "It was thought [Thomson] sprained his ankle and wrapped a compress around it for protection." Already a park veteran at age eighteen, Bice was one of the guides chosen to take Governor General Sir Victor Christian William Cavendish, the Duke of Devonshire, through Algonquin Park in 1918.

16

Notebook: Digging Up Tom's Thomson's Grave

On October 1, 1956, William T. Little and three companions dug up Thomson's gravesite at Canoe Lake. Little was a reform school superintendent in Brampton and later a provincial judge in the family court of York County, Ontario. This chapter of the Thomson story is as bizarre as any you'll see on a U.S. daytime talk show. What Little found has propelled Thomson storytelling ever since.

In his 1970 book, *The Tom Thomson Mystery*, Little said that he worked as a summer camp counselor and guide at Taylor Statten's Camp Ahmek, on Canoe Lake, from 1930 through 1940. Statten was a shameless promoter who hyped Camp Ahmek for the adolescent boys of wealthy Toronto families by nurturing legends that Thomson's ghost could be seen paddling his gray-green canoe in the lake while wearing a yellow shirt. That first summer, on August 17, 1930, Guelph High School teacher Frank Braught supervised Ahmek campers in the erection of a garish totem pole at the site of Hayhurst Point's memorial cairn to Thomson at Canoe Lake. Many who visit today describe the totem pole, a north-west Indian tradition out of place in the park, as simply god-awful. That same year, Statten hung artwork by the campers in the dining room; later, twenty-five original Thomson sketches on loan from the National Gallery would join them. He sent the guides and campers across Canoe Lake in a pirate-designed boat all summer long in search of Thomson's missing seventeen-foot gray-green chestnut canoe and cherry paddle.

Little, the other camp counselors, and the Camp Ahmek boys found a remarkable seventy-five canoes, in various states of disrepair, and brought each back for examination by experts, including old Ranger Robinson, who was called upon to tell and retell his tales of the artist's life and death on Canoe Lake in July 1917. The boys gathered around, Little said, and huddled at Robinson's feet, the smaller ones in back pressing forward to hear.

"I could hear the words of Mark Robinson...answering my query as to where Tom had been buried at Canoe Lake in 1917," Little quotes Robinson, and his enigmatic reply: "'His grave is just north of the other two.'"

Little said Robinson lowered his voice and whispered, "'I don't believe they ever took Tom's body from Canoe Lake.'"

On October 1, 1956, Little returned to Canoe Lake on a sketching trip with a friend, Jack Eastaugh, retired principal of Norseman Public School in Etobicoke. They visited Camp Ahmek chef Pete Sauvé, who had personally watched Thomson paint *The Drive*, a scene of loggers on the Petawawa River near Achray, where Thomson and Sauve worked together as fire rangers in 1916. Little and Eastaugh paddled over to Hayhurst Point to see Thomson's cairn, and then across to the Mowat Cemetery. Walking half a mile through tall grass and pine woodland, Eastaugh led the way to a large birch tree, under which a small picket fence was enclosing two marked graves. One, the subject of a long-lost Thomson photograph, contained the remains of a young mill hand, James Watson from Perry Sound, who died on his first day at work in the Gilmour lumber mill in 1897.[1] The other was a child, Alexander Hayhurst, buried in 1915 at the age of eight, a victim of diphtheria.

Eastaugh painted while Little wandered around, asking himself whether Thomson's body was still there, and began forming a plan. They walked into Mowat to see the white, tightly shuttered two-story Blecher cottage, which appeared abandoned.[2] Little provided a romantic description of the Trainor cottage next door, saying it had "teacups and saucers with hand-painted scenes showing dark spruce trees as background for water and bush subjects in beautiful colors." Back at Camp Ahmek, Frank Braught, retired from Guelph, and Leonard Gibson, a longtime Canoe Lake resident familiar with the Thomson legend, agreed to join Little in carrying out the gruesome scheme to dig up Thom-

---

1.   The headstone read, "Remember, comrade, when passing by, as you are now so once was I. As I am now so you will be. Prepare thyself to follow me." Camp Ahmek campers added a line for a show originally performed in 1927: "To follow you, I's not content, until I know which way you went."

2.   Martin Blecher, Sr., died in 1919. Louisa Blecher and Bessie occupied the main house. Martin Blecher, Jr., and his second wife, Carolyn moved into the boathouse. The 1930 U.S. Census lists him alone and unemployed, living with his mother in her Buffalo, New York, home. Blecher died of a heart attack at Canoe Lake in 1938. Louisa died in 1944, and the lease passed to Bessie, who died in 1951. The 1920 U.S. Census lists a second daughter, Louise F. Blecher, born in 1892, living with Louisa and Bessie in their Buffalo, New York, home. Canoe Lake stories never mention her.

son's gravesite. They later rationalized about the legality of opening a grave on the grounds that, officially, nobody remained buried there.[3] The circular logic of their explanation is as macabre as what happened.

In a 1935 interview recorded at Camp Ahmek, Robinson challenged whether the Huntsville undertaker, working alone by lantern light, could have unearthed and opened the outer pine box and inner oak casket, removed the body, dropped it into the steel casket, and soldered the lid in less then three hours. Only years later did rumors emerge that railroad workers doubted whether what they had lifted onto the train was anything more than sand. None ever accused Churchill publicly. Thomson's family refused to discuss the exhumation, soldered steel casket, or reburial at Leith, fueling morbid speculation that has endured ever since.

Armed with two axes and shovels, Little and crew dug up the Mowat Cemetery in a cold Algonquin autumn drizzle.[4] Working amidst the towering old birch and surrounding sugar maples, Little's crew eventually found the remains of a rough pine box, collapsed into an oak casket that in turn had given way. They found a metal plate inscribed only with the words, "Rest in Peace." They recognized the heel impression of a single woolen sock, pieces of a cotton or light canvas shroud, and skeletal remains.[5] The giddy, ghoulish crew covered the boxes and their find with tarpaper and took the body's left tibia with them to Dr. Harry Ebbs, MD, on Little Wapomeo Island, where he was spending a weekend away from Toronto with his wife, Adele, at their log cabin. Dr. Ebbs identified it as a human leg and dutifully made an official report to Ontario authorities.

On October 5, 1956, Little; Dr. Ebbs; Dr. Noble Sharpe, MD, chief of the Ontario Provincial Criminal Laboratory; and a provincial police officer motorboated over to the site. Dr. Sharpe was the most experienced forensic medical investigator in Canada. He arrived at the gravesite at about midday and began a

---

3. Under the common law of England, the United States, and Canada, there was a duty to dispose of a dead body by burial or cremation, and it was a criminal offense to disturb the remains without lawful permission. The common law recognized religious tradition respecting the permanence of a Christian burial. For example, exhumation from consecrated ground in a churchyard required permission of religious as well as civil authorities. Today, the accidental discovery of human remains triggers a complex series of legal requirements under national and provincial law. What occurred at the Mowat Cemetery in 1956 would today be considered a criminal offense.

4. In 1972, Charles F. Plewman said the original gravesite was inside the picket fence and that Little's crew dug outside. Little wrote that they found the casket "twentyone feet due north of the corner of the fence surrounding the two marked graves."

5. Investigators later observed that most textiles rot within five years. Almost forty years had passed since Thomson's burial.

thorough examination of its contents. Dr. Sharpe and Dr. Ebbs systematically removed and screened all the soil and carefully packed and shipped the skeletal remains to Toronto.

Little leaked the discovery to Toronto newspapers and eagerly awaited medical evidence confirming that he had found Thomson's skeleton. Well educated and ambitious, Little measured the gravity of his discovery. He wrote,

> The mystery of Tom Thomson's death and the location of his final resting place resembled a great jigsaw puzzle. It had taken over twenty-five years to collect the pieces with the assistance of friends, coworkers, and associates throughout the north, particularly those closely connected with Canoe Lake. How the many pieces seemed to fit into place and reveal a clearer picture of what had taken place during those final days after [Tom] disappeared on his ill-fated fishing expedition.

Chasing the story, Toronto newspapers interviewed Dixon and Churchill, the undertakers. Dixon was confused about who had issued the burial permit and mixed up over whether the casket and rough boxes were cedar or oak. Then seventy-three years old, Churchill told an outrageously muddled story of being instructed to exhume the body by Thomson biographer Blodwen Davies, who was only nine years old in 1917.

Years later, Dr. Sharpe reported that he had received several indignant telephone calls from Winnie Trainor, who insisted that she and her father were present when Churchill exhumed the body and that she was positive the body was in the casket shipped to Owen Sound, even though she left Canoe Lake, bound for Toronto, two days before Churchill arrived.

Little and the entire nation experienced dismay when, on October 19, 1956, the *Globe and Mail* reported, "Scientific investigation has established that a skeleton dug up by amateur artists in an unmarked Algonquin Park grave was not that of the great Canadian painter, Tom Thomson, who thirty-nine years ago died."

Everyone was shocked when Dr. Sharpe said the bones found were those of a five-foot-eight, twenty-to thirty-year-old "Mongolian type, either Indian or nearly full-breed Indian." Thomson was at least six-foot-one, almost forty years old, and lacking any native ancestry. [6]

Even more startling to Little, the art world, and the public was the condition of the skull in light of these facts. There was a round hole on the left temple

---

6.   Plewman said he was told that an Indian was buried in the old cemetery in 1984, as other persons probably were, too.

nearly three-quarters of an inch in diameter, approximately where Mark Robinson said Thomson's head exhibited a four-inch bruise. Dr. Howland had said it was the right temple; nonetheless, the exquisite coincidence of this finding confounded both Little and the country.

Dr. Sharpe reported, "The inner plate opening is slightly wider, showing a slight beveling. The X-ray showed no radiating fractures. There was no injury on the inner table of the skull opposite the hole....The orbital plate and nasal bones were so intact that no bullet could have escaped from the skull." Dr. Sharpe decided, after consulting with Professor Eric Linnel of the Department of Neuropathology at the University of Toronto, that the opening was consistent with a rare surgical operation called trephining of the skull for hemorrhage following a serious injury, which some physicians used years ago to relieve pressure on the brain.

Primitive trephining, or trepanning, is one of the more fascinating religious and surgical practices in human history, dating back forty thousand years. Archeologists speculate it was performed by witchdoctors to permit the escape of evil spirits, to acquire roundels (disks of bone obtained by cutting a circular hole in the skull), and later to relieve cranial pressure following an injury. It was remarkably successful. Many skulls examined by researchers show signs of healing and bone regeneration. Although trephining was largely unknown to the public, some native North American Indians practiced the procedure.

The sensational discovery of a skull with an injury to its left temple, buried in what by all evidence was Thomson's original gravesite, generated a public outcry fueled by Robinson's erroneous report of an injury to Tom Thomson's left temple and the fact that Tom's cherry wood paddle, a potential murder weapon, was still missing.

Little's investigation caused the nation to ask, "If the badly decomposed body buried at Mowat in 1917 was not Thomson but an Indian, whom, if anybody, did the family bury in the Leith Cemetery?" Thus, emerged the great myth of his death. Despite Dr. Howland's medically uncontroverted report that Thomson suffered a blow to his right, not left, temple, public controversy brewed over the next thirteen years. Tom's grave could be exhumed for verification only upon order of the Ontario Department of Justice. In February 1969, following a two-part CBC documentary, *Was Tom Thomson Murdered?* Ontario Attorney General Arthur Wishart responded to a question put to him in the Ontario Legislature:

> I have no intention of ordering that the grave be reopened at all. Perhaps if I were to get a request from some close members of the family, I would consider

it, but I would hope that nobody would disturb the situation any more than it has been disturbed.

Thomson's family opposed exhuming the Leith gravesite to verify Thomson's burial there, and that is how Little's 1956 investigation ended.[7]

---

7.   In 1996, Tracy Thomson, the artist's great grandniece, and Helen Young, a grand-niece, a told a columnist for the *Toronto Star* that it would acceptable to do DNA testing on the Canoe Lake skull she was told remained at the crime lab, but the family still opposed disturbing the Leith family plot. The columnist, Ellie Tesher, reported in 1997 that the provincial government long ago reburied the Indian's skeleton in the Mowat Cemetery. She said Dr. Sharpe's notes do refer to a skeleton being rebur-ied but do not specifically mention the skull, which, nonetheless, was never found at the crime lab.

17

Notebook: Little Falsehoods

With William T. Little, Dr. Sherrill Grace, observed, "The practice of inventing a Tom Thomson character reached new heights." Her book, *Inventing Tom Thomson: From Biographical Fictions to Fictional Autobiographies and Reproductions,* recounts Little's investigation with palpable skepticism. She notes that he resorts to narrative maneuvers and rhetorical questions in pointing the finger of guilt at Martin Blecher, Jr., and arguing with the results of Dr. Sharpe's examination of the body Little found in 1956. "Try as he might to discredit, or at least render suspect, the forensic findings, Little appears not to have solved the mystery, but to have further complicated it," she concludes.

Digging deeper into Little's book reveals that he manufactured facts crucial to his murder theory. He seized upon the national myth of Thomson's death and burial and pumped into it a story he knew was untrue but wanted to believe.

The first falsehood originates with Robinson's journal. On Saturday, July 14, 1917, Robinson, who consistently misspelled the family name, wrote, "Mr. Thompson left for his home this morning." Mrs. Addison added a footnote to her book that George Thomson "returned to Mowat Lodge on July 19 to collect Thomson's paintings and other possessions."

If George returned to the park on July 19 and personally directed the body's exhumation, Little's entire theory would have collapsed. So, instead, Little wrote that George Thomson, indeed, left Canoe Lake on Saturday "back to his home and business in New York." Little was convinced that only two passenger trains passed Canoe Lake each day, one westbound in the morning and the other eastbound in the evening. Little believed, therefore, that George could not have departed on the morning train so he altered Robinson's journal excerpt, which he reproduced as historical evidence in his book as an appendix. He wrote, "George Thomson left on the evening train."

Obviously, Little had Robinson's journal before him when he wrote his text and appendix to his book. His description of events cannot possibly be correct because George lived in New Haven and had no business in New York. George had arrived in Owen Sound from New Haven with his wife, Jean, on July 10. She stayed there while he visited Canoe Lake from July 12 to July 14 and again on July 18 and 19, returning to Owen Sound with the steel casket and thirty-three of his brother's last spring sketches.

Making a trip to New York and back to Owen Sound on July 15 to 17, not only defies train schedules and normal family relationships but also Robinson's journal, family correspondence, and newspaper reports, which reliably confirm that George made a second trip from Owen Sound to Canoe Lake.

First and conclusive is a letter George Thomson wrote on Mowat Lodge stationary dated July 19, 1917, postmarked in Mowat telling Dr. MacCallum that he was shipping a crate of Tom's unused sketching boards to him.

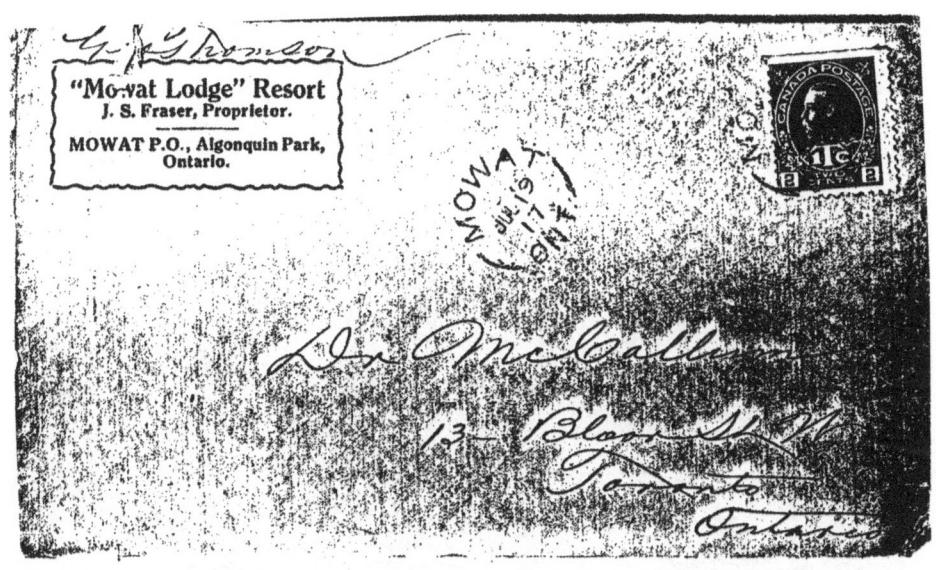

Envelope of George Thomson's letter postmarked July 19, 1917, at Mowat.

Best Trout Fishing in Ontario.
Several good Bass Lakes.
2000 lakes and streams.
Nine besides Canoe Lake within fifteen minutes to two
hours paddle from "Mowat
Lodge."

A FAMILY RESORT.

First-class Canoe and Boat
Livery, and Outfitting Stores.

MOWAT LODGE
J. S. FRASER

Mowat P.O., Canoe Lake Station
Algonquin Park, Ontario.

Telegraphic Address: Canoe Lake, Algonquin Park, Ont.
Grand Trunk Railway.

OPEN WINTER AND SUMMER.

AT CANOE LAKE Station
on the Ottawa Division of
the Grand Trunk Railway.

Starting point, and key to over
three-fourths of Algonquin
Park Lakes and Streams.

Eleven hours from Buffalo,
eight from Toronto, and
six from Ottawa to CANOE
LAKE STATION.

George Thomson's letter on Mowat Lodge stationery dated July 19,
1917.

Second, a letter dated February 9, 1918, from Tom's sister, Elizabeth Harkness, to Dr. MacCallum suggests that George made two trips to Canoe Lake. "When George came back from his *first visit to Canoe Lake* he told us that Fraser had shown him a statement of Tom's affairs with them, covering the last few weeks including the things he bought that Sunday to take with him," she wrote. [Emphasis added.] Later, in the same letter, she wrote, "When George was at Canoe Lake *the first time*, Fraser showed him your telegram offering to pay any expenses." [Emphasis added.]

Third, on July 20, 1917, the *Owen Sound Sun* said, "The body accompanied by Mr. George Thomson is expected in Owen Sound at noon on Friday...."

OWEN SOUND SUN July 13, 1917

TOM THOMSON'S CANOE FOUND ON CANOE LAKE

Efforts Being Made to Find Him Since Sunday Last—Is a Noted Artist

A telegram from Canoe Lake, Algonquin Park, received by his parents, Mr. and Mrs. John Thomson, 4th Ave. E., on Tuesday announced that a canoe belonging to their son, Thomas Thomson, the well known Toronto artist, had been found on the lake and no trace of Mr. Thomson could be found. He had arrived at Canoe Lake on Saturday and the canoe had been found the following day. Mr. Geo. Thomson, of New York, a brother of the missing man, arived here on Tuesday and left for Canoe Lake on Wednesday morning, ariving there yesterday morning and a search is now being made for any trace of the young man. A later telegram stated that, when the canoe was found the paddles were strapped to the thwarts which might indicate that the canoe had drifted from its moorings and left Mr. Thomson marooned on one of the islands. The search was proceded with all speed.

The missing man was born at Leith and attended the Collegiate Institute here and very early in life showd evidence of marked ability in drawing. He later studied art in Toronto and was with the Grip publishing company for a number of years. During the summer for many years past, he has made a practice of going alone into the wilds of Ontario with his sketching outfit and a tent and his paintings from nature have been the subject of decidedly favorable criticism. For some years Mr. Thomson has devoted his whole time to his art and in his studio in Rosedale, Toronto, is a collection of masterpieces that is not only a pleasure but an education to view.

Mr. Thomson is very well known here and everyone will hope that he will be found safe and well. The other alternative is not pleasant to consider but should it be found that he has been drowned, Canada will have lost one of her most accomplished landscape artists, and a thorough gentleman.

EN SOUND SUN July 17, 19

TOM THOMSON LIKELY DROWNE

No Official Confirmation Yet Received but Family Fears Worst, Should Know Tonight

Relatives of Mr. Tom Thomson, t Toronto artist who has been missi since July 8th and whose canoe w found on Canoe Lake, Algonquin Par received a telegram yesterday co taining the information that he h been found. The telegram howeve does not state whether he is alive, whether it is his body which has be found, but says only, "Tom found th morning." Queries were at once se back but at noon today no reply h been received. His relatives are ho ing that Mr. Thomson is safe but th will not know until a reply to the mesage reaches them. Mr. Geor Thomson, a brother, who was visiti and Mrs. Telford, and who we to Algonquin Park to search f Mr. Thomson, returned on Saturd night without the slightest clue what his brother's fate had been, b the uncertainty will likely be settl by this evening. The family fear t worst, however, as a telephone me sage, received in a roundabout wi this morning gives little hope, but th they will not give up until the answ to the telegram is received.

Owen Sound Sun articles reporting Thomson's disappearance and the discovery of his body.

Fourth, many years later, Churchill told the *Owen Sound Sun* and the *Toronto Star* that George Thomson accompanied the coffin to Owen Sound.

Finally, train schedules and the confirmed details of the exhumation and delivery of the casket to Owen Sound clearly make it possible that George returned to Canoe Lake on July 18 or 19.

The second piece of manufactured evidence also arises from Robinson's journal. On July 19 he noted, "Mr. Churchill, undertaker of Huntsville, Ont., arrived last night and took up body of Thomas Thomson artist *under* direction of Mr. Geo. Thompson of Conn., U.S.A. The body went out on the evening train to Owen Sound." [Emphasis added].

Little's re-wrote the excerpt to say, "Mr. Churchill, undertaker, from Huntsville, arrived last night (8 P.M.) and took up the body, *upon* the direction of George Thomson. The body went out on the evening train to Owen Sound." [Emphasis added].

Little also added a footnote to his book, saying, "George Thomson (deceased) of Owen Sound, Ontario, in discussion with the author Feb. 1957 and subsequently in 1962, categorically denied ever having accompanied the body from Canoe Lake or ever having viewed the body after death."

If George Thomson denied ever having accompanied the body from Canoe Lake, he was engaged in a silent conspiracy with Little, who obviously doctored his reporting of historical evidence to suit his murder theory. Both men are dead and no earlier biographers and researchers have ever raised questions about Little's excerpts of Robinson's journal. As a lawyer and judge with a distinguished career in social services, having served on numerous committees and panels on youth and family problems, it is difficult to understand why he altered them in such crucial ways unless he relied too heavily on George Thomson's denial. Had Little made a more thorough investigation, he may have confronted George and uncovered the true story. Little's book ends with a plea for the government to open Thomson's Leith grave that suggests why he let himself believe George Thomson:

> The mystery attending Tom Thomson's death and subsequent burial will never be solved short of an official opening of the Thomson family plot at the United Church Cemetery at Leith. In this grave lies the secret surrounding not only the location of his body, but possibly the facts regarding his premature death. Regardless of whether this action is ever taken, a large number of Canadians will feel that he was a man dedicated to portraying the truth and beauty of his adopted home, Algonquin Park. Many of them will be satisfied

that his remains are located where he would want to be—in a simple grave in the Park.

Apparently, Little was engaged more in defending his own actions and creating a national sensation than in seeking the truth. His zeal for unearthing Thomson's grave blinded him to his own failing to reconcile the serious personal problem Little's 1956 discovery created for George Thomson if the steel casket buried in Leith was exhumed and discovered to be empty. George's denial of making the second trip in discussions with Little after the 1956 discovery makes sense only if George did not actually witness Churchill's exhumation and he and other family member never personally viewed the body. Little's discovery certainly would have shaken whatever confidence George had that Tom was reburied in Leith.

When he arrived at Canoe Lake, George very likely was unaware of the body's earlier burial. Therefore, it is doubtful Churchill knew when he separately arrived that disinterment was required. If Churchill had refused, the expense of the trip, transport of the steel casket and value of his time would all be lost. Robinson's journal entry on July 18 notes, "Later in the day…S. Fraser [received] telegram that a steel casket was being sent in and Thom Thompson's body was to be *exhumed* and taken out, by whose orders I am not at present aware." [Emphasis added.] Some biographers assume that the telegram, rather than Robinson, announced the exhumation. However, the timing and circumstances surrounding what George Thomson and Churchill knew before they arrived at Canoe Lake indicate that they both expected to recover the body from storage in a Mowat icehouse.

He and the Churchill probably were also unaware that the body had been doubly embalmed. The undertaker, therefore, likely warned him that the body would be in dreadful condition, perhaps, unrecognizable. Also, locating and getting from Dr. Howland the medical certificate of death needed for reburial in Leith, as well as recovering Tom's last spring paintings, probably occupied all the time George had. Therefore, George's absence from the cemetery that night is understandable.

The return of death on the reverse side of the death certificate dated July 19, 1917, identifies George Thomson as the informant officially verifying Tom's body shipped to Owen Sound in the soldered steel casket. Any evidence that Churchill may not have removed the body would, if the Leith gravesite was opened and nothing found, expose the very embarrassing fact that George never viewed Tom's body. Even more dreadful for elderly George Thomson, was the possibility that Churchill had duped him into accompanying a steel casket filled with sand. So, George denied ever returning to the park or identifying the body upon its arrival in Owen Sound. It is sad but understandable that the family, who obviously knew otherwise, never corrected the record. His younger sister, Margaret Tweedale, who attended the Leith burial, was still alive in 1970 when Little's book was published.

What remains of the myth that Little's book propelled is his insistence that Churchill never removed Tom's body from the Mowat Cemetery. To accept that as true, one must believe that Churchill was crooked, that George never identified the body, that the family never opened the casket, that Dr. Howland's report of a wound to Tom's right (as opposed to left) temple was wrong, and that Dr. Sharpe mistakenly identified the body Little found as a male Indian or half-breed no older than about thirty. That is very large a pile of speculation.

The only real mystery of Thomson's death and burial arises if, as the evidence strongly suggests, Churchill removed Tom's body and an Indian was subsequently buried in his casket. If so, the likelihood is that whoever buried the Indian knew both where to dig and that Thomson's body had been removed. Otherwise, it is difficult to believe that anyone randomly digging would have found and used the casket. The chilling but inescapable conclusion is that whoever buried the Indian so was a Canoe Lake resident present at the original burial. Only one person fits that profile. Did Shannon Fraser bury an Indian in Tom Thomson's grave?

18

Tom Thomson's Last Spring Paintings

Settling at a wide oak table in the historical reference room of the Huntsville Public Library, Kristian opened his thick three-ring notebook and turned to his notes on the last spring series of sixty-two or more paintings. He removed two sharpened pencils and a rubber-banded stack of yellow index cards from his shirt pocket.

The most critical piece of the story comes from a brief essay written in the 1950s by Dr. Robert P. Little, MD (no relation to Judge Little), "Some Recollections of Tom Thomson and Canoe Lake," reproduced as an appendix to *The Tom Thomson Mystery*. Little wrote that he was at Canoe Lake from May to October 1917, staying at a cabin on Little Wapomeo Island. Little described nothing of Thomson's disappearance, the discovery of his canoe and body, or his burial and exhumation, saying he did not learn about the drowning until Charlie Scrim told him in the middle of July 1917. Robinson's journal noted that Little left for his home in Columbus, Ohio, on May 31, 1917, causing Kristian to give Little's account careful scrutiny.

Dr. Little described how he took meals at the Mowat Lodge:

> In May, Tom put all the panels he had painted that spring on the walls of the Frasers' summer dining room. They made a real art exhibit. Tom told Mrs. [Daphne] Crombie that she could have any one she [chose]. The only reason I did not take one, too, is because I did not want to impose on his generosity.

Dr. MacCallum's son, Arthur, indirectly supported by Mrs. Crombie, described a similar evening in the dining room of the Mowat Lodge occurring on Thursday, May 24, 1917.

Robinson embellished and refined his stories about the last spring series over the years in interviews and lectures. In a 1953 tape-recorded interview at Camp

Ahmek, when he was eighty-nine years old, Robinson said Thomson burst into the ranger station at Joe Creek four or five days before his disappearance on July 8, 1917. Thomson came to him, he said, with a request to hang his painting on the walls. He quoted Thomson: "'You know, I have something unique in art that no other artist has ever attempted,' I can hear him say. 'I have a record of the weather for sixty-two days, rain or shine, or snow, dark or bright. I have a record of the day in a sketch. I'd like to hang them around the walls of your cabin here.'"

Robinson's 1953 story is a much-polished version of what he had told Blodwen Davies earlier, in 1935. She wrote that the artist asked Robinson to let him hang a group of paintings in the ranger station, selected from the "mass of season's work" Robinson then put at "ninety-odd sketches." How the passing years dramatically reduced the number of sketches is neither questioned nor explained by anyone who has written about the last spring series.

Robinson told Blodwen Davies that he declined, telling Thomson he did not want to take responsibility for their safekeeping. Thomson responded, saying, "I'll take all responsibility and I'll hang them around the walls here one of these days." Robinson's journal indicates that he left the park from June 13 to June 30, 1917, visiting his wife at their home in Barrie. He never mentions any similar scene in his journal from July 1 to July 8 and notes only two Thomson visits to the ranger station, on May 3 and May 6. Piecing together all he learned, Kristian concluded that Thomson did ask Robinson about exhibiting his paintings, but that he did so before the May 24 scene in the Mowat Lodge dining room.

The other critical piece of the story of what happened to the last spring sketches arises from Audrey Saunders and, once again, Robinson. In her book, *Algonquin Story*, Saunders wrote that George Thomson recovered thirty-five of his brother's sketches from a little cabin owned by the Trainor family just below Potter Creek, where she said Tom often stayed. In his tape-recorded interview at Camp Ahmek in 1953, Robinson discussed what happened following discovery of the body and the arrival of the undertaker and embalmer on July 17, 1917: "I was instructed [by Bartlett] to go to the little house and look see what was around there, and Mr. Trainor and I found—I forget—it was forty I guess, or somewheres, maybe less, of the sixty-two pictures, or sketches, that were lying around there."

It is by joining the two stories together that we come as close to the truth as possible, because in 1917, George Rowe or Lawrie Dickson, not Hugh Trainor's family, owned the little cabin below Potter Creek, which was the subject of a Thomson sketch given the misleading name, *The Artist's Hut*. Furthermore, if the little house referred to by Robinson and others was owned by Trainor, George Thomson would have earlier searched there and found the sketches himself.

Kristian learned that the Trainor cottage in Mowat was originally constructed as a mini-headquarters in 1908 where park rangers would gather. It was equipped with a large kitchen. Later, because a Presbyterian missionary stayed there, Canoe Lake residents referred to the cottage as "The Manse." The Trainors acquired it in 1912. In his 1953 interview at Camp Ahmek, Robinson said that on the morning of July 8, Thomson retrieved his canoe and fishing tackle "from this little cottage up here that used to be known as 'The Mess,' now Mr. Trainor's." [Emphasis added]. Either the transcriber made a mistake or Robinson, an army veteran, could have been thinking about how he remembered using the building himself. Dr. Little insisted that Thomson was staying with the Frasers in the Mowat Lodge before his drowning. "Tom never lived in the so-called 'Artist's Hut'…. In early spring and late fall, Tom lived with the Fraser's as one of the family. He frequently kept his panels in the former hospital [where the Frasers lived]. [According to] Mrs. J. S. Fraser…Tom was living at Canoe Lake when the tragedy occurred. Tom was staying at Mowat Lodge." In letters to his family, Tom said he was staying at the Post Office, which was located in the Mowat Lodge. Finally, the original death certificate prepared by Dr. Ranney listed Tom's residence as the Mowat Lodge.

Robinson's story could be accurately dated to July 17 and the arrival of the first undertaker and embalmer if George Thomson returned to Canoe Lake on July 18. Therefore, the story of Robinson recovering the thirty-three panels from Winnie's room in her family's cottage fits best with all surrounding events. Robinson's journal makes no mention of this important discovery. At late age, his recollection of events might have been dim.

Charles F. Plewman added an additional wrinkle. He acted as one of the pallbearers at Thomson's Canoe Lake funeral. He wrote an article for the Ontario Camping Association, "Some Aspects of Tom Thomson's Death and Burial," and told interviewers that, while hiking up Potter Creek a few days after the burial, he found discarded pieces of Thomson sketches strewn about. Thomson typically scraped and reused panels he found unacceptable rather than discard them. If Plewman's story is true, therefore, their destruction could have been the act of a disturbed man. Plewman wrote that Fraser told him Thomson was suicidal. "The impression Shannon left with me was that Tom had come to the conclusion that a settled, married life was not for him," Plewman said. "But that he could not say so to Miss Trainor."

Kristian's first research task in the library was to confirm that Thomson painted one sketch per day over sixty-two consecutive days, based on when he arrived in the park and when he finished. From references to the weather and to the black flies, both in Tom's letters and in Robinson's journal, Kristian concluded that Thomson began the last spring series of sketches on March 23 and finished on May 24.

A letter postmarked Mowat Lodge on April 23, 1917, to brother-in-law Tom Harkness, in Annan, Ontario, mentioned that Thomson read an article in the *Owen Sound Sun* issue published on April 10, 1917. "I got a copy...and it seemed to be filled with bunk. However, the foolishness of newspaper matter is well known, and I knew nothing about it in time to have it stopped." A newspaper reporter had evidently visited Thomson's shack in Toronto a few days earlier and written an enthusiastic account of the paintings he saw there, hardly bad publicity for an artist at the beginning of a promising career. In the letter, Thomson told Harkness, "I have been here *over three weeks* and have done considerable work for that length of time." [Emphasis added.]

Thomson wrote to Dr. MacCallum on April 21, 1917, asking his friend to visit the park later that spring. "I have been here *over three weeks* and they have gone very quickly....I would suggest that you come some time around the tenth of May, as *the flies are not going properly until about the twenty-fourth*. It is likely the ice will be out sometime this month. Have made quite a few sketches this spring, have scraped quite a few, and think that some that I have kept should go the same way. However, I keep on making them." [Emphasis added.]

Kristian recognized the reference to flies with a shudder. Anyone who visits in late May through the end of June has met up with the Algonquin black fly, a small, stout pest that thrives around its lakes and rivers. Aquatic at birth and throughout the larval stage, black flies do not establish themselves on land until they reach adulthood. As adults, males feed on nectar and pose no problem to humans. Mature females, however, are energetic parasites with a decided preference for the thin-skinned necks, wrists, and ankles of warm-blooded hosts, as canoeists and hikers know all too well. Even though black flies are tiny at a tenth of an inch in length, they swarm around victims, and every little bite packs a surprising punch. Bitten areas not only itch badly but also swell up and become painful to the touch.

Robinson's journal noted break-up of all the lake ice on May 1, 1917. Early May's cool temperatures limit the population of black flies. By late May, the bright green new leaves of the deciduous trees are visible everywhere, the days warm rapidly, and black flies emerge in swarms. It is noteworthy that Winnie

Trainor, Robert Little, Lieutenant Robert Crombie of the Royal Engineers, and his wife, Daphne, all left Canoe Lake the last week of May. On May 30, Robinson noted in his journal, "Black flies very bad." Robinson went home to Barrie from June 13 to June 30.

The black-fly population does not dwindle until early July, the warmest part of the summer. Thomson's July 7 letter to Dr. MacCallum reads, "The weather has been wet and cold all spring, and the flies and mosquitoes [are] much worse than I have seen them any year, and fly dope doesn't have any effect on them. This, however, is the second warm day we have had this year, and another day or so will finish them." The clues in his letter are crucial to our knowledge of what happened. Tom said the weather was very cold, and so the lake water would have been very cold as well. Kristian found daily weather data from Environment Canada, which verified his understanding of Thomson's letter.

Mowat P.O., Ontario, July 7 1917

Dr MacCallum

Dear Sir: I am still around Mowat and have not done any sketching since the flies started. the weather has been wet and cold all spring and the flies and mosquitoes much worse than I have seen them any year and fly dope dozon't have any effect on them. this however is the second warm day we have had this year and another day or so like this will finish them. will send my winter sketches down in a day or two and have every intention of making some more but it has been almost impossible lately. have done a great deal of paddling this spring and the fishing has been fine. Have done some guiding for fishing parties and will have some other trips this month and next with probably sketching in between. Received the slip of paper a day or so ago and don't know anything about it. Would you give it to Jim McDonald or someone around the bldg. with permission to do anything about it they say if they will I will be greatly obliged.

Hoping you are well. I am

yours truly Tom Thomson

Tom Thomson's letter of July 7, 1917 to Dr. MacCallum from the Mowat Lodge.

Kristian's personal favorite among Thomson's sketches that last spring is *Northern Lights.* In handwritten notes from 1930, and in a 1953 interview, Robinson said he recalled this painting.

> I did not see Thomson again until the spring of 1917. He had arrived a few days ahead of my return. Tom and a young man named Charles Scrim called at our cabin. We spent the afternoon recalling past events—the following evening, Tom walked in quite excited and referred to a very unusual display of northern lights. A few mornings afterwards, a very cold northern sky, what we get here, and it were cold. It was below zero that morning, and the sky had all the green colors, all over the north here. Tom came bolting into our house and walked up and down the floor...he said, "I want that, you see the sky, I want the black spruce, the raggest-looking old tops you find on them."

A few nights later, Robinson said Thomson produced a second northern lights painting. Robinson did not arrive at Canoe Lake until April 11, 1917, according to his journal. Robinson does not mention either event in his journal and notes only two visits by Thomson to the Joe Lake Creek ranger station on May 3 and by Thomson and Scrim on May 6. Thomson is never mentioned again until July 10. Kristian therefore doubted Robinson's later stories about when Thomson painted the northern light sketches, although the aurora borealis, or northern lights, does appear over Algonquin throughout the year.

Kristian settled on March 23 as the starting date and May 24 as the ending date and set about tracing the sixty-two paintings in the last spring series. The assumption that Thomson did one sketch each day for 62 days coincides with the day Thomson's letter warned Dr. MacCallum that black flies would be in full control of the park.

On July 7, 1917, Thomson wrote to Dr. MacCallum, saying, "I am still around the Frasers and *have not done any sketching since the flies started.*" [Emphasis added.] Evidence for the accuracy of the dates Kristian selected included a 1993 interview given by Arthur MacCallum, fixing the date of his father' visit to Thomson at the Mowat Lodge as May 24, 1917. A few days later, on May 28, Dr. MacCallum wrote to Thomson, saying, "You had better send down a lot of those sketches of yours as soon as you start in guiding and see if I cannot sell some of them and increase your account...."

Thomson's paintings lined the walls around the dining room, perhaps in honor of Dr. MacCallum, who carried home to Toronto the better of the two northern lights paintings, which he bequeathed to the National Gallery of Canada in 1944. Tom's family recovered the other. Kristian noted the two paintings on yellow index cards, moving one to the left and the other to the right.

Thomson had dinner that evening with Dr. MacCallum and Winnie Trainor. They talked about the last spring sketches. Remarks by Dr. MacCallum, Winnie Trainor, or both may have prompted the sensitive artist to stroll about the room inviting other dinner guests to view the collection, comment, and carry away the work of their choice. The lodge had twenty rooms. If fully occupied, and if other guests came from around Canoe Lake, upwards of fifty persons may have dined that evening.

From *Tom Thomson: The Last Spring*, Kristian learned that Dr. MacCallum took away several other paintings from the Mowat Lodge before leaving for his cottage on Georgian Bay. One of these paintings he put on consignment with William Beatty, who had a shop near the Scotia Junction station. Beatty sold *Winter Thaw in the Woods* to William J. Ard a few days later for twenty-five dollars. Dr. MacCallum mentioned the sale in a letter to Thomson on May 28, 1917. Evidently, MacCallum took *Winter in the Woods, Tea Lake Dam, Swift Water*, and *Portage Ragged Lake* for himself, all of which he bequeathed to the national gallery. It is odd indeed that Dr. MacCallum claimed these four panels as his own, unless the circumstances that evening at Mowat Lodge were inconsistent with their relationship as artist and patron. Kristian added notes to five more cards and added them to the pile on the right.

During the early months of 1917, Lieutenant Crombie and Daphne had an extended stay at the Mowat Lodge, leaving on May 25. Lieutenant Crombie was recuperating from tuberculosis in the clear, cold air of Algonquin. At the May 24 exhibit in Mowat Lodge, Thomson offered Daphne her choice of paintings. In 1977, Mrs. Crombie told an interviewer that she selected a panel Thomson said was "of the pathway that you and your husband used to go over to the other lake." Years later, Mrs. Crombie sold *The Path behind Mowat Lodge* to a Vancouver collector. During a January 1977 interview with Algonquin Park Ranger Ronald Pittaway, she was so embarrassed at mention of the sale that Pittaway was constrained to turn off the tape recorder before she continued. Kristian noted his finding on a blank index card and added it to the pile on the right.

Winnie Trainor died in 1962, owning at least thirteen of Thomson's panels. For many years, she kept them wrapped in old newspaper in a six-quart basket, tied with a cord. Later, at the urging of her physician, Dr. Wilford T. Pocock, MD, she acquired a safety-deposit box in North Bay, where they remained at her death.

"If she traveled, she would carry the basket across the street to the home of Addie Sylvester, a telephone operator who lived alone with dozens of stray cats," wrote Toronto newspaper columnist Roy MacGregor, Winnie Trainor's grand-nephew by marriage, in a May 2003 article for the *Globe and Mail.* "Addie would stash them in the back of the stove to keep them away from curious cats."

Before her death on August 12, 1962, Winnie told Terrence T. McCormick, younger sister to Marie's son and sole beneficiary of the estate, that a leading Toronto art dealer was holding four other Thomson panels for appraisal, in addition to the thirteen found in her safety-deposit box. Terrence McCormick quietly probated his aunt's estate, and whether he recovered the other four is unknown. Joan Murray verifies that Miss Trainor once owned *Canoe Lake*, a painting of a wintry sky over an icy lake, undoubtedly done that spring. Some of the seventeen reputedly depict scenes in downtown Huntsville. Kristian counted off thirteen slips, adding them to the pile on the right.

Shannon Fraser took *Early Spring, Canoe Lake.* Fraser and his wife, Annie, set aside at least two others from the dining room gallery that evening because, according to Joan Murray, they offered to sell three Thomson sketches to Hart House, a student activity building at the University of Toronto, in 1928. It bought two for $125 each. They later sold the other to the Art Gallery of Ontario. Kristian noted his finding on three cards in the pile to the right.

Howard Hancock's story Friday night explained the disappearance of four more panels. Margaret Rose O'Gorman, Mrs. Edwin Thomas, Rose Thomas, and Jack Riddle each took one. Kristian made notes on seven cards from the pile to the right.

Sometime that evening, Thomson asked Shannon Fraser to mail one of the panels to his good friend Dr. McRuer, in Denver, Colorado. Kristian added one more card to the pile on the right, picked them up, and counted.

"Twenty-eight," he murmured.

Kristian went back through three other books of Thomson prints: *Tom Thomson: Design for a Canadian Hero*, by Joan Murray, Dennis Reid's massive 386-page *Tom Thomson*, and *Tom Thomson: The Silence and the Storm*, by David P. Silcox and Harold Town. He found thirty-three panels from 1917, which were either owned by the Thomson family or held by museums and private collectors, to whom Dr. MacCallum had sold them in the name of the estate. He noted each one on the pile of cards to the left.

He recounted the cards to the right.

Kristian added and double-checked his figures.

"Sixty-one," he sighed.

Kristian reached the end of his research, accounting for all but one of the sixty-two panels painted by Thomson in the last spring series. He tossed his pencil on the table, disgusted, realizing he would never find the last panel.

Both Kristian and Ms. Murray fell far short of finding the "ninety-odd sketches" earlier reported by Robinson to Blodwen Davies. She wrote,

> The series, of which he was so proud, was broken up and scattered. Even yet, someday it may be possible to assemble the spring sketches in one of the galleries and catch something of what he intended to say. It would be an epic of spring, in which Thomson would seem to be poet and musician, as well as painter, so well did he unite his rhythms and harmonies in color.

Given his remarkable achievements over his last five years, many biographers argue that Thomson could not have been so depressed that he was considering suicide. Not only does this completely disregard the medical nature of mental depression, but also Kristian began to see Thomson's actions from a different angle as he pored over his notebook and pondered.

Thomson painted exhibition canvases from these little sketches. Giving away all sixty-two from the final weeks of spring 1917 left him with nothing to paint from the following winter. An artist paints to be seen, a writer to be read, and a musician to be heard, but first an artist, writer, or musician works for the sheer joy of creating. The passionate life is not outwardly but rather inwardly directed. The commitment comes not from anything he or she knows but from an abiding faith in what he or she does not know—and without which the work is unfulfilling. Kristian tried unsuccessfully to reconcile the incongruity of what Thomson did that evening to his last spring series of paintings with the attitude of a healthy artist whose faith and commitment to painting was firmly established.

19

Notebook: Alice Elinor Lambert's Version

In 1934, Alice Elinor Lambert wistfully described her summer romance with Tom Thomson through the fictional hero of her third and final Dell paperback novel, *Women Are Like That*. The twenty-two-year-old character is Miss Juliet Delaney, a chestnut-haired beauty with red-brown eyes and straight, level brows. Capable, kind, and wise about the world beyond her tender years, the character seemed a word-for-word description of Ms. Lambert herself. Alice was adapting her own experience to the needs of her book. Three remarkable passages describe for the discriminating reader, in her own words, her summer romance with Tom Thomson thirty years before:

> For one disturbing year, she had been desperately in love with a tall, dark boy named Tom, a commercial artist, who in the summer used to take her on streetcar rides to Alki Point and in the wintertime to the musty dimness of the public library, where he would pore over prints and reproductions of the masters. When, finally, darkly morose and determined to succeed, Tom had gone east, the girl, unversed as she was in the art of pursuit and capture, had let him go, powerless to hold him or call him back. Not once after he had left had she been able to pass Pioneer Square with its ancient gaudy totem pole, where they had been wont to meet, without tearing pain in her heart. When later she learned that Tom drowned while on a sketching trip in Canada, she sealed up a section of her heart, never again to open it. Tom had been tall and slender, with thin, nervous hands and flashing eyes. Instinctively, since his death, Juliet had avoided men of similar build and appearance.

A few pages later, building Juliet's character on a date in a roadhouse with a roaring, great fireplace of four-foot logs, Alice recalls a similar scene from her own past with Thomson.

"It's the fire," Juliet said softly, slipping out of her coat, for in spite of the chilly night outside, the crackling logs threw out abundant heat. "It's the campfire. It reminds me of something I used to do. A boy I knew a couple of years ago. He—he's not alive any more. He used to take me to Alki, and we'd get our supper at a place there on the boardwalk, and then we'd go down on the beach and build a little campfire, and just sit and talk. Until the last car, I guess. I love picnics. And campfires."

Her book's final reference to Thomson suggests that they were hardly intimate lovers. When her date takes Juliet home from the roadhouse, he "caught her up roughly, his arms drawing her close—closer—so that when he released her she was shaken and breathless."

'There," Carter said, his hands on her shoulders. "That will teach you a lesson, young woman. When I kiss them, they stay kissed."

But Juliet did not stay to hear. With a little sob, she turned and ran up the stair, flung open the door, and closed it, leaning against its inner side, breathing heavily.

"Tom," she whispered through trembling lips. "I wish it had been you. Just once, if you'd kissed me that way, I could have borne this—this waiting. Oh Tom," and fighting back the tears which would not stop, she went, a trifle stumblingly, up to her room.

Tom left Seattle a short time after meeting her. Two stories emerged of what happened between Alice and the artist, ten years her senior. One version is that he proposed marriage, to which she, perhaps startled, laughed or, more crudely, snorted in derision. The other suggests that Alice was flirting all summer long with Horace Rutherford, who confessed to Tom that he was engaged to her in marriage. Alice claimed in a 1971 letter to Joan Murray,

Tom packed [Horace] up and…went east to save me. I used to long to write him, or find him, but a miserable experience prevented me—I married a man with whom I had no communication whatever.[1] But I never put Tom out of my heart. We were two star-crossed young and innocent people who never should have parted.

Blodwen Davies's original biography, *A Study of Tom Thomson*, privately published in 1935, is quite rare. Only 450 copies were published, Consequently, it could not have had any influence on the public. The book sold so poorly that in 1957 Blodwen Davies told Little in a letter that dealers had copies still available at twelve dollars each. She offered to sell him one for seven dollars. Nonetheless, the book guided later Canadian biographers with three sentences of purple prose.

> Who met Tom Thomson on that stretch of grey lake, screened from all eyes, that July noon?
>
> Who was it that struck him a blow across the right temple—and was it done with the thin edge of a blade?—that sent blood spurting from his ear?
>
> Who watched him crumple up and topple over the side of the canoe and sink slowly out of sight without a struggle?

She offered no evidence of murder and evidently had no medical knowledge regarding cold-water drowning victims. Years later, she asked A. Y. Jackson to republish the book. He did so following her death, inexplicably excising these three sentences and a few others discussed in detail by Sherrill Grace. In 1930, Blodwen Davies wrote a thirty-five-page pamphlet titled *Paddle and Palette: The Story of Tom Thomson*, which may have received wider sales.

Ms. Davies book analyzed Tom's relationship with Alice, as well as the relationship's ending. Ms. Davies wrote,

> The mistake so many make [in lost love] is in regarding this cosmic urge as a means of personal gratification and as a culminating experience [that] ends in negative happiness. Because of this misuse of a cosmic force intended for the evolution of man into a creative being, the race is doomed to learn its lesson in sorrow. And so we see so many loves frustrated in a personal sense in order that the lover may use his power impersonally. From those who learn the lesson we have our truly creative class whose vision is universal.
>
> He who refuses to regard his love for another individual as anything but a right to demand devotion, sympathy, and service in return is shriveled up by its fire when it is denied an outlet. Because of the results in Thomson's life, we

---

1.   Alice married Joseph E. Ransburg in 1912. She took his name. They had two daughters, Victoria, born in 1914, and Josephine, born in 1916. According to Joan Murray, she separated from Ransburg in the 1920s, moved to San Francisco, and wrote an advice column called "Alice Elinor" for the *Examiner* newspaper. According to the 1930 U.S. census, they lived together in Seattle. In 1931, she again separated, moving to New York. She returned to Seattle the following year. During these years, she wrote three novels. Ransburg died in Hawaii in 1955. Alice E. Lambert died in Marysville, Washington, in 1981.

know the quality of his love. He did not waste its force by blaming the woman but set to work to alter the currents of his life.

Neither Alice nor Blodwen Davies probably reached the true story—these two artistic souls simply passed, mingled, and departed on their separately destined paths of life. Thomson never spoke of Alice again.

20

Notebook: Tom's First Trip to Algonquin

Before he could unleash his creative genius, Tom Thomson had to escape from his overbearing older brother, George, and from Alice Lambert. When he arrived back in Ontario, he was at least as relieved to be away from them as he was glad to be on Canadian soil. It was at this time—1905 to 1913—that Thomson began his formative years as an artist; however, biographers know little of Thomson between ages twenty-four and thirty-three. He joined a commercial art firm in Toronto, the Legg Brothers, drawing eleven dollars per week. He also enrolled at the Central Ontario School of Art and Design. The master, William Cruikshank, taught many of Canada's artists. Thomson traveled home to Owen Sound on summer weekends, consistent with the trickle and, later, the floods of Toronto residents whose northward trips each summer weekend culminated in Ontario's official three-day summer holidays.

In 1908, Tom made the crucial move of his artistic career: he joined the staff of Grip Limited, where many of Canada's eventually famous painters toiled on commercial photoengraving projects. The senior designer was James E. H. Mac-Donald. Already working there were Frank H. Varley, Franklin Carmichael, Frank Johnston, and Arthur Lismer, all of whom would become widely admired post-impressionist painters of the Canadian landscape. They influenced each other, sharing the varied experiences they had received at European art schools. Joining with A. Y. Jackson and Lawren S. Harris in 1919, they formed a school of artists known as the Group of Seven, which exhibited together beginning in 1920, heralding the new style of Canadian landscape art in the early 1900s. Johnston moved to Washington and Alfred J. Casson took his place in 1926. Thomson worked at the Grip as a formal design artist for the commercial print industry. He drew on this experience to create his paintings, giving them a formal cathedral-window quality, capturing the wild expanse and power of Algonquin Park.

Not until 1910 did Thomson venture north to paint. He was best man at Dr. John M. McCuer's wedding the preceding year in Huntsville, forty miles west of the park, making where he made a few seminal sketches at Fairy Lake, twenty miles west of Algonquin Park, establishing a pattern he would follow the rest of his life. In the autumn of 1911, Thomson made sketches that Canadian separated him from his peers, according to Canadian art critics today. In 1912, he took up oil painting. He and artist friend H. B. "Ben" Jackson paddled up the Oxtongue River into Canoe and Joe Lakes. They portaged over into Smoke, Ragged, and Big Porcupine Lakes and back down the Oxtongue River to the Tea Lake Dam, a favorite site of Thomson's for painting and fishing. Later that summer, he made a three-hundred-mile journey down the Mississagi River with another friend, William S. Broadhead. Here, they were upset in the rough whitewater rapids on the Audinandong River and lost many sketches. Back in Toronto, at the Arts and Letters Club, Dr. MacCallum happened to see some of the salvaged sketches. He was impressed enough to begin buying Thomson's work, taking him under his well-endowed financial wing.

That winter, Thomson joined an exodus of Grip artists to Rouse and Mann, Ltd., a commercial art firm, where he began an annual practice. He painted a magnificent oil canvas, *A Northern Lake*, for the annual spring exhibition of the Ontario Society of Artists (OAS). It sold in early 1913 to the Provincial Government of Ontario for $250. Thus began his career as Canada's greatest landscape artist. In following years, Thomson spent more and more time at Algonquin in the summer and fall, returning to work and paint in Toronto in the winter and spring. In May 1913, he quit Rouse and Mann to take up work as a park ranger in Ontario's Mattagami Reserve, south of Timmins. Along the way, Thomson met Mark Robinson, who suggested he visit the Mowat Lodge. Later that year, after Thomson urged him to visit Algonquin and share his tent on the north shore of Canoe Lake, Arthur Lismer spent a glorious fall season there. Thomson painted during this time, and his new seventeen-foot keeled chestnut canoe arrived from New Brunswick. Thomson painted it with a distinctive mix of dove gray and cobalt blue oils, which he purchased in tubes costing two dollars each.

Lismer recognized Thomson as a gifted angler, who could make his own flies for the brown trout and spooners for deep-fishing lake trout, still a spring sport there today. Some biographers say Thomson's favorite book was *The Compleat Angler*, by Isaak Walton. First published in 1653, Walton's book celebrates the art and spirit of freshwater fishing in prose, verse, anecdotes, and commentaries on catching and preparing everything from carp to trout. Robinson observed later that Thomson "was capable of swimming the length of Canoe Lake easily." However, it seems unlikely Thomson would have spent the hours it would have taken to swim across cold blue-green lake.

In 1914, with the financial guidance and encouragement of Dr. MacCallum, Thomson pursued success as an artist, moving into the newly built Studio Building overlooking the Rosedale Ravine, sharing space with A. Y. Jackson. That summer, Thomson visited Dr. MacCallum's home on Georgian Bay, traveled to Lake Nipissing, and paddled solo up the South River and down the French River, an arduous trip. He and other Toronto artists Varley, Jackson, and Lismer traveled together, working on 8.5"-by-10.5" birch shingles. The autumn colors were exceptionally brilliant that year. Sometimes he painted on the back of earlier works he had completed. For example, he painted *Autumn* on the back of *Rounded Hill and River*.

The *Globe and Mail*'s "Arts and Artists" column reported in November 1914,

> Mr. Tom Thomson has just returned from a sketching trip to Algonquin Park, where he had gone to follow the autumn color into winter. He brought back a great many fine studies, particularly remarkable for color and originality of design, and the subjects range from studies of full autumn color right through the fall of the leaves to white frosts and deep snows.

He participated in three art shows that winter, including the Royal Canadian Academy's Thirty-sixth Exhibition, where he showed *A Lake, Early Spring*, and *Frost Lake after Rain*. Thomson put two canvases into the OSA show that winter, *Morning Clouds* and *Moonlight, Early Evening*, each of which the National Gallery purchased that year for $150. Thomson was elected a member of the OAS. He exhibited five small paintings in a show at the Art Gallery of Toronto. The exhibition assured his fame as an artist.

The next winter, 1915, he entered three paintings in the OSA show, including one of his more famous ones, *Northern River*, which Ottawa's National Gallery purchased for the remarkable sum of five hundred dollars. In April 1915, he went back to Algonquin, setting up camp at Hayhurst Point on Canoe Lake. Thomson visited Winnifred Trainor at Canoe Lake and in Huntsville, where he painted his first-floor room a vivid red, mixing the color himself. She later let the room out to tourists, bragging for years about his handiwork. He traveled from Canoe Lake all over Algonquin, heading as far north as Kawawaymog Lake. There he gave Ranger Tom Wattie a sketch called *Sand Hill*. In November, Tom visited Owen Sound, where his parents now lived. He returned to Toronto for the winter, when he completed and contributed two major canvases, *Forest Undergrowth* and *Spring Ice*, to the OSA art show. Again, the National Gallery purchased both.

In the spring of 1916, renowned artist Lawren Harris, Dr. MacCallum, and Thomson visited Cauchon Lake. Harris wrote,

> I remember one afternoon…when a dramatic thunderstorm came up. There was a wild rush of wind across the lake and all nature was tossed into turmoil….When the storm broke, Tom looked out, grabbed his sketch box, ran out into the gale, squatted behind a big stump, and commenced to paint in a fury. He was one with the storm's fury, save that his activity, while keyed to a high pitch, was nonetheless controlled. In twenty minutes, Tom had caught in living paint the power and drama of a storm in the north.

Thomson took a job as a fire ranger, reporting to Achray, a train station on Grand Lake on the south branch of the mighty Petawawa River. He followed the Booth Company log drive down the Petawawa River, painting a sketch for *The Drive*. Fellow Fire Ranger Edward Godin said Thomson visited the Ottawa River near Pembroke, where Thomson made the sketch used in his famous canvas *West Wind*.[1]

Over the winter of 1916, Thomson completed one major canvas, *The Jack Pine*, but failed to enter it or any others in the 1917 art exhibitions. "I did not send any paintings to the OSA Exhibition this year and have not sold very many sketches, but I think I can manage to get along for another year at least," he wrote to his father on January 23, 1917. Thomson was working on several canvases that

---

1. Many friends and acquaintances of Thomson claim personal knowledge of where he made the sketch for *West Wind*. Robinson offered the tallest tale. In one of his taped Ahmek interviews, he insisted that Thomson painted the sketch at Achray on Grand Lake, offering the panel to him at the Joe Lake Ranger Station in 1915. Robinson claims he refused on artistic grounds. "Tom, I think you had better put it on canvas!" Robinson allegedly demurred. "I know you cannot afford to throw them away anymore than I could, and for that reason, you've got something good there." Dr. Robert P. Little, MD, said that the Reverend Mr. Arthur Reynolds of Annan, Ontario, told him Tom painted it at Fairy Lake. Winnifred Trainor said it was painted at Cedar Lake. Tom Wattie believed it was done at Round Lake. In a letter to Miss A. L. Beatty, secretary to the curator of the Art Gallery of Ontario, dated May 14, 1937, MacCallum wrote, "It may interest you to know…that the *West Wind* was done at Lake Cauchon. Thomson, myself, Lorne [sic] Harris, and his cousin Chester were up there. It was blowing very hard, and Lorne Harris was painting farther up the shore. The wind blew down the tree of the picture, and Harris first thought that Thomson was killed, but he soon sprang up, waved his hand to him, and went on painting."

Dr. MacCallum said he never finished, including *The Drive, Woodland Waterfall,* and *The Pointers.* He began work on the *West Wind* canvas. That last winter, he worked on it under MacDonald's guidance for many weeks. MacDonald said Thomson's problem arose from its combination of two styles—a formalized tree against a natural background. How Thomson would have resolved this frustration remains the second biggest mystery of his life, since he left the canvas unfinished in his studio in mid-March 1917, when he ventured forth on his last spring trip to Algonquin Park. thinking, perhaps, of the closing line from Percy Bysshe Shelley's poem, *Ode to the West Wind,* "The trumpet of a prophecy! O, Wind, If winter comes, can spring be far behind?"

21

Kristian Attends His Ex-Wife's Funeral

Kristian sped southbound on M-65 from his house in downtown Romeo. Tragic, gut wrenching, unthinkable though it was, he needed to know more. Wasn't he entitled?

He often marveled at how fast his relationship with Tess had ended. In one moment of excruciating intimacy, he told her he was planning to leave, and the next they were embarrassed strangers. She shut up the bedroom, relegating him to the living room sofa. It turned out to be more comfortable than the bed he shared with her. She also started shutting the bathroom door. So did the girls. He had taken showers with her and baths with them, up to ages three or four, when the girls got too big to go in the tub with him. Never again did she talk with him. She did talk *at* him frequently, demanding money and transportation for their daughters. These demands—for payment, delivery, and pick-up—escalated in subtle, indirect ways. After he moved out the first Monday in February, his younger daughters called daily seeking money and automobile rides to the mall, the movies, or fast food restaurants. As they did, Tess coaxed audibly in the background.

Kristian's oldest daughter, Shelley, called him at 4:38 P.M., according to the clock on the stove. He turned to record the moment in his mind, out of habit. Her voice cracked, tinged with bitter anger and profound sorrow.

"Dad, I got to tell you that Mom died."

"What do you mean?"

"She killed herself."

"What?"

"I don't know. Aunt Beth Ann is over at the house for the girls. I don't know very much."

"What do you know?"

"She was dead in the bathtub."

"Bathtub?"

"They'd already taken her away. The police said Mom called 9-1-1 but didn't say anything. She left the phone off the hook. Sheriff's deputies came and found her."

What could he say?

"I am sorry, Shelley," he said. "Where are the girls?"

"The school says the buses are on the way. Aunt Beth Ann is there waiting."

Kristian said he was going and hung up. Bob Francis was Aunt Beth's wife and Kristian's best friend, as well as the best man at his wedding. Kristian's mother, however, prevailed on him with threats to boycott the wedding, insisting his brother be the best man instead. Even now, speeding seventy-four miles per hour, he reflected on his regret at making this choice. What difference did it make now? he thought, pushing it aside again. He wondered what the funeral etiquette was for an ex-husband following his ex-wife's death by suicide. Obviously, you had to go to the funeral for the children. Can you ask about arrangements? Do you send flowers? Where do you sit at the funeral? What do you say to her parents? What do say to your daughters?

He passed Twenty-five Mile Road doing eighty-three miles per hour. He decided to slow down and pull off at the M-34 exit to get some coffee. He sat for a while with the coffee and went up to get another cup and a donut, which he gulped down. He went to the restroom, puked, and puked again. After turning off M-34 at Van Dyke and going south two miles, he stopped at a 7-11 and picked up a fifth of good Scotch, Johnny Walker Black, something he had often shared with Bob over the years.

"I'm not going back there today," he reminded himself, having completed his intensive outpatient alcohol recovery program at Maplegrove Hospital only seven weeks earlier. When he arrived at Bob's, his friend was grateful for the gift, and the gesture of forgiveness, and although he was disappointed at the loss of a long-time drinking companion, he was proud, or at least respectful, of Kristian's resolve. Kristian sat for hours late into the night, drinking coffee, talking about his intense guilt, and bemoaning that there was nothing he could do except say he was drunk one night and decided to get divorced because Tess did not love herself or him anymore.

Bob stood by his side the next night at 7:43 P.M., a Wednesday. Kristian was wearing a cleaned and pressed white shirt, black suit, subdued blue tie, dark socks, and shoes. That is what you do, he said to himself, getting ready. He removed his wedding band for the last time. Not much for fine grooming, he shaved himself twice. He checked closely in the mirror, loaded a new razor blade, and shaved a third time. He wanted to look his best, having not seen his daughters and in-laws for months. Kristian also used underarm deodorant—the stick—a Christmas gift from Shelley, which he had never used before that evening.

His ex-wife's family ignored him. Despite his calls, Kristian's family stayed away. His daughters stayed away from him, too, huddled together around the oldest sister, Shelley. They moved around the entry room to the chapel, the four of them representing twenty-four straight years of kindergarten to twelfth grade, daily homework, Saturday ballet lessons, Brownie and Girl Scout meetings, early morning marching band, afternoon volleyball, track meets, evening choir performances, weekend swimming, and gymnastic lessons. Much of that ended when he filed for divorce. Sheila had been an A student since fourth grade. She started skipping school, flunked Spanish, and dropped out of band. Between them, the two younger girls dropped out of band, choir, Brownies, ballet, and gymnastics. The youngest enrolled in martial arts. Less affected was Shelley, away at college in Ypsilanti at Eastern Michigan University. Still, she had not spoken to him for seventeen months before making her call late Monday afternoon. All of his daughters were lean chestnut-haired beauties, getting their mother's good looks, her sharp, dark eyes, high cheeks, perfect nose, rosy complexion, gently prominent chin, and graceful, long neck over strong shoulders. These defiantly self-confident and independent girls clung to each other at the funeral home, not because they lacked strength, but because they knew they at least had one another now that Tess had abandoned them too.

"Whose idea was it to conduct the funeral service at night with a private burial the next day?" he asked Bob, who shrugged. Nobody else told him, nor did he ask. Tess's family didn't say a word to him. He had not seen any of them since the day he left Tess. He knew all of them personally, gotten drunk with them, celebrated the Fourth of July, Easter, and Labor Day weekends at sister-in-law Karen's, where she always served the same uninspired buffet consisting of hamburgers, hot dogs, plain and smoked Kielbasa, sauerkraut, ribbon Jell-O, cheesy potatoes, and Caesar salad for her father. Thanksgiving and Christmas Day, perpetual sore points between Tess and Kristian, were always celebrated at her parents', Dean and Lena Christopher, with a turkey, which Lena cooked and Dean carved. Tradition was unbreakable with them, and Kristian's decision to follow it left his family dumbfounded every year. The only explanation he could offer was that he wanted to get along with his wife. Kristian thought back now to the sacrifices he had made visiting her family all those years. They had never invited any of his family.

For them, family was forever defined as parents, children, and later grandchildren. All others were outsiders. Today was the last of such gathering that Kristian would attend.

Lena swayed and moved unsteadily on Dean's arm. Kristian never gave any thought to what was obvious to everyone else who knew her. Lena was not only a lonely homemaker but also a well-protected alcoholic. Dean kept her stocked up with bottled, never canned, Blatz beer, an economy brand. She refused to drink anything else. Blatz recycled its bottles and Lena's looked especially well worn. If he had realized it sooner, he would have figured out why they spent all holidays at her home, why Dean isolated her from everyone, including her sons, daughters, sisters, and brothers. He would know why Tess often bitterly complained that her mother never went out to lunch, never invited her to go shopping or to do anything else together. Kristian concluded that Dean was a facilitator—gruff outside and angry inside that Lena's drinking had ended his automobile-industry career. Dean took an early retirement five years ago, a few months after the last of the Christopher children left home, Kristian remembered. Lena needed closer watching because, living alone, she was going through Blatz bottles at an alarming rate.

Determined to know more about the suicide, Kristian set out to maneuver Shelley to one side and away from her sisters. He gestured clumsily to her, and Shelley responded by wagging him away. Forlorn, he stood quietly with Bob. The entry room to the chapel hummed around him, Aunt Elsie and Uncle Kirk murmuring about the missing brother-in-law, crack-addicted Brian. He heard Shelley say something about a luncheon tomorrow after the burial. Kristian's face flushed red with embarrassment, and the pounding in his ears drowned out the din. He knew all these people from earlier family funerals. His exclusion from the lunch was wrong.

He, Bob, and Beth Ann went into the chapel. Beth Ann sat by Kristian and touched his shoulder. Beth Ann was a suicide victim social worker at Detroit Receiving Hospital. They talked. She told him most suicides were younger men between twenty and thirty-five and middle-aged women devastated by who knows what, though severe depression, other psychiatric disorders, and terminal illness were the leading causes.

In the United States, there are nearly thirty thousand suicides per year, the eighth leading cause of death. Seven percent of female suicides are by drowning. Male drowning cases are somewhat rarer. The numbers may well be higher for women since it's easier to disguise suicidal intent by drowning than by the more common methods—gunshots, hanging, and poisoning. Over ninety percent of drownings occur in freshwater lakes, while bathtub drownings account for seven percent of the total.

"Suicide by drowning is often described as a slow, agonizing way to die, but it's actually effective and quick, usually taking between four and ten minutes. Less than half succeed though," she explained. "That's because once the lack of oxygen reaches a certain point, survival instincts take over, until all the person can do is try to get air. All effort at drowning is instinctively abandoned. That's why alcohol or drugs are involved in the majority of drownings. Two-thirds of adult males who drown consume at least some alcohol."

Kristian raised his eyebrows quizzically.

"As far as I know, Tess took nothing," Beth Ann said.

"There are actually two types of drowning," Beth Ann continued. "Eighty-five percent are wet drownings, in which the victim aspirates large volumes of water. Dry drowning occurs because of a sudden closure of the airway caused by cold water in the throat, a laryngeal spasm."

Beth Ann paused, and her eyes grew moist.

"She filled the tub with six bags of ice."

"Why?"

"If the water in the bathtub was below sixty degrees, she may have suffered cold-water shock and died instantly. Or within minutes, she would have been rendered unconscious. When she slid under, she probably did not even know. It could have been an accident."

"Accident?"

"That's why in fifteen percent of drowning cases, the cause of death cannot be determined solely by medical examination. Deciding among murder, accident, or suicide requires a thorough investigation of all of the circumstances, including evidence of other injury. When a person drowns in a lake or a river, the body always assumes a face-down position, with the arms, legs, and face dragging against whatever is down there. It's common to find wounds and scrapes to the face, arms, and hands. It is particularly difficult to know when a wound occurred, since they bleed more readily due to the marked fluidity of the blood. Hemorrhages in the middle ear are also common in drowning cases, contributing to bleeding."

Kristian listened.

"Also significant is whether the victim is undressed—suicide victims normally don't want to be found naked—and the presence or absence of a suicide note."

Kristian raised his eyebrows again.

"She was fully dressed," Beth Ann said.

"Did she leave a note?"

"No," she responded. "Do you think she wanted anyone to know?"

"Yes."

At the time of her death, 2:36 P.M., Kristian was at Coney Island, across the street from the Macomb County courthouse, he remembered, reading the *Detroit Free Press* and munching two Coney Island hot dogs with everything, along with chili fries and a Diet Coke. Instead of heading home, he had walked there after signing the divorce papers and lingered over a newspaper. He stopped by the law firm, looked over his e-mail, returned two voicemails, and filed the paperwork to end his marriage. One of the senior partners looked in and told him to go home.

He then left, drove sixteen minutes north to his home in Romeo, and took Shelley's phone call. A Romeo police officer called him seven minutes later, offered condolences, and asked where he was that afternoon between noon and three o'clock.

"Getting divorced and eating hot dogs at Coney Island across from the court-house in Mount Clemens. I stopped by the office too."

Silence.

"Can we call if we have more questions?"

"Of course," he said. "I may go out of town tomorrow for a few days. I will be back next week."

"Okay, then. Sorry for your loss."

As Reverend Buss stood to conduct the service, the gathering shuffled into the chapel. Much had collapsed around Kristian since he packed up his books, clothes, a dresser, and a few CDs, moving away from Tess and stealing away from the girls, breaking his marital vows.

Her younger brother, David, who had been a frequent weekend dinner guest along with his attractive wife, Brianne, and two young sons, gave himself up to cocaine after the invitations from Kristian and Tess dried up.

Her younger sister's marriage failed, and her older brother filed for divorce again.

Kristian's younger brother got divorced out in California.

All that was stable and sure in the family crumbled away in the wake of his drunken resolution seventeen months ago to get divorced. Guilt overwhelmed him for months and lingered because he still had no explanation for her death.

Reverend Buss finished his sermon and the pallbearers moved solemnly to the front. Kristian stood helpless at the rear. The church was full of people, young and old. As they came up the center aisle, his four daughters sobbed. Kristian followed the procession into the entry room and shuffled off to the side. His knees shook with the weight of his guilt.

Shelley appeared behind him and whispered, "Dad, what do you want?"

"What happened?"

"I told you."

"Not how, or why?"

She looked at him for a while, shook her head, and cleared her throat. Shelley enjoyed teaching him lessons.

"Mom's cancer was terminal, and you divorced her anyway."

She slid away into the crowd.

"I didn't know," he whispered. "Nobody ever told me."

He had thought to ask, often. However, his daughters had pushed away all of his inquires.

"You have to ask *her*, Dad."

"We don't talk about that with you, Dad."

"I don't know what you mean, Dad."

"Can you take me to the movies, Dad?"

His bottom slapped into a nearby bench. Everyone heard him drop. He sat with his head drooped, eyes closed. A few minutes later, Bob grabbed his shoulder and helped him up as the chapel quieted.

"Time to go," Bob said. "You have done what you needed to do. Come on. Come on. They are all gone. All gone away, and you should to go home."

Kristian stood on shaky legs, pulling up his arms and body once again, feeling as if he was leaving something, some part of himself, there in the chapel.

"Stand and go," Bob urged.

"She is going home, too," said Beth Ann, her eyes glistening with tears.

Kristian left the funeral alone and stopped to pick up a fifth of vodka, and then he drove to his apartment, committed to developing their relationship again during the night ahead.

He fell off the dining room chair trying to get up for some more. He pulled himself to his feet and wandered around the apartment. He played Michael Hedges on the stereo, the guitar wailing as he wailed deep in his heart. The refrigerator's freezer held but two empty ice trays and a half-gallon of chocolate ice cream, untouched since the weekend visit of Mollie (Bob's daughter) and Sarah. Nothing but mustard, pickles, and old salad dressing jars lined the door of the fridge.

Kristian closed the refrigerator at 11:47 P.M., noting the time on the stove. He left out the back and headed over to a bar on Main Street, where he wanted to get something more to drink and a hamburger. The grill was closed, but the bar was open until 1:46 A.M., when the bartender, who refused to talk, eased him out the rear into the alley. He stumbled back to the apartment.

His mind stumbled, too, in a drunken daze of disparate, rambling thoughts and images. Reverend Buss did not know Tess and said nothing of the years she spent with Kristian. Reverend Buss never mentioned the trips to the Breakers Hotel in Palm Beach, Barbados, the U.S. Virgin Islands, Atlanta, New Orleans, Los Angeles, Disneyland, and San Francisco. He did not talk about the delicious beef sandwich, along with the news of his law-firm partnership, that he brought to Tess in their bedroom the night they brought home their fourth daughter. Sherry was the youngest, most talented, and most fiercely independent of his daughters. She had stood there, age six, with her sisters at the front of the church. She turned to glare at him, eyes filled with tears.

He cried, too, for them and for himself. Tears streamed down his face now as he remembered facing her coffin. His mind filled with this last picture of her, eyes sleeping, lips closed, hands clasped across her lower chest, wearing a dress he did not recognize, a sunflower print, notes from their daughters resting over her left shoulder against the back of the coffin.

Tess had gotten nothing out of doing this to all of them. She had wanted everything out of him yesterday in the divorce, and she had gotten it, the one-sided negotiations stretching into the early afternoon.

"The marriage is already dead," he told his lawyer. "Let's end the divorce, too."

Had be been too eager to get it over with, to hear whatever she was trying to say?

"What did she really want?" he asked Bob in the funeral home parking lot.

"I don't know."

"Did she love me?" he thought, stumbling down the sidewalk behind the Old Towne Bar.

As he slid into bed, Kristian saw his Tom Thomson poster on the wall—Thomson, who slid into the waters of Canoe Lake in 1917 without a word to those who loved him, not his family, not Winnie Trainor, not his drinking buddies or colleagues in the Toronto art community he had cajoled into accompanying him on trips to Algonquin. Kristian studied the painting, trying to understand Thomson's death. He saw past the artist to the park's wilderness, a sacred place where he might find forgiveness and redemption for his loss of commitment to Tess.

"I'm going to go back," he decided. "I need to get the camping gear together."

Kristian swung up and around, attempting to put his feet on the floor; instead, he fell against the wall. The Thomson poster crashed to the floor, the glass shattering. Startled, Kristian fell back, hitting his head on the nightstand, knocking himself unconscious and sending an alarm clock and paperback books flying. He awoke at dawn, having vomited in the spot he had fallen on the floor. He looked at the fifth he had bought coming home last evening, which was dead empty, and then he loaded himself into the car for a trip to Algonquin Park.

22

Notebook: Tom and Winnifred

Winnifred Trainor was the older of two daughters born to Mr. Hugh Trainor, a logging supervisor with the Huntsville Lumber Company, and his wife. Winnie worked as a bookkeeper in Kearney. She infrequently visited her parents at their summer cottage on Canoe Lake, the third and farthest south of Mowat Lodge in 1917. Logging was a winter trade—the hauling of timber depended on roadways cut through forest made passable only by winter ice. Lumberjacks spent their summer off work, while bookkeepers worked year round.

During Thomson's first visit to Algonquin Park, in 1912, at age thirty-four, he spent two nights at the Trainor winter home and boardinghouse in Huntsville. There he began a friendly relationship with Winnie, age twenty-eight. There is no evidence of an intimate friendship between them, except for one short, provocative passage from a letter she allegedly wrote to him shortly before his death. "Please, Tom," she allegedly wrote, "you must get a new suit, because we'll have to be married."

It is this letter, if it ever existed, that prompted the rumor of Thomson's suicide. The rumor began with Shannon Fraser and his wife, Annie. In 1977, Mrs. Daphne Crombie, then in her nineties, told two interviewers that Annie Fraser had confided to her in November 1917 that she read this remarkable statement in a letter on Thomson's dresser at the Mowat Lodge in July 1917. George Thomson did not find any letters in his thorough search after the disappearance, nor did Mark Robinson gather such a letter during his visit to the Trainor cottage a few days after the drowning. Mrs. Crombie's full statement to the two interviewers is part of a longer story of love, pregnancy, shame, pride, money, and murder that she waited sixty years to tell, securing her place among the myths and legends of Thomson's life and death.

A second, verified letter written by Winnie, however, offers some insight into her feelings about his death, even if it does nothing to illuminate her relationship with Thomson. In a letter rife with enigmatic implications that she wrote to the

Thomson family in September 1917, she said, "If I see you, I can tell you all...after I knew what was going on at Canoe Lake, I did all in my power to get things righted—I was told it could not be done....The Frasers were money grubbing as usual, but it will all come back to them....As far as good faith is concerned, [Fraser] has none....Mark Robinson hates him."

Winnie Trainor died in 1962, saying nothing more to anyone who came forward. Ottawa newspaper columnist Roy MacGregor, whose great uncle, Dr. Robert R. McCormick, married Winnie's younger sister, Marie, wrote a book in 1980 entitled *Shorelines*, which has since been republished as *Canoe Lake*. In this fictionalized account of Thomson's death, a pregnant character based on Winnie Trainor confronts Thomson, demanding marriage. Leaving the actual cause of his drowning for readers to decide, MacGregor's book then follows her over the next nine months, to a Philadelphia home for unwed mothers, where she gives birth on Easter Day to a daughter, who returns as a young woman to Algonquin Park in search of her mother and father.

In a poignant article originally published on June 9, 2002, in the *Ottawa Citizen* (and which was added as an author's note to the second edition of the book), MacGregor acknowledged his family's connection to Winnifred Trainor and offered personal glimpses into her character, his book's speculation about her pregnancy having ended any ongoing relationship with at least one member of her side of the family.

> She was intimidating and opinionated and frightening to the neighborhood children, who called her a witch," he wrote. "[After her death in the] summer of 1963, when I was fifteen, I helped clean out her old house in Huntsville and her cottage on Canoe Lake, both of them packed to the rafters with saved magazines, knickknacks, and trinkets, her bathtub in Huntsville filled...with empty paint tins. She came by her reputation for eccentricity honestly.
>
> I have no proof. All I know is what I was able to find in the 'Personals' section of the *Huntsville Forester*, which had a handy habit of recordings the comings and going of every person in town during those years. On November 12, 1917, the *Forester* reported that Winnifred and her mother...returned to Huntsville after spending several weeks in Northern Ontario, where they visited with Mrs. James Bradley in New Liskeard, Mrs. Jago in Haileybury, and Miss Lottie Laing, who had been ill, in North Bay.
>
> In the same edition, it was reported, farther down in the personals, that Mrs. Trainor and [Winnie] had left for Philadelphia, where they would spend the winter. The *Forester* does not record their return until Easter of 1918...Upon the return of...Winnifred to Huntsville, Hugh Trainor immediately moved his family north to Kearney, where the Trainors stayed until

Hugh Trainor's death late in the winter of 1932. Only then did Winnifred Trainor return to Huntsville to live the remaining thirty years of her life.

MacGregor explained in a lecture at the Tom Thomson Museum that the Trainors had no relatives in Philadelphia and that his uncle, later a New York State physician, and aunt, Marie Trainor, who studied nursing, would have known where to send Winnie if she was pregnant. MacGregor wrote:

> When this book was first published in the spring of 1980, there were still people alive who had known Tom Thomson and been at Canoe Lake that fateful summer of 1917. I personally know nothing of what truly happened. I only know, for sure, that this book so upset certain members of my family that it cost our relationship. I understand their response.

The article seemed as much an apology to the family as a tantalizing look at a possible motive for Thomson's death. MacGregor acknowledged in the original book, *Shorelines*, that her physician, Dr. Wilford T. Pocock, MD, doubted she had ever been pregnant. In 1920, Dr. Pocock set up a medical practice in Kearney, many miles northeast of Huntsville. He did not meet Winnie Trainor until a few years after July 1917. However, pregnancy would explain her long visit to Philadelphia. She left Canoe Lake on May 25 and did not return until July 17 for Thomson's burial. Therefore, the existence of a letter to Thomson makes sense only if she had been pregnant before leaving Canoe Lake. If this was the case, why did she not leave Huntsville until November 12, 1917, and why did she stay in Philadelphia until April 22, 1918?

An article by S. Bernard Shaw in the winter 2002 issue of *Pinecone* magazine reported on notes of an interview that Dr. Pocock gave to Park Ranger Ron Pittaway. Shaw wrote, "She told him they could not afford to marry....Winnifred had no categorical answer to the mystery of Tom's death, but they appear to have agreed that a heart attack could have caused his canoe to upset."

Even if she had delivered a baby and put it up for adoption in Philadelphia, there remains the question of what drove them apart a few weeks before Thomson's drowning in Canoe Lake, unless we accept the explanation that he refused her pleas for marriage. More likely, knowing what we do about their personalities, Winnie realized Tom had no intention to marry; instead, he planned to venture out into the Canadian Rockies.

In his 2002 article, MacGregor theorized that a pregnant Winnie Trainor wrote Thomson pressuring him to confront Shannon Fraser over the repayment of $250, which Fraser used to purchase two canoes. MacGregor came to this conclusion based on a 1977 interview Mrs. Crombie gave to him for the *Toronto Star*.[1] Her tape-recorded conversation that same year with Ron Pittaway, in which she tells the same story, is republished in Joan Murray's book, *Tom Thomson: The Last Spring*.[2] In the Pittaway interview, Mrs. Crombie gave a rambling and garbled version of troubling events the night of July 7, confided to her by Annie Fraser, who had since died. It is the story of a drunken Saturday gathering at Rowe's cabin on Potter Creek. Thomson, Fraser, Blecher, Dickson, Rowe, and a few others were there, she said.

"They were all tight," she said.

Robinson noted in his journal on June 30, 1917, that he visited trains at Canoe Lake that day "and looked over three barrels of beer (2.5 [percent]) for Martin Blecher. Passed it as okay. It being for personal use."

Mrs. Crombie continued, "I could start in by Annie and I having a walk, and about the letter she had read, and about Winnifred's desire to come up the following week. She said, 'Please, Tom, you must get a new suit, because we'll have to be married.'"

Thomson, she said, confronted Fraser over the repayment of the $250 loan.

> Tom asked Shannon Fraser for the money that he owed him because he had to go and get a new suit....Anyway, they had a fight and Shannon hit Tom, knocked him down by the fire grate, and Tom had a mark on his fore-

---

1.   The text of MacGregor's book, *Shorelines,* implies that a local man, Russell Pemberton, who was in love with Winnifred Trainor and jealous of Thomson, was the killer. MacGregor explained that Pemberton is entirely a fictional character, but the book, otherwise written with remarkable fidelity to the true story, casts doubt on Mrs. Crombie's version of events. Highlighting this conclusion is the curious fact that MacGregor never mentioned Annie Fraser's confession to Mrs. Crombie in an author's note to the book dated 1979. MacGregor replaced that author's note for the book's republication as *Canoe Lake* in January 2002 with Mrs. Crombie's story but he ended by quoting a conversation he had with a man described as one of Huntsville's oldest and most respected citizens, Frank Hutcheson, on a Christmas Eve in the Anglican Church.

> "He only had one thing to say to me."
> "That book you wrote," said the old man, then in his nineties.
> "Yes, sir."
> "Well, that's pretty much the way it was."

MacGregor said that, by doing so, he did not intent to cast doubt on Mrs. Crombie's story.

head....My conception is that he took Tom's body and put it in a canoe and dropped it in the Lake....I believe that Annie helped him pack the canoe and he went off into the lake with Tom's body, because she always helped him pack his canoe quite often.[3]

MacGregor fretted over the details of Mrs. Crombie's story, suggesting that when Thomson returned from his Sunday fishing trip, no one noticed him except Fraser, who killed him—perhaps accidentally—and, with Annie's help, disposed of the body in Canoe Lake by tying weights to his ankles with copper fishing line. One of the many unexplained details in this version of events is the sighting—by Martin Blecher and his sister, Bessie[4]—of an overturned canoe two hours after Thomson set out from the Mowat Lodge dock. Blecher and his sister so testified under oath at the inquest. MacGregor and other biographers uniformly doubt Blecher's explanation, arguing that anyone living at Canoe Lake would have recognized the overturned canoe as Thomson's and investigated. Blecher, MacGregor points out, did not even report the sighting to anyone until the morning of Monday, July 9.

MacGregor downplayed another detail too. His Aunt Winnie told the Thomson family that although he had indeed lent Fraser $250 in 1915, Tom "got it all

---

2. Joan Murray also interviewed Mrs. Crombie. She wrote, "All I can add is that, when I interviewed Crombie about Thomson in 1971, she was a careful witness. She did not seek notoriety for her version of Thomson's death, saying, "Indeed, she did not mention one word about it, though, of course, as a serious art scholar, I did not ask."

3. Why Annie Fraser would make such a startling confession to Mrs. Crombie in November 1917 is especially puzzling because she and her husband were then corresponding with Dr. MacCallum, Tom Harkness, and George Thomson regarding whether she and her husband had circulated Thomson suicide rumors, which they denied. When she returned to Toronto, Mrs. Crombie brought Annie Fraser's confession to Dr. MacCallum. "The first thing that Dr. MacCallum said was, 'You don't think he committed suicide, do you?' I said, 'Utter bosh, rubbish.' He was getting all excited about his paintings because they were being recognized. He told me with great big round eyes that he'd just sold one to the government for five hundred dollars. He was all up in the air about his paintings." Not before 1918 did the National Gallery buy *The Jack Pine, Autumn's Garland*, and twenty-seven other sketches. Mrs. Crombie may have met Dr. MacCallum at the Thomson art exhibition at the Mowat Lodge on May 24, 1917, but otherwise, when, where, why, and how she looked him up in Toronto to tell the story is very difficult to understand. More troubling, however, is why neither Mrs. Crombie nor Dr. MacCallum ever informed park rangers or provincial police.

back." A letter to Dr. MacCallum from Tom's sister, Margaret Thomson, dated September 9, 1917, said,

> I might say I met Miss Trainor of Huntsville in Toronto....I asked her if Mr. Fraser had paid Tom the two hundred and fifty dollars that Tom spent in buying canoes for them. She said she had asked Tom this spring if he ever got that money, and he said he got it all but in very small amounts....She said that he had warned her not to put anything in her letters that she wouldn't care to have them read, as they always seemed to know his business.

Regarding marriage plans, Little wrote that Winnie Trainor's nephew, sole beneficiary of her estate, found letters offering "indisputable evidence that Tom and [his] aunt were engaged to be married." Nevertheless, Little expressed only the nephew's opinion, because he produced none of the letters.[5] Little also wrote that an innkeeper outside Huntsville told A. Y. Jackson that Thomson wrote a letter inquiring about reservations for two persons in the late summer of 1917 at one of her cottages in the Billie Bear Resort on Bella Lake. However, weighing heavily against this letter as evidence of Thomson's intention to marry Winnie, a few weeks before the drowning, Thomson shipped all of his camping gear to Tom Wattie for a planned summer trip. The July 1, 2004, issue of *The Raven*, visitor's newsletter of The Friends of Algonquin Park, reprinted excerpts from an article in the now-defunct *Toronto Telegram*.

> Some years ago, another friend of ours, Mrs. Newton Pincock, had a summer cottage beside North Tea Lake....There she became acquainted with a park ranger named Tom Wattie....Tom Wattie told Mrs. Pincock that it was while

---

4. Bessie Blecher was a thirty-year old Buffalo elementary school assistant principal in 1917, an unlikely accomplice or witness to Thomson's murder. She never married and was listed as living with her mother and Martin, Jr., in the family home in Buffalo, New York, in the 1930 U.S. Census.

5. Terence Trainor McCormick's credibility is suspect not only because he refused to produce the letters for Little or anyone else but also because he stated to Little, "The one thing that amazes me is that never has much been written with regard to my aunt and Tom Thomson, but upon his death, condolences poured in to her from all over the province and the States." Little's book emphasized an important fact on which all biographers agree—nobody knew whether Winnie and Tom were engaged. Under the circumstances, then, why would people "from all over the province and the States" send her their sympathy at his drowning? McCormick, born December 9, 1927, and his wife, Elaine, of Vestal, New York, refused to respond to several written and telephone requests for an interview.

Thomson was about to start on his annual pilgrimage to the northern corner of Algonquin Park in 1917 that he was drowned in Canoe Lake. Wattie was expecting him and had made plans to give his friend a cordial reception. It was many days later when he learned of the tragedy.

Whatever plans he had, evidently he was not preparing for a summer honeymoon. Margaret Thomson's letter to Dr. MacCallum about her conversation with Miss Trainor casts final doubt on any engagement. "She said that he was intending to leave [Canoe Lake] in a week or so," she wrote. "And that he didn't want [the Frasers] to know where he was going as they were so curious about everything." In letters sent to his father on April 16, 1917, and to Harkness on April 23, 1917, Thomson said he was planning to leave Algonquin Park to visit the Canadian Rockies when the last spring series was finished.

Furthermore, in the spring of 1917, another woman visited him at Algonquin, Toronto painter Florence H. McGillivray, who also visited his studio over the winter of 1916–1917. Born in 1864 in the same town as Thomson's father—Whitby, Ontario—Ms. McGillivray was widely admired in Toronto art circles. Her parents were close friends with Thomson's grandmother, Elizabeth Brodie. Her grandfather, Charles Fothergill, was a naturalist and bird painter. Thomson and Ms. McGillivray had much in common. In his book, *Tom Thomson: The Silence and the Storm*, David Silcox said Ms. McGillivray visited Thomson at the Mowat Lodge while he was working on his last spring series. We can peg the precise time of her visit to later in the period: her calling card and an invitation to her 1917 art show were found in Thomson's sketch box after his death. Whether or not the fifty-three-year-old painter—who Thomson told Mark Robinson was "one of the best"—enjoyed an intimate relationship with Thomson, gossip about the visit would have reached and disturbed an affianced Winnie Trainor. The complete absence of Ms. Gillivray's visit from Robinson's journal and the stories of Canoe Lake residents suggests that their activities went unnoticed, at least, in part, because he and Winnie were not engaged.

Winnie Trainor learned firsthand of Thomson's great fame in Toronto later that summer. In her September 9, 1917, letter to Dr. MacCallum, Tom's sister, Margaret Thomson, wrote, "I met Miss Trainor of Huntsville in Toronto. She told me she had known Tom for four years.... [She] spoke as though she thought a great deal of him." Her niece, Mrs. Fisk said she met Winnie at the Canadian National Exhibition, held in Toronto from August 25 to September 10, 1917, where Thomson's *West Wind* and five of his Algonquin Park sketches were exhibited publicly for the first time. There, Winnie Trainor would have realized that the thirty-three sketches Robinson had taken from her family's cottage had significant value. Winnie was gone when they were taken, working at her bookkeeping job in Huntsville at least six weeks before the drowning. She may have taken the thirteen others with her when she left on May 25. Winnifred was a stiff and aloof person. Mrs. Irene Ewing, who was eighteen years old during the summer of 1917 and got to know Thomson at that time, said many years later, "Tom could see beauty in the old shoe left on the road. That is one thing...I will never understand—as Winnie could never see beauty anywhere—she and Tom were miles apart in this respect."

Nonetheless, the strength of her friendship with Thomson, as evidenced by his visits to her in Huntsville over the years, did not escape the notice of some. When Harold E. Emery of the Huntsville Public Library wrote to Harrison O. McCurry at The National Gallery of Canada on February 24, 1933, he described her as "a personal friend of (and I believe engaged to be married to) the late Mr. Thomson."

One of the least mentioned of Thomson's works is *Figure of a Woman*, the cover photo of MacGregor's first edition. MacGregor insisted that the woman portrayed was not Winnie Trainor, but his publisher thought the painting would help sell the book. Sadly, he said, the painting did not. In her book, Sherrill Grace identifies the woman as Laura Meston Worsfold, from its name card in the McMichael Canadian Art Collection, Kleinburg, Ontario. Gallery records do identify her as the original owner, but nobody knows whom Thomson painted. Posed in a wilderness setting on a sunny afternoon, the female figure faces right, before a pine stump, seated on a large rock above the water beyond. "The molding of the figure is awkward," Grace wrote, "but what interests me in the image is the degree to which the figure is abstracted and, thereby, merged with the surrounding sky, water, tree, and rock." Her dark hair is pulled back, some flowing below her neck. In three photographs, Winnie wore her hair up, in a tight, flat bun.[6] The woman in the painting and the woman in the photographs are similar, their figures tall and thin. Whether the painting is of Laura Meston Worsfold or of Winnifred Trainor is for biographers and arts critics to debate.

---

6. Mrs. Fisk identified the woman in two photographs taken by Thomson as Winnifred Trainor, according to Dennis Reid, curator of post-confederation art at the National Gallery of Canada. Mrs. Fisk met her only once in 1917, and she did not find the photographs until fifty years later. Terence Trainor McCormick insisted that the woman is not his aunt, according to MacGregor. If it is Winnie, nobody can explain the two or three rings on the third finger of her left hand. The third photograph—a more delicately featured woman—appears in Little's book.

Mark Robinson offered a fascinating tidbit of information about Winnie Trainor's relationship with Tom Thomson in a 1953 tape-recorded interview about his search of the Trainor cottage on July 14, 1917.

> There was several letters. Most of them was from Miss Trainor. They were just ordinary boy and girl letters. There was nothing extraordinary about them and there was nothing in any way to think there was anything wrong about them, so I read them. There was one still to be opened. I opened it and handed them back to Mr. Trainor. I said, "Your daughter's letters to Tom." I said. "Keep them. Give them to her."

This last, unopened letter is a possible key to understanding Thomson's death. Letters to Thomson from Winnie Trainor found in the days following his death could have proved crucial pieces of evidence regarding his cause of death. Neither their existence nor their contents interested the coroner. First, Robinson lamely explained later, "We never asked for them afterwards, for there was nothing in them in any way to cause any feelings of any kind, one way or the other." If what her nephew said is true, Robinson obviously characterized them falsely. Second, Harkness told Dr. MacCallum in a letter dated November 3, 1917, "I at last received the burial order from the coroner at North Bay, and I am going to write him about the *letters produced at the inquiry.*" [Emphasis added] Nonetheless, the letters mentioned by Harkness, produced at the inquest, failed to persuade Dr. Ranney of a motive for suicide, and nobody except Mrs. Crombie ever said anything further about them.

An unopened letter from Winnie Trainor to Tom Thomson would have raised so many dramatic possibilities that Robinson, who often wrote about his recollections for regional publications and lectured at the Taylor Statten Canoe Lake children's camps, could have failed to appreciate its implications. The artist drowned in the waters of Canoe Lake as it sat in her family's cabin. Miss Trainor would have personally delivered any letter she had already written before she departed Mowat on May 25. Therefore, Robinson would not have found any such letter after May 25. Moreover, more likely than not, Robinson, whose Thomson storytelling grew exponentially over the years, found no letters at the Trainor cottage from her to him. If so, how and why would she have gotten the letter back?

In addition, a letter disclosing her pregnancy would contradict what we know about her character. Such a private person never puts into writing anything of a personal nature. Moreover, since her cottage was a brief walk away from the Mowat Lodge, where Tom was staying, she would be even less likely to do so. If

Robinson found any letters at the Trainor cottage, common sense suggests that they were from him to her and written before May 24. It would not make sense for Thomson to have sent anything to the Trainor cottage after the twenty-fourth, because she was gone.

If the letter Annie Fraser told Mrs. Crombie about ever existed, it would have been found at his room in the Mowat Lodge, not at the Trainor cottage. Neither Fraser, Tom's brother George, nor Robinson found any letters among Tom's few remaining effects. Finally, nobody—not even Robinson, who said he opened it, read it, and handed it back to her father—was ever bold enough to tell an eager biographer or a dining hall filled with Canoe Lake campers about the night Winnie Trainor sat by the dim light of a lantern in her room writing a letter that could solve the mystery of Thomson's death in Algonquin Park.

Perhaps more telling than anything else, if there was any truth behind rumors of her pregnancy or her claim in 1956 to Dr. Sharpe that they were, indeed, engaged to be married, is her conspicuous absence from Robinson's daily journal from July 8 to July 16. He makes one mention of her on the night of the funeral and burial: "Tuesday, July 17: Miss Winnifred Trainor...went out on the evening train."

George Thomson's mention of her in a letter to Dr. MacCallum on December 23, 1917 suggests that she may have returned while he was there before the burial. He said, "I spent a few hours in her company, and I think that even in that short time I formed a fairly accurate estimate of her worth and attractions." Nonetheless, a woman pregnant or engaged or both would likely have returned, frantic and distraught, when news of his disappearance reached Huntsville. If so, her conversation with George Thomson would have made a greater impression on him. Furthermore, if she were his lover, she would probably not have made a businesslike exit from the scene of his death and burial.

In 1917, Mr. and Mrs. Edwin Thomas and their daughter, Rose, lived in the Canoe Lake Station. In 1927, Thomas built the Kish-Kaduk Lodge in the northern part of Algonquin, which Rose operated until her death in the late 1970s. Rose Thomas told an interviewer in 1976 that nine days after Thomson's disappearance, in the late afternoon of Tuesday, July 17, 1917, she stood by the train platform when Winnifred Trainor arrived back from Huntsville, wearing a beige coat and big beige hat, her long black hair woven into braids.

"She come up after he was drowned and got off the train," she said. "I asked her in, but she said she'd not. So she went and stood on the bridge....I can always remember her standing on the bridge and looking down into the water."

That ten-year-old Rose invited her in to the family's home is likely an exaggeration, but the arrival of Winnie Trainor late in the afternoon before his burial fits into what we know about her character. Winnie felt a duty to come not out of love, but out of enduring respect and friendship. Whatever loss she suffered, surely it was not their planned marriage, as constrained, unemotional, and unsentimental as she was. She said as much in 1954. Winnie wrote,

> Tom Thomson was the man that made me happy, and then vanished. If I saw you, I could say things that I will never write. His friendship was as true as ever when he went on to the great beyond. I still have his small pictures. And what I have gave up for him I should have had some of his others; but I was not treated fair, and [had] nothing to do with his death. Now my time will soon be in too.

Winnifred Trainor never talked about the things she never wrote. More plausible than any other reading of her letter is that what she gave up was the thirty-three panels taken by Mark Robinson from her family's cottage. If it were their child, given up for adoption in Philadelphia, she would not have suggested soothing such a wrenching loss with getting some of his other paintings. Winnie never married and never let go of her Thomson paintings, living without hot water or electricity in her Huntsville home rather than sell them.

Little's book provides the most poignant story to emerge over the years of this tall, wiry woman, her hair pulled back and tied behind her head, visiting the little Mowat Cemetery alone on summer evenings, bending, picking up, and tossing away wild flowers that admiring Camp Ahmek boys had strewn across his grave.

Winnie Trainor called Dr. Sharpe several times in 1956 and 1957, following the incredible exhumation of Thomson's Canoe Lake gravesite. "She was indignant and insisted that she and her father were present when the undertaker returned and are positive the body was in the casket, but I couldn't get her to say they had actually looked in," Dr. Sharpe told a CBC interviewer for an investigative program broadcast on February 6, 1969.

Little asked why, if she knew the body was not in the grave, she bothered removing the wild flowers. Little failed to ask the more basic question of how she could have been there to see the exhumation on July 19, 1917, when she left on the night train on July 17, 1917, according to Little's own account, bound for Toronto, where she stayed for six weeks with Mrs. Irene Ewing and her husband. Little's account of a six-week Toronto visit immediately following Thomson's Canoe Lake burial explains how she came to meet with Margaret Thomson and Jessie Fisk at the Toronto exhibition of his paintings in late August. Mrs. Ewing was a newly married eighteen-year-old, according to Little, and Winnie Trainor was thirty-three years old. Mrs. Ewing never mentions engagement, pregnancy, or anything else that might help explain her relationship with Thomson, except to remark that Winnie Trainor "was most upset by the death."

Mark Robinson's journal noted that Winnie left immediately following the burial on the evening train with "Miss terry"[7]—a clever pun playfully inserted into Thomson lore and never before mentioned by his biographers. Clearly, the companion was Irene Ewing. If what Little said about her trip to Toronto with Irene Ewing is true, he knew that Winnie Trainor was lying to Dr. Sharpe about being at the gravesite for his exhumation.

Regardless, Winnie Trainor would forever avoid the true story of what happened between them, perhaps because she blamed herself for Tom Thomson's death. As years passed, and as his fame as a painter grew, it is possible that Miss Trainor's bitter guilt grew brittle. One could suppose that she never resolved—with herself or with his family—what happened between them on May 24, 1917.

---

7.   Robinson's journal used a small *t*. Reproductions of the entry in many biographies use a capital *T*. Consequently, finding the pun in his original handwriting is especially amusing.

23

Howard Hancock Finds Another Thomson Painting

Hancock opened the double doors to Laura's closet and pulled the string connected to the light bulb overhead. Coats, dresses, blouses, and pantsuits filled the space, hanging from the sturdy six-foot wooden rod crossing at eye level. Shoes neatly placed in matching pairs took up most of the space on the floor to the left. Shoeboxes were piled four across and four high against the right wall, each labeled with big block letters.

"Laura's doing," he muttered to himself.

She had marked the top box "Bills." The next four were "Coupons," "Coupons," "Bank Statements," and "Birthday Cards." He heard a knock at the front door. He thought it must be Dr. Beckley coming by to help sort out Laura's things before Mr. Hancock's appointment at the legal offices of Andrews & Andrews in Huntsville. Mr. Hancock poked his head out the bedroom door and called out.

"Come on in. I'm back here."

Hancock stacked the top four boxes in his arms and carried them out to the kitchen table, where he pushed them across it and against the windows.

"Hi, Howard. How are you doing?"

Dr. Beckley wore a white crew-neck T-shirt, a blue V-neck sweater tucked into his pants, and crisply creased khaki trousers with a bright red belt and a military-style brass buckle. He noticed Howard's astonished stare. Beckley stepped back and spread his arms.

"Think I'm ready for the Memorial Hospital's golf outing this afternoon at Gravenhurst?

Howard smirked and huffed. "You're gonna make a statement. Just what, I do not know. Back home, wearing red, white, and blue casts a middle-aged duffer like you as gay, Republican, or both!"

Dr. Beckley laughed.

"Where do you want to begin?"

"Coffee!" Howard responded, dreading the imminent task of sorting through his dead wife's history.

"I'll take a cup, black."

Dr. Beckley looked out across Canoe Lake to Big Wapomeo Island. Four canoes were passing, three old clanking aluminum Grummans and a one sleek green Kevlar, heading up to Joe Lake. This old Joe seemed to be doing well with Laura's dying last week, he said to himself.

"What are these?" he asked, gesturing at the shoeboxes.

"Oh, just the bills. She took care of all that for us. I'll probably wait until next month to see what she paid and what she didn't. Betcha' everything is up to date, though. Wasn't much."

Howard smiled inwardly.

"Health and car insurance, phone, electric. I'll need to call about her pension and the 401K, I guess."

"Let's get started," Dr. Beckley urged, pouring himself coffee from the pot on the stove.

Howard went back to the bedroom and started pulling out the twelve remaining shoeboxes: eight "Taxes," three "Important Papers," and one "Wills." He took the last four out to the kitchen and put them on the washing machine by the back door so he would not forget to take them for his appointment this afternoon with Clark A. Andrews, who did their wills. Laura told him where to sign. That was all he knew.

"Are you going to keep the clothing?"

Howard shook his head.

"Let's get some plastic bags. I'll take them over with me when I leave. Memorial Hospital has a Ladies Auxiliary that can use them."

It took fifteen minutes to transfer Laura's things from the closet and dresser into eighteen bags and then load them into Dr. Beckley's motorboat. Howard was silent the whole time.

Cardboard banker boxes lined the back wall of the closet, every one labeled in Magic Marker: "Laura's Closet."

"Never knew they were there," Howard said.

Dr. Beckley moved the first one onto the bureau and lifted the lid.

"Books."

Howard brought over the second. More books. Then he brought over ten more boxes of old paperbacks, mostly romance novels. Across the top of one were three Alice Elinor Lambert books, *Women Are Like That*, *Hospital Nocturne*, and *Lost Fragrance*. On the floor across the back, propped up against the right wall, was a one-inch-thick, twelve-inch-wide, seven-foot-long cardboard box. Dr. Beckley put the last box on the bed.

Howard tossed the lid aside and looked inside. He saw a few knickknacks, wrapped in paper towels and held in place by wide rubber bands. He removed them carefully, one by one, and lined them up on the windowsill in their wrappers. In the bottom of the box was the Thursday, July 12, 1989, issue of the *Toledo Blade*, a supermarket flyer from the Safeway Market back in Defiance, Ohio, and six unopened pieces of mail. Howard recognized four bills and a renewal notice from AARP, but not the envelope from Tresslander, Harkins, and Everingham, Solicitors and Barristers, Toronto, Ontario, postmarked July 10, 1989.

"I think they handled Margaret Massey's estate," Howard told Dr. Beckley. "Margaret O'Gorman, whose parents originally owned this place."

Inside he found a postage-paid return envelope folded neatly in thirds, a brief letter, and an estate's administration form captioned "Receipt of Heirs." The items listed included Furnishing, Canoe Lake, Peck Township, Ontario; Fishing rod and reel; Black cherry paddle; and Unsigned birch panel painting ("Tom Thomson 8 July 1917" noted in pencil on the back). At the bottom right of the estate administration form was a signature line for Laura T. Hancock.

"I'll be darned," Hancock exclaimed. "Pull out that box in back there."

Dr. Beckley brought the long box over to the bed where Howard sat. The UPS label was from Toronto, to Laura T. Hancock, 7117 Claremont Avenue, Defiance, Ohio, 43512. Howard fetched a pocketknife from the upper drawer of his dresser, carefully slit the packing tape at each end, and opened the box. Inside, packed in peanut-sized pieces of foam, were an old fishing rod and reel and a well-worn canoe paddle. At one end was another eleven-inch-by-seventeen-inch plain cardboard box, fitted tightly and taped in place. Howard cut the tape and sat the box on his lap. Dr. Beckley leaned over, watching without saying a word.

Howard slit two more pieces of cellophane tape and opened the box. Inside was a bubble-wrapped package, crisscrossed with masking tape. He fumbled with the tape for a moment, finding that one end was open. He pulled the tissue-wrapped inner item out and set all the packing items aside. It, too, was taped. The tissue tore apart easily, revealing an unframed, oil-painted birch wood panel, about four and a half by six and a half inches. It was the same early-spring scene on Canoe Lake depicted on the same-sized panel on the mantel. Howard carried the panel out into the living room, setting it on the far right side of the fireplace and moving aside Laura's old violet plant. Indeed, they were identical—a gray-green canoe positioned the same way at the same location in Canoe Lake north of Big Wapomeo Island. Howard looked at the new addition to his mantel and was overwhelmed by Laura's indifference to everything except his care these past few years on the shores of Canoe Lake. He wept a silent tear standing on the porch overlooking Big Wapomeo Island.

24

Notebook: Winnie Trainor's Cottage May 24, 1917

Shannon Fraser nudged Thomson's shoulder.

"Tom!" he said loudly.

The whiskey bottle was empty. Fraser grabbed a nearby half-full glass and emptied it into his mouth.

Thomson snorted. Fraser shook him again. Thomson's upper body shuffled. He grunted low and deep but did not stir.

"It's time to close the dining room," said Fraser, his voice rising. "You have to leave. Let's get you and your sketches up to your room."

The warning woke him.

"Come on…there you go," Fraser urged.

Thomson rolled his neck and struggled to lift his head.

"What time is it?"

Thomson's head rose slowly. He reached for the whiskey bottle and felt that it was empty. He swished it back and forth.

"Empty."

Fraser stepped back and went off to the kitchen. Thomson's eyes looked left and right across the table, looking for more whiskey. Seeing none, he scanned the rest of the dining room. Dr. MacCallum and Winnie Trainor were gone, along with many of his sketches. His mind struggled with what he had done that evening. Thomson stood by the chair and turned to stare at Fraser as he came back toward him. Thomson looked around the dining room again. The room was empty. The lanterns and candles were burning low. He tried to focus his eyes on the walls.

Thomson asked himself, "Did they take them all?"

Fraser returned with a dishtowel and bucket. Thomson turned and asked, "Are they gone?"

Fraser looked about the room, seeing nothing. He dropped the iron bucket on the table and said again, "We're done for the evening. Go on up to your room."

Thomson struggled to see the two *Northern Light* paintings he remembered placing on the north wall, the four paintings of ice he had done across from Hayhurst Point on the south wall, and the two of beech trees budding across Potter Creek. His eyes went back and forth. And where was the one for Winnie he had finished that morning? The moment stood still. Thomson stood shakily, stretching his stiff back and shoulders, rubbing his eyes, and looked again about the dining room at what remained of his sketches from that spring. The energy, warmth, and vitality he had known for a few weeks drained away.

"Where is Winnie?"

"She left for Huntsville."

"Dr. MacCallum?"

"Upstairs."

"Tom Thomson?"

"Mowat Lodge dining room."

"My sketches?"

"Whatever wasn't taken is here."

Shannon Fraser went to the kitchen, returned, offered him an empty fifty-pound flour sack, and ushered Thomson around the room.

"What were you doing?"

"What do you mean?"

"You gave away all those sketches."

Thomson did not recall.

"Huh," he mumbled. "I, huh, thought…huh…I am leaving Algonquin Park."

They went around the room removing the remaining panels, those that nobody had wanted. He spun around the room, and it spun around him in kind. He staggered as they moved from panel to panel. The room seemed smaller, the lanterns dimmer, the candles burning out. Their light, flickering off the walls, made it even more difficult for Thomson to recognize which ones were gone. He was still drunk and remembered nothing of what had happened. What had Dr. MacCallum and Winnie Trainor said to him? What had he said to them?

Dr. MacCallum had chided him for failing to submit any canvases to the prestigious OAS exhibition. Dr. MacCallum wanted him to come back to Toronto to finish *West Wind* and his other Algonquin canvases before even considering a trip out west. Dr. MacCallum was aghast at Thomson's idea of venturing off to the northern Canadian Rockies. "You don't have the funds for a trip," he pleaded. "Come back to the shack, where you can work from any of the sketches there."

Thomson picked up Winnie's glass and gulped down a mouthful of whiskey. He stared at Dr. MacCallum for a moment, filled with anticipation.

"I am going out to the Rockies."

Winnie no longer kept her silence. Her relationship with Tom had prospered these last few weeks despite rumors that another woman had been there a few days earlier. What was this talk of his leaving for the Rockies? She let loose on him. "You've wasted your time and mine here these many weeks!" Winnie burst out. "What is there out west for you?"

She stood and rested her hard knuckles on the table.

"You are drunk. You don't know what it is you're doing."

She took him over to the east wall, where she found the panel Emily Thomas would eventually take.

"Those are two women?"

"Huh?"

Thomson tried to remember the scene. Winnie was going by them too fast. She pointed at the nearby panel of a canoe in the lake. He gasped.

"What is this gash of color in the water?"

He turned back to their table, his eyes moving toward the bottle and the half-empty glass. His eyes ran and around the room of Mowat Lodge guests, who chattered and splattered wine and whiskey in the cool May breeze drifting across the dining room. Tom suddenly recalled that snow covered the ground this morning, melted away in a short time, and all the birds were singing gaily during the afternoon as he finished the painting.[1]

"It's for you," he murmured.

"Keep it," Winnie replied, turning away.

He could not feel the depths into which he sank, merely water whisking by his face too quickly. Tom staggered back to the table and sat sluggishly. She followed.

"You got to get a hold of yourself," Winnie scolded, beginning to weep. "You want to get away from here? I do not know what you have been doing all these months. Look at what you're doing to yourself. Look at what you are you doing to me!"

"Winnie, this is all for you," he whispered.

Winnie was indignant.

"Tom, I have to go. I'm leaving tomorrow. Back to Huntsville. If you do need to get on, get up and go. Good-bye."

---

1.   The weather description comes from Robinson's Journal entry on May 24, 1917.

She left him alone with Dr. MacCallum and Arthur, the heels of her shoes clicking on the wooden floor as she strode out the back double doors and away forever.

"I know," he said in a barely audible whisper, the water washing by his eyes as he dropped, letting go of her and everything else. He joked to himself whimsically. "I am drunk today, and it will be okay tomorrow."

He refilled his glass as Dr. MacCallum rose to leave, gesturing to Arthur.

"Goodnight," was all the art patron said.

A few hours later, Tom stood with the flour sack, protesting to Fraser that others would come tomorrow to see what he had done these many weeks, these many months, these many years.

What had he done? He had seen the park, Canada's North Country, in a way no other painter could. Spring brought few visitors to its cold campsites, but it was a time of renewal and change. The forest shivered with awakening. His brush, stiff with cold, captured the slow running of winter into spring. Time comes and goes at Algonquin as long as the water and earth mix, growing the marsh weeds into bogs. The bogs flower and sprout trees that spread, die, and grow again thicker and taller, time giving them strength and space year after year. His stiff brush wore away over the last sixty-two days.

"Oh, no," he thought, recalling that Winnie had not taken the sketch he made for her.

"Alice!" he shouted.

Hearing himself, he called softly, "Winnie."

The word drifted away.

One more time he tried, his voice dropping, "Winnie."

Shannon Fraser, ignoring his old friend, whose affection for this frigid woman he never understood, stuffed the last few panels into the flour sack as Tom sat back down. Tom's mind whirled with images of the northern lights and snow and ice flowing south off the lake. The whites and purples and the dense greens of the pine across the lake filled his mind, and he saw again his vision of what was there: dry frost on his palette, vapor crystals of his breathe freezing on the panel if he did not look away.

Shannon Fraser helped him up and out the back. Tom wandered toward the lake. His canoe was out there, and he thought about paddling out and dropping them away, going deep, and never coming back. Instead, he decided to deposit the whole bunch at Winnie's cottage, dragging the flour sack and leaving a trail of crushed grass and weeds. He stopped along the way, reached into the sack, and pulled out a panel, trying to recall when he had done it. His mind wove and dove, his eyes straining to focus in the moonlight. Tom shook inside. He swung his arm in a wide arc and whacked the panel against the trunk of a nearby birch. The panel cracked and fell into three rough pieces. He reached into the sack again and cracked two more panels against the tree, sending echoes of the crash across Canoe Lake. He turned and looked across the lake, fell to his knees, and then dropped onto his face in the scrubby grass and weeds, unconscious.

Twenty minutes later, Thomson woke and struggled to his feet. Straight ahead, he saw the wooden bridge rising up over Potter Creek in the moonlight and realized he had taken a wrong turn from Mowat Lodge. He opened the sack and sorted through the panels; he pulled one out and dragged all that remained to the front steps of the Trainor cottage, where he heaved them onto the porch. He then stumbled back to the Mowat Lodge, never to see them, or her, again.

25

Notebook: George's First Trip to Algonquin

George Thomson played a crucial role in shaping his brother's artistic legacy. He was the obedient first son of a father who was demanding and unloving and of a mother who was loving and undemanding. Preferring to improvise, Tom had great difficulty following the script the family had set before him. His bouts of mania and depression baffled and exasperated his mother and father. They often turned to George, whose insight, experience, and position as the oldest brother gave him some influence.

Despite all his talents and achievements, even as co-owner of one of the largest private business schools in the United States, George never felt personally satisfied. Following graduation from the Canada Business College in Chatham, he spent a year in Detroit working for a lumber company. In October 1892, he formed a partnership with Francis McLaren, and they left together for Seattle. Early in 1893, he married McLaren's sister. His only child, George M. Thomson, was born on February 1, 1894. Six months later, his wife, Margaret Euphemia McLaren, died of diabetes. George raised the child as a single father, not remarrying until 1914, by which time his son had rejected admission to Yale University and moved to Regina, Saskatchewan. "On my leaving," he said, "Father advised me not to write home for money and not to chase after strange women."

All of the Thomson brothers followed him to Seattle upon reaching age twenty-one. In Seattle, law-school classes and studies surrounded tense administrative staff meetings in the morning and faculty committee meetings in the afternoon, to discuss the academic needs of student immigrants from Hawaii, Japan, China, and Polynesia. George Thomson needed some other fulfillment. Before his youngest brother, Fraser, followed, George left for New York City in 1906, taking his son, his law degree, his business fortune, and his budding artistic ambition with him.

In New York, George started his life anew, taking painting lessons at the prestigious Art Students League. In 1907, he moved to the first widely influential American impressionistic art colony of Old Lyme, Connecticut, and in 1908 moved to New Haven, where he went to work as bookkeeper for the Union League, a Republican Party men's club, which occupied the historic Sherman Building. There, George settled uneasily into an existence far from that for which he yearned. George wanted to return home to Owen Sound overlooking the vast, blue waters of Georgian Bay. He kept himself busy in Connecticut, involving himself with politics and studying accounting and painting. He was a member of the prestigious Quinnipiac Club of New Haven.

Since 1915, the family regularly sent Toronto newspaper clippings about younger brother Tom's success as a painter of Canadian landscapes. He received the news with a sense of family pride and personal regret. George did all that was formally required of an educated artist, while Tom, his younger brother, who did nothing of the sort, was earning popular attention back home. In 1934, George he wrote a brief autobiographical sketch, in which he mused over why he made a radical change in his life, but he never mentioned his famous brother.

"Sometime along in his early thirties he saw a good modern landscape in oil color," George wrote. "It surely was a revelation, as he had never before seen anything of the kind done by a first-class artist. It was possibly at this time that a regret entered his mind that he had not become an artist."

Little claimed in his book that Bartlett reached George by telephone at a commercial art studio in New York City on Tuesday, July 10, 1917, immediately upon hearing the news of the overturned canoe and Thomson's disappearance. Bartlett had one of the only telephones in Algonquin Park at the time. In 1911, he had arranged for telephone lines to be strung from his headquarters at Cache Lake to the ranger stations at Rock Lake, Lake of Two Rivers, Rain Lake, and Joe Lake, using telegraph poles located along the Grand Trunk railway. However, George never kept a commercial art studio in New York City, New Haven, or anywhere else.

On late Tuesday afternoon, July 10, 1917, following Robinson's initial investigation, which would have consumed most of Monday and Tuesday, Shannon Fraser telegraphed Thomson's family in Owen Sound about the disappearance. Coincidentally, George Thomson and his wife, Jean, were visiting Owen Sound. George arrived that day to visit with his wife's brother, Colonel Alfred Telford, and his wife, Nellie. His father prevailed on vacationing George immediately to depart for Canoe Lake. John Thomson's somber instructions were for George to learn all that he could about the disappearance, assist in the search, and retrieve Tom's belongings.

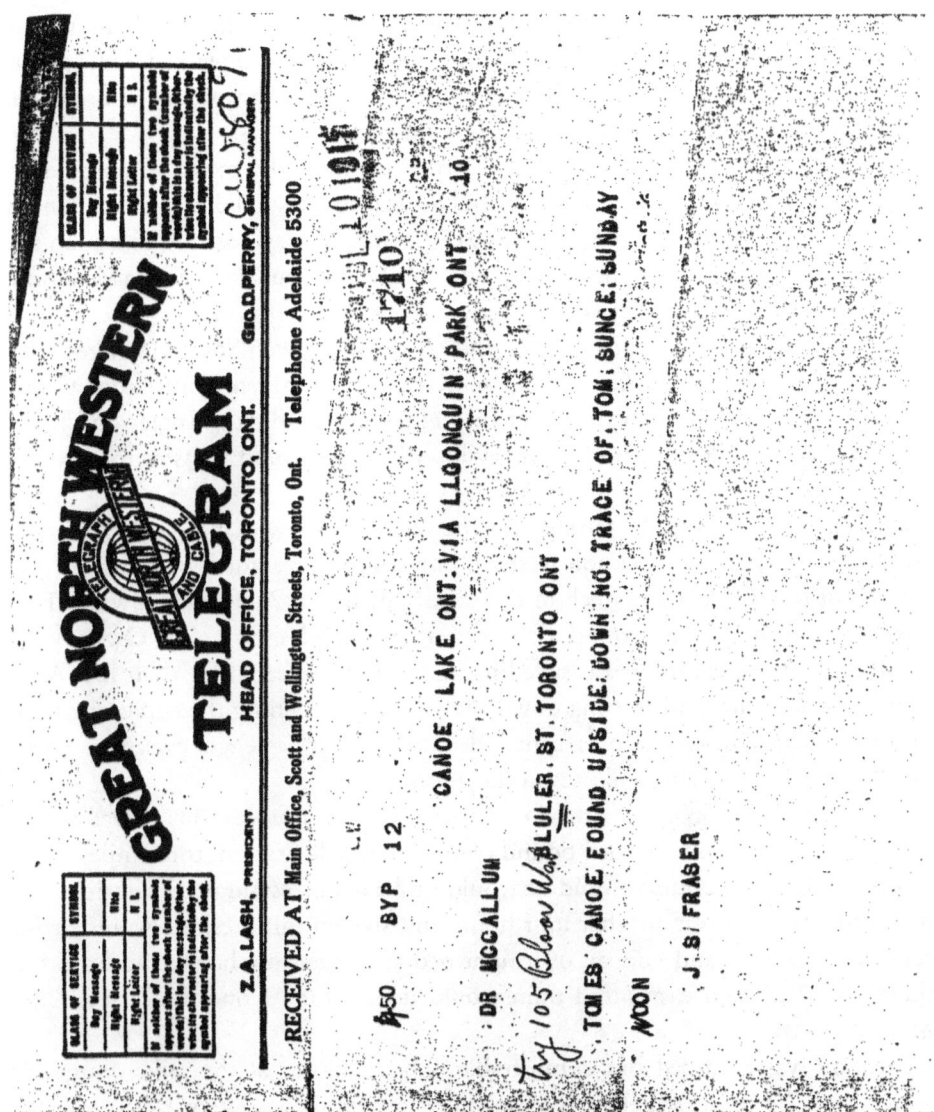

Shannon Fraser's July 10 telegram to Dr. MacCallum. He sent a similar telegram to the Thomson family in Owen Sound.

"Tom spent the spring in Algonquin Park, painting sketches of the snow, ice, water, trees, and sky around Canoe Lake," George's father explained. "His paintings have found an appreciative and generous market in Toronto. If he drowned, these last spring sketches certainly will be valuable."

Tom had always been a bothersome little brother and a much better painter. George troubled over the fuss, because he learned that Tom had written to brother-in-law Harkness on April 23, 1917, saying, "I may possibly go out on the Canadian Northern this summer to paint the Rockies but have not made all the arrangements yet. If I go it will be in July or August."

Because there was no direct eastbound train from Owen Sound to Algonquin Park, George boarded a Canadian Pacific train that rolled south from Owen Sound in the early-morning hours of July 11, 1917, heading to Inglewood Junction, seventeen miles south of Orangeville, where he would transfer to a north-bound Grand Truck passenger train.

A frequent visitor to his family over the years, he knew that in 1907 the troublesome steep grade and famously sharp horseshoe curve north of Cardwell was the site of the worst train wreck in the history of Bruce Peninsula railways. Two passengers from Owen Sound debarked that fateful evening at Orangeville, claiming that the engineer was speeding and that they feared for their life. After leaving Orangeville and starting down the grade approaching the curve, the train jumped tracks. The engine overturned, destroying four passenger cars. Seven people died and 114 suffered injuries in the wreck.

At Inglewood, George waited for the next Grand Trunk train. It was a one-hour, forty-seven-minute northbound trip to Allandale Station, three miles south of Barrie, where a conductor said he would find a good restaurant. The trip north to Scotia Junction was another four hours and sixteen minutes. He would arrive there at 1:45 A.M. and take an overnight bed at the railway house and breakfast there for $1.25. An eastbound train would depart for Algonquin Park at 9:00 A.M.

Seating was cramped but comfortable. The clanking of the rails, the gentle swaying of the train, which may have lulled others to nap, kept George awake with his thoughts and a book. If Tom drowned, George worried, the drowning would have been his younger brother's own doing. His brother was a big drinker. Twice in Seattle, George had finagled Tom out of police custody. The first arrest arose from a bar fight that Tom threw himself into, not knowing any of the principal combatants. The second involved the disgruntled older husband of a young wife who, loose downtown without her wedding ring for the evening, fell under Tom's charm. George was not interested in the who and what of his brother's drunken follies; his only concern, as it was now, was getting him back home safely and protecting the Thomson name from disgrace. Tom's romance of Alice Lambert was a hoot. Since Tom's leaving, having run through all the available Owen Sound boys, including Horace Rutherford and Tom, she'd taken up with a bevy of men in Seattle. These included a gold miner, a lumberjack, a salmon boat captain, two whalers, an ice company accountant, and who knows whom else. Seattle had been good to George, but it was a town that neither he nor Tom would ever go back to again.

In the morning, George sat in the Scotia Junction Railway House reading a collection of stories by Anton Chekhov. One short story was called simply, "Art." It pushed him toward a powerful realization. Chekhov wrote, "One creates; the other helps him. In himself, a nonentity, a sluggard, a drunkard, and a wastrel, but when he creates something with his tools, he is at once something higher, a servant of God."

George thought had Tom squandered his gift for painting these last five years with wasteful and self-indulgent adventures as a fishing guide and fire ranger in the wilderness of Algonquin Park. George thought he should have stayed in Toronto, putting in diligent full-time work at his commercial art firm, earning a good living, taking art classes from the masters in Toronto, developing skills, and gaining experience. His painting was unharnessed by self-discipline and artistic resolve.

The blast of a train whistle, a warning of its impending departure, startled George. He turned, knocking a water glass to the hardwood floor with a crash. Rising suddenly in response, George pulled the stiff cotton tablecloth with him, spilling everything else onto the seat across from him, including the Chekhov story collection. George left it behind, rushing onto the Algonquin-bound train with his briefcase.

It was two hours and thirty-four minutes to the Canoe Lake and Joe Lake stations. A conductor recommended that he stay at the Hotel Algonquin, which was operating under new owners Edward and Molly Colson. According to his pocket watch, the time was 11:34 P.M. as he stepped out. The sky was overcast, the air hot and moist.

Park Ranger Mark Robinson had a cabin at Joe Lake. Robinson came to Algonquin in 1907 because of a serious respiratory illness. His doctor advised outdoor work in northern Canada's fresh, clear air. He joined the staff of the Algonquin Park Rangers. In October 1915, Robinson enlisted in the Canadian Army. He returned to the park from service overseas on April 11, 1917, holding the rank of major and suffering from wounds received during a German artillery assault on the army's Simcoe Foresters at Vimy Ridge, France. Robinson, age forty-nine, described himself as frail and perhaps unready for the physical and emotional ordeal that the search for Thomson would prove to be, but he gave to it all the military pomp and circumstance he had learned.

Robinson greeted every passenger who debarked at the either the Canoe Lake or Joe Lake station, which were a half-mile apart. The army often stationed soldiers at railway bridges and stations to guard against saboteurs and spies. On May 24, 1917, he noted in his journal, "A large troop train went east this afternoon carrying a fine bunch of men." Robinson checked for poachers, issued fishing permits, and offered lodging suggestions, but he had never before greeted anyone from the United States who was there to search for a missing family member presumed drowned in the park.

Robinson stepped up to the visitor, an intimidating forty-nine-year-old character sporting a well-trimmed mustache. He was finely dressed in a dark pinstriped suit, his vest draped with a solid gold pocket watch chain and a smooth red silk tie. He carried a large brown briefcase with highly polished brass hardware. Station hands unloaded one piece of rich leather baggage. "Good morning," he announced. "Welcome to Algonquin Park."

George stretched out his right hand, noticing that his greeter walked with a limp. The man wore a rumpled gray hat, a woolen lumberjack shirt, plain white suspenders, and thick khaki trousers. He sported a stiff, full mustache and carried a military officer's whistle around his neck.

"I'm Ranger Mark Robinson. This is my son, Jack. What brings you to Algonquin Park?"

Robinson brought eleven-year-old Jack with him everywhere. The boy never spoke unless spoken to and did so only with his father's permission. "Yes, sir," "No, sir," and "I don't know, sir" was the extent of his replies.

Thomson introduced himself, and Robinson apologized. "Of course, I am sorry for what's happened."

Robinson recounted the events since Sunday, asked George where he was lodging, and arranged to take him into Mowat after lunch.

"Meet me at my cabin, which is just beyond those trees," he said, pointing between the passenger cars. "The Colsons will show you the path."

"I appreciate your efforts," Thomson said. He then departed on a wagon arriving from the Hotel Algonquin. Before he left, he addressed the boy.

"Have a good day, lad," Thomson said to Jack.

Looking at his father, who nodded, Jack responded, "I don't know, sir."

The afternoon of July 12, 1917, was hot and damp. A cloud-covered sky hung over the park as they bobbed along Joe Creek in Robinson's motorboat to Mowat Lodge. George remained quiet during the trip, having already learned there had been no news of his brother.

"No," Robinson said. "No, I'm sorry to say."

Robinson tied up his motorboat at the lodge dock, where he showed George his brother's gray-green canoe, its two portage paddles tied tightly but awkwardly in place.

"I'm the man that turned that canoe over. There was none of his equipment in it, and the paddles were tied in for carrying. His paddle he used for paddling was not there. If he had it with him, we never found it."

After examining the canoe at the dock, they went up to the rustic Mowat Lodge. Shannon Fraser greeted them in the dining room and took George and Robinson up to see his brother's bare second-floor room. Shannon Fraser was tall, with bright red curly hair and freckles. He was a well-spoken, good-natured talker. That afternoon, he wore a blue suit, shirt, tie, and fedora.

"Where are his things?" George inquired. "Are you holding them under an innkeeper's lien for the cost of his room and board?"

"No, of course not," Fraser answered indignantly. "Tom has a few dollars on account. We moved his belongings downstairs into storage for safekeeping. There was a plaid overcoat, blankets, some other old clothing, handkerchiefs, a new pair of shoes...I think that was it. I have a list on my desk. Nothing worthwhile. We cleaned up a bit—there were a few empty liquor bottles and some rags and newspapers strewn around."

"New shoes?" George asked, incredulous. "What was he doing with new shoes up here?"

"Snowshoes," Fraser responded, shrugging.

Years later, some Canoe Lake residents would accuse Fraser of keeping the snowshoes and trying to sell them.

"Where are his paintings? Where is his paint box and palette?"

Fraser shrugged again at George's question.

Robinson reminded Fraser that he'd brought up to the lodge some other personal items Thomson left behind at the dock—three old tin pails, a pair of buckskin moccasins, an axe, and three trolling spools.

One of the lesser mysteries of Thomson's story arises in the family's angry correspondence with Shannon Fraser that autumn and winter of 1917—namely, what happened to the missing palette and these items? Thomson's sketch box eventually ended up in the hands of Thomson's niece, Mrs. Jessie Fisk of Owen Sound, who sold it to the National Gallery of Canada in 1947. She was the daughter of Tom's sister, Elizabeth, and Thomas J. Harkness, who administered the estate. In 1910, Thomson painted a sweet and delicate portrait in pastel on paper of a teenage Jessie dressed in a deep rose-colored smock. In the sketch box, Thomson preserved a watercolor original signed by Perce Cuthbert from 1912, showing a cello player lost in reverie. On it is a stanza of poetry.

> Sweet strains rose from the cello,
> Soft, almost melancholy,
> Vibrating in the memory,
> Awakening the inmost soul.

Mrs. Fisk also came into possession of his studio palette, donating it to the Tom Thomson Museum in Owen Sound in 1964. Still later, in 1967, she found among his belongings a small bundle of forty carefully preserved photo negatives that Thomson had made himself. How they eluded earlier discovery is also a mystery. In a letter dated September 12, 1917, Harkness warned Fraser that he was "suspicious that [he was] not dealing square" and queried him about many issues, including repayment of Tom's loans to Fraser for the purchase of two canoes, the reason why Tom had only sixty cents when he recently made a bank withdrawal and been paid a guiding commission, and the whereabouts of Tom's personal belongings.

A subsequent letter from George Thomson dated December 25, 1917, accused Fraser and his wife, Annie, of giving evidence at the inquest that suggested Thomson's drowning was a suicide:

> You have apparently done your utmost to fasten this terrible stain upon his memory using as evidence for this purpose some trivial incidents, innocent enough in themselves, and fashioning them to suit your theory....When I was at Canoe Lake, you showed me various things belonging to Tom. You will recall that you promised to hold them subject to the wishes of whoever should act as administrator. This as you know was undertaken by T. J. Harkness of Annan. He now wants every article belonging to Tom boxed and sent COD to his address at Owen Sound.

The Frasers may have found the sketch box, discarded or hidden away by Thomson, and shipped it to Harkness, although it is not listed among a bundle of personal items that Elizabeth Harkness described in a letter to Dr. MacCallum as eventually receiving from Fraser. Dr. MacCallum probably recovered the studio palette and negatives from Tom's Shack in Toronto and sent them to Harkness, whose own estate may have passed them to his daughter upon his death in 1925.

All we know about the photographs is that during August and September 1912, Thomson and William S. Broadhead took a canoe trip through the Mississauga Forest Reserve. In a letter written to friend Dr. John McRuer, MD, Thomson wrote, "We got a great many good snapshots of game—mostly moose and some sketching, but we had a dump in the forty-mile rapids, which is near the end of our trip, and lost most of our stuff—we only saved two rolls of films." Housed today at the National Gallery of Canada Library, the negatives are stained by water. Among them are two portraits of Winnifred Trainor and an eerie photograph of the James Watson headstone in the Mowat Cemetery, inscribed, "Remember, comrade, when passing by, as you are now, so once was I. As I am now, so you will be. Prepare thyself to follow me."

Fraser, George, and Robinson walked back downstairs to the sitting room's robust fieldstone fireplace. Archways to the first-floor rooms interrupted the north and south walls. A wide doorway led into the thirty-by-forty-foot dining room, with its double doors in the back open wide, allowing sunshine to fill the rough-hewn space. The walls on either side were empty. The three men sat at one of the eleven tables and Fraser continued his story.

"I thought Tom was depressed these last few weeks. He spent the spring painting, adding a new panel to the floors here and downstairs every day for more than two months. In late May, when Dr. MacCallum arrived, he brought them all down to the dining room, and we displayed them all around the walls here. Tom pointed them out to everyone who came in. Then he went over to each table and invited everyone to take whatever they wanted."

Annie Fraser came over and joined them.

"Me and Annie got one of his paintings ourselves that night. Anyway, the guests looked them over and took whatever they wanted. A few walked away empty-handed. Tom grew more and more disturbed during the evening. He sat with Dr. MacCallum and Winnie Trainor. You know them?"

George nodded.

"They sat right over there by the double doors. They had a fifth of good whiskey, and Tom was drinking steady. About 9:30, Winnie got up and left. She thanked me for dinner and told Annie she was taking the morning train back to

Huntsville. A few minutes later, Dr. MacCallum went up to his room with his son, Arthur.

"I helped Tom pick up the remaining panels later that night; what he did with them, I don't know. He did ask me to pack up a favorite and send it to his friend, Dr. McRuer, out in Denver, Colorado, which I did. Sad to say, a few weeks later, toward the end of June, we got a telegram from Toronto that Dr. McRuer had died. Tom was best man at the doctor's wedding in 1909 over in Huntsville. Dr. McRuer practiced medicine there until he fell ill with consumption in 1913. Tom spent a lot of time in the days after we got the telegram brooding up in his room and away on the lake."

George Thomson thanked Fraser and asked him to send over any guests that were around. Lieutenant Crombie and his wife, Daphne; Mr. and Mrs. Thomas; their daughter, Rose; and a few others offered hopes and prayers but no information. Robinson then took him by the Blecher cabin, where George spoke with Martin, Jr., and Bessie. Nobody answered the knock at the Trainor cabin.

They toured around the lake in a steady rain, stopping to interview several others, including Charles Scrim, who found Tom's canoe across from Big Wapomeo Island. Robinson frequently and furiously blew his officer's whistle as they cruised the shoreline. That evening, after dinner, Robinson gathered six members of the returning search teams at his cabin.

First, Mr. Blecher, Sr., and his son told George of their search of the lake's west shoreline, around the islands and bays south of where Tom's canoe was recovered.

"We found nothing," Mr. Blecher, Sr., concluded. "It's slow going. We'll work our way down to Bonita Lake in a day or two."

Fire Rangers Albert Patterson and William MacDonald had seen no sign of Tom along the lakes east shoreline. At George's urging, Robinson instructed Patterson to leave immediately on the evening train to Huntsville to find out whether Winnie Trainor knew anything about Tom's disappearance. George Thomson pressed Dickson and Rowe about the disappearance and their finding of Tom's canoe.

"It's a mystery," Rowe said.

Over the years, two mutually exclusive rumors grew regarding Thomson's Canoe Lake legend. The more startling of the two surfaced many years after Thomson's death, arising from separate interviews Mrs. Crombie had given to MacGregor and Pittaway in 1977. She said that in November 1917, Annie Fraser confessed that her husband, Shannon, had punched Tom during a drunken brawl at Rowe's cabin the evening of July 7, 1917. They fought, she said, over the repayment of a $250 loan to Fraser. Apparently, Thomson needed the money to buy a new suit for his marriage to Winnie Trainor. During the scuffle, Thomson fell and struck his head on a fire grate. Thinking him dead, Fraser hauled the unconscious body to his boat and, with Annie's help, motored out and pushed the artist over into the lake, Mrs. Crombie said.

If a fight had broken out at Rowe's cabin, George certainly would have learned of it during his interrogations of Rowe, Dickson, or one of the others who were there, and Robinson would have arrested Fraser and charged him with murder. However, none of them said anything to implicate Fraser in Thomson's death. An entry Robinson made in his journal on July 19, 1917, confirms only that Shannon Fraser drew the attention of Bartlett and others in the provincial government. "I have received instructions this morning to have Mr. S. Fraser have no more booze come in," he noted. "Also to have a plan and lease of his house prepared at once to be submitted to the Department of Lands, Forests, and Mines." [1]

The other murder theory grew out of a truth bathed in the prejudice of war. The Canadian Army Corps enjoyed its greatest victory of World War I, the final capture of Vimy Ridge in France on April 9, 1917, where Robinson had earlier fought and been wounded. Of the 10,602 Canadian casualties there, 3,598 died during years of brutal trench warfare. For Canada, the final attack on Vimy Ridge marked a turning point in the country's march toward distinct nationhood. One of the country's greatest painters, capturing her rugged wilderness spirit, was Tom Thomson, who himself never served in the military.

Following his death, family and friends insisted that Tom tried to enlist several times during the Boer War. They said the army rejected him, citing problems with his feet. Posthumously, his artist friends, chiefly A. Y. Jackson, who enlisted and went to Europe in late 1914, insisted that Thomson had also tried to enlist for duty in WWI, but that the army had rejected him in 1914 and again in 1915.

Martin H. Blecher, Jr., age twenty-six, was of German descent and spoke with an accent. He said he was a private investigator with the world-famous William J. Burns International Detective Agency in Buffalo, New York, from which speculation grew that he had fled to Algonquin Park with his family to avoid imminent military service in the European war.[2] The United States declared war against Germany in April 1917. The U. S. was calling up young men across the country under the Selective Service Act, adopted in May 1917. The American Expedi-

---

1.   It is noteworthy that neither Ottelyn Addison nor Little reproduce in their books this part of Robinson's journal entry.

tionary Force began arriving in France in June 1917. Speculation that Blecher was a draft evader proved unfounded. Robinson's journal noted that Blecher went home on November 14, 1917. The Adjutant General's Office in Washington, D.C., confirmed for Blodwen Davies in 1931 that Blecher registered for military service in Buffalo on November 27, 1917, a few days after he returned from Algonquin Park.

During the Saturday, July 7, 1917, drinking party at Rowe's cabin, Thomson and Blecher allegedly exchanged hostile words over the war, Thomson calling Blecher a deserter. Leaving for the evening, he warned Thomson, "Don't get in my way if you know what's good for you." The suggestion was that Blecher met Thomson on the lake Sunday afternoon and killed him.

This version of events was fueled by Robinson's speculation that Blecher was a German spy reporting on military troop movements by train through the park. On May 14, 1917, Robinson wrote, "Martin Blecher, Jr., left this morning for St. Louis. I am of the opinion he is a German spy." A few days later, on May 18, he noted, "Martin Blecher, Jr., returned today to Canoe Lake via Renfrew."[3]

Others gossiped about the spicy possibility of a love triangle between them and Winnie Trainor, adding romantic jealousy to Thomson's Canadian patriotism as a point of contention between him and Blecher. In this version of the story, Thomson's antagonism toward the German-American embodied his own nation's fierce, independent spirit, highlighted by his Canadian lover.[4]

George Thomson's own version of what Dickson, Rowe, and the others related to him hardly supports the either murder theory. Recounting what George reported to the family, youngest brother Fraser Thomson told the *Toronto Telegram* in an October 12, 1956, interview,

---

2.   Blecher's career with the detective agency apparently was short lived. The 1910 U.S. Census describes him as an assistant with a newspaper. He is missing from 1920 Census records. In 1930, unemployed, he was living with his mother and sister in Buffalo, New York.

3.   Unless Robinson was referring to Mount St. Louis, Ontario, these geographic references, when coupled with the brief four-day span between Blecher's departure and return, are difficult to reconcile. Furthermore, Mount St. Louis is southwest of the park and Renfrew is far across Ontario, southeast of the park.

4.   According to Ralph Bice, Blecher was married in 1917. "The fact that [Blecher and Thomson] quarreled over Winnifred Trainor," he said, "that is the most ridiculous slander, because Martin Blecher had a wife who was much, much prettier than Winnifred Trainor."

I know that there had been ill will between a German…and my brother. Tom had been trying to enlist and the German…said something to him. There was a quarrel. Then Tom was found dead soon afterwards. Who knows what happened? His death will always be a mystery.

George Thomson, a sharp-minded businessman and well-trained business and law-school graduate with many years of political and civic experience, would have told his family a much more alarming story from the direct, firsthand accounts he heard if there were any truth to these rumors.

"Six and a halfwit makes seven," George said to himself, the halfwit being Robinson, who blew his officer's whistle repeatedly as they struggled with Jack across the portage trail to Sam Lake earlier that afternoon.

George remained worried that the upturned canoe was Thomson's own drunken doing, or that mania had driven his brother to flee for the Canadian Rockies. Although he was convinced that searching the vast Canoe Lake area was futile, he decided against mentioning his doubts to these sincere men, lest they grow even more discouraged. Darkness settled over Algonquin Park as the meeting ended. George enjoyed the cool night breeze coming off Joe Lake as he walked back to the Colson's hotel.

The next morning, he arose early and hiked over to Mowat, where Hugh Trainor answered his knock, standing square in the doorway.

"Can I help you?"

"My name is George Thomson. I'm Tom's older brother," he said, handing the slightly older, burly man with a barrel chest and thick wrists and fingers a slightly worn business card. George was carrying his dark leather briefcase.

"I've come about Tom's paintings."

"So you have."

George waited for a further response, learned from his legal and business experience. ("Give them time to respond when you think they might be hostile. Hardly anyone can resist the urge to fill the silence arising from an unresponsive answer.") Trainor, however, was an exceptional man.

"You'll have to speak to my daughter about that, and she's not here."

Hugh Trainor pushed the door closed with a thump.

That afternoon, and the next day, George visited all of the other cabins around Mowat and out on the three islands, inquiring about his brother and the missing sketches. Many recalled the evening Thomson displayed them in the lodge dining room and gave them away. Emily Thomas showed George the panel she had taken and offered her opinion.

"Tom was drinking too much," she said.

George went back to ask Mr. and Mrs. Fraser again about the panels' whereabouts. Neither had any information, and suggested that he speak to Winnifred Trainor.

"She would know, if anyone," Annie said. "Miss Trainor works as a bookkeeper in Kearney and lives in Huntsville. She spent a few days here last spring. Been gone, since Dr. MacCallum was here. She can't know anything."

George said that he helped organize search parties, sending them across Canoe Lake, scouring its islands and portages. Nevertheless, in an angry letter to Dr. MacCallum on December 29, 1917, Shannon Fraser claimed he had received no help. He said, "George Thomson ought to be the last one to say anything, as he came up here and did not do anything to find Tom's body, didn't help the men to grapple, went back home, and left everything for me to do, and the people were talking about him wondering if he had no money."

Fraser later told artist John W. Beatty that, before departing for Owen Sound, George bought a seventy-five-cent box of cigars and asked him to divide them among the park rangers and guides who joined in the search. Thomson's brother-in-law, Harkness, however, reported to Dr. MacCallum that George's itemized expenses included a more expensive $1.80 box of cigars.

That Friday, Robinson and his son, Jack, continued their search across the lake's west portage trails and Bertram Island. They portaged over to Gauther Lake and Gill Creek, turning west to Gill Lake, where they found the Colson canvas canoe.

"Found no traces of any person having been there for some time," he wrote in his daily journal.

Who took the Colson canoe to Gill Lake and how they traveled anywhere else from there are two of the many mysteries of Canoe Lake. "We returned to Canoe Lake having called on Mr. Fraser and Mr. Thompson. We also called on Mr. Lawrie Dickson and Fire Ranger MacDonald, then returned home and met evening train."

George Thomson was up at five o'clock the next morning, Saturday, July 14, 1917. He dressed and walked briskly through the woods to Robinson's cabin, finding him gone. Dejected, he returned to the hotel, deciding he could do nothing further. A train was departing for Scotia Junction at 9:02 A.M. A carriage left him at the Joe Lake Station thirty-four minutes early.

Why George left Canoe Lake on the morning of July 14 while the search for his brother's body continued has perplexed biographers ever since.[5] One possible explanation is that Tom's missing belongings—tent, sleeping bag, fishing gear, paint box, and paintings—convinced George that his mania-disturbed brother secreted away with them to the Canadian Rockies. Another is that George was not suited to the physical demands of Algonquin Park travel—crossing the waters, walking the portages, and enduring the social demands of Canoe Lake's less sophisticated residents and guests.

A few minutes before the train arrived, Robinson and Jack appeared.

"Nothing new about your brother," Robinson announced peremptorily. "Ranger Patterson found nothing in Huntsville. He never got to see Miss Trainor. I don't think that matters now."

Robinson paused.

"Tom was a licensed guide, an expert canoeist, and a fine friend. I pray he'll turn up with his paddle, fishing pole, and empty kit bag looking to load up again for some new adventure in the park."

---

5.   In *Tom Thomson: The Silence and the Storm*, David P. Silcox wrote, "I have never understood or read any plausible explanation why George Thomson visited Canoe Lake immediately after Thomson's disappearance, and then not only left with while everyone else continued the search for his brother, but took most of Thomson's sketches away with him. If he presumed him dead, why did he not take all of Thomson's belongings? And if he thought that he might be alive, why would he not have helped with the search, and why did he take away work that Thomson might have wanted? His behavior was odd, to say the least."

Silcox's first complaint is incomprehensible. George dutifully came on behalf of the family. All of the others presumably had work, children, or other responsibilities and could not make the trip. He was visiting from New Haven and could spare the time. His father was seventy-seven years old. Moreover, George's father could easily have prevailed upon him to do so, as George was the oldest son who had lived away for many years. Silcox is also wrong in saying that George took away most of the sketches. George took nothing back from this trip to Canoe Lake.

26

Lucky Haskin's Desperate Decision

Lucky Haskins stuck a key into the ignition of the Ford pick-up. The starter groaned. He pumped the gas pedal in a well-practiced motion and the engine roared, spewing a cloud of blue smoke into the parking lot as he sped away onto Route 60, kicking up gravel.

"She'll get my truck, too," he growled.

Haskins squinted at the road ahead. Mary Alice's cabin was four miles away, her driveway marked by a tiny hand-painted black-and-white sign reading, "Native Canadian Jewelry." A faint arrow across the bottom pointed the way. Well off the road, the sign was sheltered in a grove of aspen trees that Haskins offered to chop down the past fall, when business at his shop slowed. Mary Alice did not seem to care one way or the other. Haskins wished that he had done the job, because he did not want to miss the driveway again.

Suzy's telephone call was unexpected. Never before had she stood up to him. He remembered her always looking down at the floor, getting out of his way, ducking out the back door, spending weekends at her sister's house in South River, and, finally, fleeing to Vancouver seven months ago. That was what Suzy did. Taking his two sons was bad. Removing the deed from the safety-deposit box was nasty. Burning the deed was treacherous.

Haskins had worked for Suzy's father since before he was nine years old, cleaning and polishing lawnmowers, tillers, power saws, and post hole diggers rented by the hour, day, or week at Red's Rent-All. The old man paid him in cash all those years, bought him lunch most days at the Bar, and let him use the new pick-up truck to take Suzy to the Huntsville High School prom in May. Haskins failed to graduate. He dropped out in late March when Sue Ellen's father collapsed of a heart attack in the tool crib.

Seventeen years old, Haskins took over the business as the old man spent eleven days at Memorial Hospital and seven more months at home. Sue Ellen missed much of the last eleven weeks of school, but she graduated, since the principal let her take final exams later that summer, a privilege he denied Haskins.

"Son of a bitch hated me," an intoxicated Lucky muttered, as a speeding semi-truck and trailer passed on his left, shaking the pick-up truck and startling him.

The rental business prospered over the summer, and Harold Haskins earned his nickname the weekend after Labor Day. Suzy's old man came into the shop Mondays and Fridays to collect banking and sales slips for the bookkeeper. Haskins had been out in the yard with a Toronto real estate broker who wanted a snowmobile and trailer for his family's cottage across the Lake of Bays, near Norway Point. Haskins had maneuvered the hi-lo carefully, lifting out a model 700 from the top of a stack of four piled up against the garage wall. He lowered the cardboard crate and pallet into the open bed of the broker's pick-up truck, put the hydraulic lift in neutral, pulled the parking brake, jumped down, and scampered around the side of the truck. Harold climbed into the bed.

He was pulling the snowmobile off the pallet onto the truck bed when a giant truck wheel rolled into the yard from Route 60 doing forty-seven miles an hour, heading straight for the lift vehicle. It crashed into the wide side with a violent thud and a crunching noise. Harold looked up to see the lift vehicle fall over.

Harold and the broker, standing by the passenger door of his truck, looked at each other and out toward Route 60 and back, following the dust cloud brought in by the truck wheel, which continued on its course. After bouncing off the lift vehicle, it continued into the open garage door and bashed off the far wall directly under the payphone, leaving a wide black scuffmark that was still there today. The wheel spun over on its side and came to spinning rest.

The dust cloud dissipated in seconds, and a green and white soot-belching flatbed tractor-trailer followed into the yard slowly, coming to a stop.

"Did you see a truck wheel come in here?" the teamster shouted down.

Right behind, in his late-model Ford pick-up, came Suzy's father, who had seen the truck wheel break loose from the flatbed on the curve about a hundred yards east of the shop. Edward "Red" Wilkins watched as the wheel bumped, straightened, and sped down the hill before turning gracefully into the yard past the "Red's Rent-All" sign by the side of the highway. Red Wilkins braked to a stop next to the flatbed and looked around.

"What the hell happened?" Wilkins said, completely baffled. "Where'd it go?"

Haskins told the story to the *Huntsville Forester* later that afternoon and posed by the scuffmark next to the truck wheel under the payphone for a front-page photograph, which he later pasted on the wall. "Lucky Haskins!" read the head-line, and the nickname stuck.

Haskins was not feeling lucky as he pulled into Mary Alice's driveway. He was feeling desperate. Mary Alice knew all about the deed Wilkins handed Suzy at the wedding two months after the truck wheel accident. She also knew Sue Ellen took it with her to Vancouver, along with his two sons and a busy late-spring weekend's receipts. Haskins pulled to a stop on the lawn, leaving the engine running and headlights shining. He patted his left collarbone, feeling the holstered revolver he had purchased two days after Sue Ellen disappeared.

"That'll never happen again," he told the gun dealer.

Haskins bounced up the steps, stumbled right, and threw the screen door onto the front porch floor with a crash. The inside door to the showroom was open. He picked himself up and went directly in, shouting, "Mary Alice! Mary Alice!"

He found her in back, putting a kettle on the stove.

"Lucky, what are you doing here?"

"I need your property."

"What?"

"I have to move the shop."

"What are you talking about?"

"Sue Ellen burned the deed. I have to move everything over here, starting now."

"Not here, you're not," Mary Alice insisted. "Now, get out. Turn around and get out."

She pushed his shoulders with both hands, feeling the gun with her left.

Haskins stepped back and reached under his jacket.

"Mary Alice, I got no choice."

"You got one choice, and that is to get out."

His sweaty right hand brought out the revolver, which he wagged out toward the front porch. Haskins did not know whether he could shoot her, but he knew he would never be able to talk Mary Alice into doing something she didn't want to do, gun or no gun. She was a tough, stubborn woman. He was going to have to show her how serious this was for both of them.

"This way," he said, shaking the revolver again toward the front porch. "We're in this together, like it or not. Come on, this way."

Mary Alice wanted him out of the house, so she went.

27

Notebook: George Returns to Owen Sound

"George, how are you?" asked his father, seventy-seven-year-old John Thomson. Anxiety and tension gripped his voice. George was tense and anxious too. He had come back without his brother or any good news. The businessman and lawyer in George had rehearsed his greeting for hours on the train. All that he had practiced now escaped him. He never understood how his father managed to affect him this way.

"I am..."

He coughed, shook his head broadly, and took in the air coming off Georgian Bay, which was soothing. George hesitated, reminding himself to be circumspect. He responded formally.

"I'm sorry to say, father, that he has not been found."

"What?"

"Tom is gone."

"Gone?"

"They dragged the lake, searched the trails and the nearby lakes. Park rangers and guides went up and down the bays and rivers. They cannot find anything—his paddle is gone, his dunnage sack and—"

"What?"

George decided he would never tell his family everything he knew. George himself had not yet fully grasped all of what he had learned at Canoe Lake. Family and friends are often unable to judge one another fairly, even when the facts are plain. On the train back to Owen Sound, he had reviewed his notes and organized his thoughts from the last three days. He had tried to think as a lawyer, sifting all of the evidence before arriving at a conclusion.

"Tom left little behind when he disappeared—a crate of unused wood panels. His room at the Mowat Lodge was empty of all valuable personal belongings other than a new pair of snowshoes. Missing items included his sketch box, paints, brushes, and palette. All of his paintings are gone, too."

George went on to explain that on May 24, Tom gave away many of his last spring sketches to Dr. MacCallum and other guests at the Mowat Lodge.

"Tom delivered the remaining sketches in a flour sack to the Trainor cottage late that night or the next morning," George said. "Winnifred Trainor left for Huntsville on May 25. I didn't get to talk to her about what she knew. I tried to talk to her father, Hugh Trainor, just yesterday morning. I suspect that she may have his paintings."

"What happened to Tom?" John asked.

"Last Sunday, July 8, 1917, at a few minutes before one o'clock, Tom went out in his canoe alone, taking a week's worth of food supplies with him, leaving behind the axe he would need to cut firewood. Two hours later, his overturned canoe was seen floating on the lake southeast of Mowat Lodge. Two days later, they found his canoe overturned on the southwest side of Big Wapomeo Island, a thousand feet farther down the lake. The canoe was undamaged, with a rubber cloth stuffed into the bow protecting a large tin of maple syrup, berry jam, some cooking equipment, and utensils. Two paddles were lashed across the gunwales so the canoe could be carried. Two guides told me they were knotted in a most unorthodox way, as if a much less experienced canoeist had tied them. As an experienced canoeist, woodsman, and licensed guide, they told me, Tom would have told Park Ranger Mark Robinson if he was meeting a party of park visitors. Tom did not check in with Robinson before setting out on Sunday.

"I talked to everyone there," he explained, pausing again. "Tom's disappearance is a mystery to all."

John Thomson scanned the platform. George's luggage had been unloaded onto a cart. He saw a tall, heavy man wearing a rumpled blue railroad coat and a gold badge standing over a nearby cart awaiting instructions.

The Thomson's father stood erect—a full six foot one and 263 pounds—his beard graying and bushy this hot, damp July afternoon.

"You have none of his personal things?"

"Everything valuable was gone!" George insisted. "Also, he might return. I did not want to take the pitiful few remaining things."

The distressing implications settled on John's mind, and he sighed.

Worrying about Mother, George thought.

"Let us go, George. Your mother will need to be reassured."

George gestured to the station hand. His father stepped up behind the older man, who pushed the cart off into the shade of the station overhang, the right rear wheel clanking and whizzing gaily as it bumped along. George followed, feeling cranky and wheezy himself.

George's father had hired a two-horse carriage for the journey to and from the station in Owen Sound. It was a ten-minute ride to the family home. As the carriage pulled up in front of the house, George regretted his decision to visit Owen Sound this July.

"Thanks, again," George said. The driver gently whipped the reins and the team pulled forward, around in a tight circle, and away on the narrow street. Father went ahead into the house with the flour sack. Tom Harkness came out and retrieved the crate. The overhead sun was hot, the air still and heavy. George's mind swirled. He needed to brace himself as he ascended the front steps into the small, quiet, conventional brick house.

His mother stepped back from the doorway.

"George," she said.

He struggled through the screen porch door with his leather bag and briefcase, dropped them in the foyer, and came forward to embrace his retreating mother, kissing her on the cheek.

"So sorry, Mother."

She did not reply, merely stared with red and blurry eyes.

He edged around her and went straight to the telephone to call his old friend, Colonel Telford. He asked about his wife and announced that he would return for dinner in an hour. His mother edged away, too, back to the kitchen, where a stew was simmering on the stove. She busied herself in the kitchen until her husband called her into the home's small parlor.

"We have no good news of Tom from George," John Thomson announced to the gathered family members. "We hoped, but it was not to be. They are still searching for Tom. He will be found. I know it."

Late Monday morning, July 16, 1917, a telegram arrived bearing Shannon Fraser's terse message: "Tom found this morning." John Thomson immediately ordered a telegram sent back for confirmation. The next morning, a constable came to say they had received a telephone message from the provincial police in North Bay, saying Tom had been found at Canoe Lake but neglecting to mention whether he was dead or alive.

Late Tuesday afternoon, July 17, 1917, another messenger came to the Thomson home with another telegram from Shannon. Elizabeth Harkness signed for the envelope and carried it solemnly to her father in the parlor. It confirmed Tom's death. In a letter, also dated July 18, 1917, Fraser wrote from Mowat Lodge,

Dear Sir:

We found your son floating in Canoe Lake on Monday morning about nine o'clock in a most dreadful condition, the flesh coming off his hands. I sent for the undertaker, and they found him in such a condition he had to be buried at once. He is buried in a little grave overlooking Canoe Lake, a beautiful spot. The doctor found a bruise over his eye and thinks he fell and was hurt; that is how the accident happened.

Yours truly,
J. S. Fraser.

28

Notebook: George's Second Trip to Algonquin

Promptly after receiving the telegram confirming his son's death, John called George at Col. Telford's home and asked him to go back to Canoe Lake and bring the body home for burial.

"Your mother will not relax until Tom's brought home. Now, you go make arrangements. I will speak to her, and then the rest of the family."

George and his wife hurriedly took Col. Telford's carriage to the family undertaker, who called the local station manager of the Canadian National Railroad for instructions on transporting the body from Canoe Lake. He learned that a soldered steel casket was required. The undertaker, unfamiliar with steel caskets, called the railroad's national office to protest. They referred him to an experienced Huntsville undertaker named Franklin W. Churchill. The station manager offered to arrange transfers at Scotia and Inglewood Junctions as well as send two telegrams: to Churchill, to arrange recovery of the body, [1] and to Algonquin Park, to obtain the death certificate needed for reburial at Leith.

Meanwhile, George boarded the Tuesday-evening train bound for Inglewood Junction, praying for good connections so he could get to Mowat Lodge by Wednesday evening. There, he would meet Churchill.

After arriving at Joe Lake late on Wednesday afternoon, George sent his baggage down to Mowat Lodge and visited Robinson's ranger station to inquire about the death certificate. Robinson and Jack were gone. He got on the telephone, which connected directly to the superintendent's office at Cache Lake. Bartlett's wife answered and said he was away. George explained who he was, and Mrs. Bartlett asked if she could help.

---

1.   The family did not arrange for the services of an embalmer, as had Shannon Fraser. This indicates that they never anticipated viewing the body and is why they later disputed Dixon's bill for embalming services.

"Can you get a connection to an undertaker in Huntsville?" George asked.

"No," Mrs. Bartlett answered crisply. "We can reach Ottawa government offices. From there, they have a connection to the provincial police and county crown attorney in North Bay." Frustrated, George asked her to have Bartlett telephone back as soon as he returned. George waited there until dusk, when the telephone rang. Bartlett explained that Dr. Howland had examined the body; the coroner decided Tom had accidentally drowned, and the body was now buried in Mowat Cemetery.

"Buried?"

"Yes, sir. Your brother received a Christian burial on Tuesday afternoon."

"Why? On whose authority?"

"Upon my authority, as superintendent of the park, and that of the crown coroner. Mr. Thomson, the body was badly decomposed, since Tom drowned on the afternoon of July 8. He was not found until the morning of July 16, and he spent the next thirty-six hours in shallow water covered with a blanket. I ordered burial out of respect for the man."

"Is there no icehouse here?"

"The lake water is still quite cold, and we thought the coroner would arrive earlier, but he was detained by other matters and came in on the Tuesday-evening train."

"What about the death certificate?"

"We have none. Dr. Ranney left on the morning train yesterday. He will send the necessary documents by mail to Park Ranger Mark Robinson upon his return to North Bay."

"The family sent me here to bring the body back for burial. What am I to do?"

Bartlett paused, and then suggested that George obtain a certificate of death from Dr. Howland and immediately remove the body.

"Dr. Howland was staying at a cottage on Little Wapomeo Island. He is the only person who can prepare the necessary papers. Whether he is still there, I cannot tell you."

"Are Tom's belongings still at the Mowat Lodge? Have any of his paintings been found? Will you order Mark Robinson to search the Trainor cottage?" George asked in rapid-fire order. "Everything I learned points there. This is ridiculous."

"Let me answer your questions one at a time, please," Bartlett responded calmly but firmly. "I know nothing of Tom's belongings. I presume they remain at the Lodge. I directed Mark Robinson to search the Trainor cottage on Tuesday. I don't know if Mark found anything. Is he there with you?"

"No."

Bartlett agreed to speak with Robinson about the matter when he returned.

George walked across to the Canoe Lake Station to wait for the eastbound 8:00 PM Grand Trunk train, upon which he expected the Huntsville undertaker to arrive. Meanwhile, Shannon Fraser hitched up his horse-drawn hearse for the ride up to the Canoe Lake Station to meet incoming guests, including an undertaker, whose telegram that afternoon advised that he would be coming with a steel casket for Tom Thomson's body.

George heard the train announce its arrival with a rumble as he continued walking along the mild half-mile grade up from Joe Lake. In the distance, he saw a tall man dressed in a long, dark coat and bowler hat greeting Shannon Fraser on the platform in front of the station. The two men talked briefly as baggage handlers loaded a casket onto a hearse.

"How fitting," George mumbled.

As Fraser bounded into the station, George stepped up.

"Good evening. Are you the undertaker from Huntsville?"

"Yes, sir. You would be George Thomson. Please accept my sympathy for your tragic loss."

"Thank you," George said.

"I have to tell you, they already buried your brother's body."

"I know," George said, repeating what Bartlett had told him. "Are you prepared to do what's required?"

"Mr. Thomson, I am a professional with many years of experience. I carry out my responsibilities fully. I would want you to know that the condition of Tom's body could be highly distressing for loved ones such as yourself. While I would understand your need to satisfy yourself about its identity, I warn you that the removal of the body will be especially unpleasant."

"Mr. Churchill, I trust you to do what's necessary, promptly and efficiently. I want to return to Owen Sound by tomorrow morning. Are the payment arrangements for your services satisfactory?"

"Yes, sir, and they are confirmed by the family undertaker in Owen Sound."

The two men discussed their arrangements. Both would take rooms at the Mowat Lodge. Churchill would exhume the body and bring it to the train station for the trip back to Owen Sound as soon as possible, while George searched for Dr. Howland.

"Here is the necessary medical certificate-of-death form. On the reverse side is the return of death," Churchill said. "Dr. Howland fills out the certificate in his own handwriting. He will sign and return two copies to you. I keep one; you take the other with you to obtain the burial permit."

Late that evening, George heard a knock on the door of his second-story room, recently occupied by his brother.

"Mr. Thomson," the undertaker said. "I have removed the body, reburied the casket and holding box, soldered the casket, and delivered it to the Canoe Lake station. Have you the signed death certificate?"[2]

George brought Churchill his copy.

"Again, please accept my condolences, and rest assured that your brother's body was as well cared for as possible under these tragic circumstances. Good evening."

In the early-morning hours the next day, George spoke with Fraser about Tom's remaining belongings and arranged to ship an unused crate of sketching boards to Dr. MacCallum, sending him two letters on Mowat Lodge stationery. He paid for his room and rode Fraser's hearse up to the Canoe Lake station, where the dull steel casket basked in bright July sunlight.

George walked across to the Joe Lake ranger office. Again, Robinson and Jack were gone. The morning westbound train signaled its coming in the distance. George decided against departing without first talking with Robinson about the missing sketches from Tom's last spring series. George spent the day at Joe Lake, had lunch at the Hotel Algonquin, and chatted with the Colsons, asking every person he met where he might find Mark Robinson. As the westbound evening train's arrival drew near, he returned to the Joe Lake ranger office and left a note on Robinson's door.

---

2.   Part of the controversy of Churchill's exhumation that evening arises from assumptions that nobody can confirm. According to accounts attributed to Fraser, Churchill borrowed a shovel, crowbar, and two lanterns. When they arrived at the cemetery, Churchill sent Fraser away and completed the task alone within three hours. Some speculate that Churchill could not have removed the body so quickly. Churchill later said Robinson sent four men to help, while Fraser and Robinson said Churchill proceeded alone. Churchill may have asked Fraser to stay and, failing that, to leave the horse and hearse. Churchill certainly warned Fraser, as he would have warned George that the exhumation would be an unpleasant experience. Moreover, the fee for doing what he did that late night is the greatest an undertaker ever receives. Digging up the fresh grave and opening the box and casket might not have been that difficult, because the easiest way to remove a well-embalmed corpse, which is what Churchill found, was to wrap a rope around the chest and drive the hearse ahead ten feet. Nobody has ever mentioned George's presence at the gravesite.

Seven minutes before the train rumbled into Joe Lake, Robinson, and Jack stepped up to greet George.

"Fine evening," he announced.

"'Tis so," George replied brusquely.

"Your brother's body?" Robinson gestured toward the steel casket.

"Yes, sir. I am taking him home to the family."

"Your note asked about your brother's paintings," Robinson said, hesitating as he decided whether what he would do next would ever cause him trouble.

"Here," he continued, pointing to Jack. "I went to the Trainor cottage on Tuesday. These are all that I found. Tom dropped them on the porch the morning Winnifred Trainor returned to Huntsville. Mr. Hugh Trainor and his wife they said they wanted instructions from Winnie. I, ah…I persuaded Mr. Trainor to turn them over for safekeeping."

George nodded gratefully.

"I give them to you on your honor as his brother."

Robinson gestured to Jack, who bowed and pushed his loaded arms toward George. The boy hefted a heavy flour sack into George's arms as a train chugged into the Joe Lake station. That day, Robinson forever preserved a major piece of Canadian art history. He gave to the family, and the world, thirty-three of the remaining spring series of paintings.

"Thank you," George said, looking at the boy.

"Yes, sir."

As he waited for the train to depart, George pondered why Tom had given away his last spring series of paintings that night at the Mowat Lodge. George knew his brother used the sketches to prepare larger canvases. Without them, there would be no winter painting for the next year's art shows. Putting the last of them into Winnie's hands must have been the beginning of a deliberate plan, begun at least seven weeks earlier as Tom and Fraser packed them up in a flour sack at the Mowat Lodge dining room.

Eighteen hours later, on Friday afternoon, July 20, 1917, brother-in-law Harkness and the local undertaker greeted George at the Owen Sound station and collected the flour sack, George's baggage, and the soldered steel casket, which they brought home and put up in the parlor. When the undertaker finished polishing the steel casket and arranging flowers in the room, John Thomson gathered the family. He stepped over and picked up the flour sack from a cabinet behind him in the dining room.

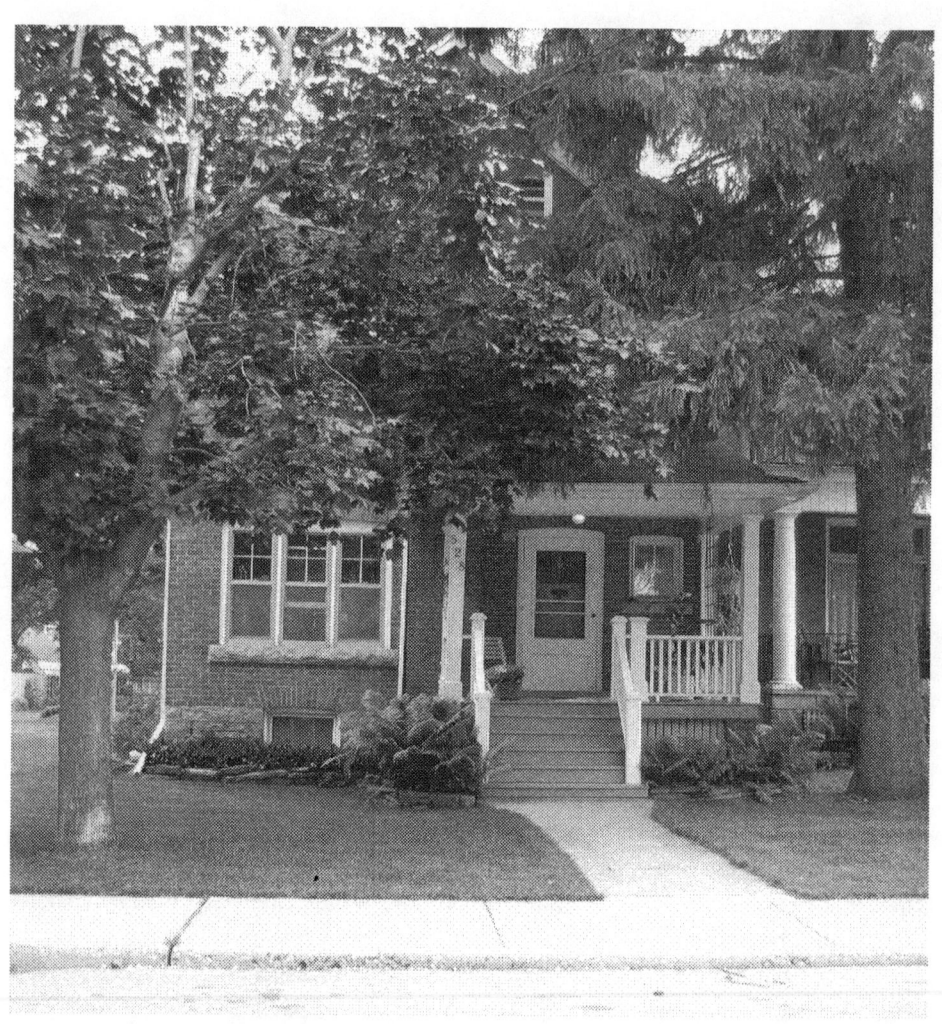

The Thomson family home in Owen Sound as it appeared in 2004.

"George brought these back."

John Thomson untied the flour sack and removed each panel of the last spring series. He handed them around one by one. They were stunningly bright and beautiful. Harkness, a sensitive man of thirty-four years, was amazed as Tom's living presence filled the room. His wife, George's sister Elizabeth, held the back of her right hand hard to her cheek at their beauty.

George stood by the fireplace, still and quiet. Sister Margaret Henry stared and leaned in. George's wife, Jean, dropped his hand and leaned back. She was breathless. Mother Thomson sprang from the room clumsily. Minister Arthur D. Cornett of the Knox United Church in Owen Sound was there as well. He later presided over Thomson's funeral and burial at Auld Kirk, now called the Leith Church Heritage Cemetery. Reverend Cornett stepped back, silently prayed for God's grace and mercy on the family, and followed Mrs. Thomson into the kitchen.

"Shingles?" Margaret said, calmly examining one of the sketches. "He painted on roofing shingles?"

John turned to George and asked, "Are there no canvases?"

"No," George said. "He painted those in Toronto. We need to ask Dr. MacCallum about what is there."

Tom Harkness arranged the sketches on the dining room table in neat rows, five across, six down, with three in the last row. George rearranged them by the changing of the season, putting the frigid *Northern Light* sketch in the upper-left corner and ending with *Spring in Algonquin Park* in the lower-right corner.

"These may be Tom's last paintings," George said to his incredulous father, spreading his arms across the table. George especially admired the last one, which his father gave him in January 1928.

"There were many more," John said. "All you have is thirty-three. Where are the others?"

"This is all we found. Winnie Trainor's father turned these over to Park Ranger Mark Robinson. I talked to everybody I could. Tom gave many of them away to guests one evening at the end of May in the Mowat Lodge dining room. Dr. MacCallum was there and took away several, I was told. Many, many others were taken, too. We will have to talk to Dr. MacCallum about what happened."

No family member ever said the steel casket was unsoldered so Tom's body could be identified. A letter from Thomson sister Margaret to her sister Minnie, dated July 22, 1917, confirmed this, saying, "None of us wanted to see him even if the body had been fit to see."

Relatives attended a simple private funeral service at the Knox United Church on Saturday, and the casket was buried in the Leith Cemetery. The stone reads, "Tom Thomson, Landscape Painter, Drowned in Canoe Lake July 8, 1917." Reverend Cornett wrote of him in the Church Register of Deaths, "Thomas Thomson (Artist), Accidental Drowning, Canoe Lake, Algonquin Park, July 8, 1917, age 39 years, Born August 4, 1877, Buried at Leith, Ontario, July 21, 1917, Talented and with many friends and no enemies, a mystery."

29

Notebook: Canoe Lake July 8, 1917

Tom Thomson awoke to a brilliant Algonquin Sunday morning, song of robin and cedar waxwing rising up from the pin cherry trees to his second-floor window on the front of the Mowat Lodge, which looked down toward Canoe Lake. He blinked as he pulled the blanket up across his shoulders and turned toward the open window. He breathed in the damp air that filled the room. Thomson groaned, recalling his agreement to fish that morning with Shannon Fraser at Joe Lake Dam. His head pounding, he yanked himself up and planted his feet on the rough wood floor. The night's gathering at George Rowe's cabin left a bad taste in his mouth—or maybe it was the drinking he had done. He coughed, trying to clear his head, and stood shakily looking for his whiskey in the dim light. Thomson drew the bottle to his lips and drained the last few ounces into his throat, let it sit until the burning quieted, shook his head, and swallowed. A few lines of poetry ran through his mind.

> But though I have wept and fasted, wept and prayed,
> Though I have seen my head (grown slightly bald)
> Brought in upon a platter;
> I am no prophet—and here's no great matter;
> I have seen the moment of my greatness flicker,
> And I have seen the eternal footman hold my coat,
> And snicker. [1]

He reached down beside the bed and pulled on a pair of well-worn woolen socks, a frayed gray woolen shirt, and some khaki trousers before adjusting his suspenders and tying on a pair of grimy white canvas shoes. He checked his

---

1.   T.S. Eliot, *The Love Song of J. Alfred Prufrock* (1915).

dresser, finding his pipe, a pouch of rough-cut tobacco, and a silver nickel. Thomson took a wad of the tobacco and stuffed it into the pipe as he looked about for a match. Finding none, he dropped the pipe into his shirt pocket and tucked the pouch and silver nickel into his empty right pants pocket. Standing in the hallway, Thomson looked back into the dull room, reminding himself that he would never again spend an empty night here, alone. He closed the door and went downstairs to find Shannon Fraser.

The two old friends hiked up to the bridge across Joe Creek and up to the dam as the overcast sky brightened with the rising sun. They fished together below the Joe Lake Dam often, standing on the rocky west shoreline as water spilled hard into the center of the creek, leaving a wide circulating pool where a wily old trout resided, one that had eluded them since spring break-up.[2] Thomson sat quietly tying a mayfly to his leader as Shannon Fraser watched. Thomson reached back and, with great precision, floated his line out and across the deep pool, the mayfly skimming lightly over the water. Tom's eyes gleamed, his jaw tense with concentration. Shannon Fraser sighed as he saw a shadow flicker up toward the surface near the center of the pool and dive sharply away. As it did, the mayfly danced, following Thomson's deft choreography. Thomson reeled in the line, keeping his eye on the shadow turning slowly toward the dam on the far side of the pool. Thomson steadied his casting arm and waited as the shadow rose back toward the surface. He flung the line out and skimmed the mayfly across the water in a figure eight. The shadow burst up through the surface, twirling, and fell back into the water with a great splash as Thomson yanked back on his pole.

"You've got him!" Fraser cried.

The big trout dove and drove toward the big rocks below the dam, where the current ran faster. Thomson let him take the line for a few seconds and dropped his pole low, reeling in the slack. The big trout turned and twisted back, letting Thomson take the line before diving again toward the rocks. Thomson gave back some and the trout took it all, pulling the line taut, bending the long pole sharply.

Up across the top of the dam, Mark Robinson and his son were watching. They saw the pole bend and the line flash, knifing through the water below and away. Robinson had hooked this big trout himself, seven days ago, in morning light. Last evening, he'd told the story at George Rowe's cabin. Thomson scoffed, saying there was no trout on Canoe Lake he could not land, promising a morning

---

2.   On July 5, 1917, Robinson wrote in his journal, "Quite a number tried to capture the Big trout at the Dam, but all failed to entice the Big to fool himself."

trip out to the Joe Lake Dam with Shannon Fraser to prove himself. Robinson had decided to come and see.

"Darned if he hasn't hooked him," Robinson told his son.

The line darted back and forth, as the two combatants measured each other. Thomson lowered the pole, the line quivering in response as the big trout circled back to shore, coming toward the surface. Thomson lifted his pole smartly as the line fell slack across the water. Suddenly, the trout dove and twisted back, taking the line out and down into the rocks, where it snagged on a log and snapped. Thomson felt the line go lifeless and groaned as the big trout steadied itself deep in the center of the pool, under the protection of a sunken, overturned canoe.

"That old guy got away again," Shannon Fraser hooted. Robinson laughed too, and he waved, but neither Thomson nor his friend heard or saw him as they busied themselves with Thomson's fishing gear.

"Tell you what," Thomson said. "This afternoon, I'll take my canoe out to Tea Lake Dam, Gill, or West Lakes, where the big trout are easy to catch. We'll leave it on Mark's doorstep. When he asks, you tell him it was the one that got away from him. That'll put him in his place."

Thomson told Fraser he wanted to visit with the new owners of the Hotel Algonquin and get some late breakfast before setting out on his next fishing expedition. He asked Fraser to arrange for some food supplies, including a fresh loaf of bread. Thomson clapped him on the back and headed up to the dam and across, where, in the distance, he saw Mark Robinson and son walking north on the road to Joe Lake.

"How do you do?" Thomson shouted. He waved as Robinson turned and waved back.

30

Notebook: Night on Big Wapomeo Island

Dickson and Rowe had paddled with Tom Thomson many times. To them, his death was no mystery. They and almost all other Canoe Lake regulars knew Tom as a reclusive, angry, and impulsive man who was less than an expert canoeist, as well as a poor swimmer and a drunk. Dickson and Rowe concluded that he had gotten drunk, fallen out of his canoe, and drowned in the lake water, which was colder than any they could remember in July.

"Ten minutes out there tonight would kill anybody," Rowe observed. "Lake trout are still at the surface."

Dickson shook his head with the resigned fear of an Algonquin Park veteran. His own father had drowned here years ago, according to what Rowe had told him a few years earlier on his twenty-first birthday, after they had both gotten drunk.

Thomson's bloated body was face down at the shore, in the shallows, tied to the roots of a scraggly Jack pine, as the two sat by a campfire. Stars pierced the blackness—single, chilled points of light in the night sky. North and southbound freight trains passed through the park many times each night, their low rumbles and station whistles flowing down Potter Creek and Joe Creek a few minutes apart.[1] Regulars on Canoe Lake learned to keep time by the trains. Rowe said the next one came at 11:30.

Dickson said, "No, it's closer to 11:45."

Rowe, pocket watch in hand as he tried to stay awake, won the first round.

Dickson and Rowe faced each other across the campfire. Thomson's body glistened, reflecting the light from a left-handed moon that climbed across the sky.

---

1.   As many as 120 trains passed through the park each day, carrying soldiers, wheat, war materials, and other freight.

Dickson was twenty-four years old. His own father had died in a lumberyard accident before he was born.

Rowe, who was much older, at age sixty-seven, had faced death two years earlier at a fire across from Brent station. He had rescued a railway worker from a burning dormitory. He thought little of it here in the park, where death was an everyday occurrence.

"Death is maybe today or tomorrow. The only thing certain is that it was not yesterday."

"Death looms large here tonight." Rowe said.

Dickson heard the 11:30 train first, knew he had lost, and thought to make a new bet.

"12:26 next?"

Rowe replied, "12:10! Wanna' bet on it?"

Dickson wondered whether Rowe was bluffing. What was the sure thing to do? Rowe was groggy and tiring of the game. They waited. Dickson heard a train whistle and tossed a shot of whisky on the logs, which erupted in flames.

"Unless I'm not correct, 12:10," he said to this younger man he loved.

"What did I say, 12:05?"

"No, 12:26," said Rowe.

"Who's keeping time?"

"The trains keep time."

Rowe checked his pocket watch.

"12:10," he said. "Next train at 12:59. Want to bet?"

"The *Times* you get at the Canoe Lake Station every morning from Ottawa," Dickson joked.

"What times?" Rowe responded.

"Bad times."

"The *Ottawa Times*."

"You spend too much time reading the *Times*."

"What time is it here on Big Wapomeo Island, poor Tom down there in the water?" Rowe asked.

"We have whatever time we need," Dickson replied. "He has none. All we can do is watch and wait and pass the time." Dickson heard a train whistle come down Joe Creek at 12:59.

"You lost the bet," Rowe said, adding, "Time took him down and time brought him up again."

Rowe knew from earlier drowning experiences that when a man drowns in forty feet of cold water—the water is always very cold down there—he will spend some time on the bottom until the natural process of decay cause gasses to build in his body. The sun's heat spreads through the water, and as summer continues, the ever-moving surface water separates from the lower water. Rowe knew that from fishing lake trout, which spend their summers in the deep, cold water.

"1:17," Dickson said.

"No, later than that—1:37."

"We wait until it's time to take our friend up and out again to be buried."

Dickson let his head fall back against the bedroll he had fixed up.

"We wait as they wait out there in the park, waiting his time, wondering whatever happened to Tom," Rowe said.

"Where do you find a man like Tom? He is going to go where he is going to go. What could we do about it?"

Rowe fell silent for a moment as a train whistled away from Joe Lake Station at 1:37.

"Either you or the train was late," he suggested, apologizing for his string of wins that long night.

Dickson admired Thomson. Dickson had grown up in the park, the stepson of a park ranger who took him everywhere he went from the time his new parents decided the boy could eat what they ate. His mother had died of dysentery when he was four and his stepfather had drowned off Rosebary Lake in an October storm when Dickson was six. Rowe's family took him in, and this man's love was all he could remember.

"What did he want?" Dickson mused. "Tom never said much to me. He did what he did. He had a few drinks and he went to sleep until the morning was new. I do not know what happened or why we're here and he's there. God bless him and grant him peace. I thought well of that man."

Dickson knew as much and as little as anyone about Thomson. During these past few months of 1917, he knew that Tom was mostly off with his sketch box.

"Tom painted. He knew no time."

Dickson had watched him sketch a scene toward the end of May, of a canoe heading south of the dock from Mowat Lodge lacking a paddler. Thomson put the panel aside, paused to suck on his pipe, blew a cloud of pale blue smoke and recited, "We have lingered in the chambers of the sea by sea-girls wreathed with seaweed red and brown. Till human voices wake us, and we drown." [2]

---

2.   T.S. Eliot, *The Love Song of J. Alfred Prufrock* (1915).

Dickson fell asleep thinking that what he wanted was to spend more time with George Rowe. He had the time. From the train across Potter Creek going northbound, he remembered it was after 1:37, and Dickson feel asleep.

The last two train whistles he remembered that night stayed with Rowe for years. They came down Joe Creek and Potter Creek into Canoe Lake—four bright snorts, two long bursts, and one final, mournful gasp of steam at 4:07 A.M., and again at 4:11 A.M.

Dawn rose over the island, bringing a mist that spread across Canoe Lake. The water was still, and the park was silent before the birds awoke. Dickson slept. Rowe stood and yawned, taking a long, deep breath. He tucked in his shirt, shook his left pant leg down, and bent to pick up his cap. Beaded dewdrops rested on the leaves and grasses. White ash covered the firewood, and a pencil-thin column of cool blue smoke drifted straight up from the corner of one log.

"Damn fine day," he said to himself. He then set about getting another fire going, for a breakfast of fresh coffee and fried bacon.

31

Oxtongue Rive Chase

Kristian was running out of time. For as long as he could remember, he could sense the trickle of time inside his head. Librarian Ruth Ubley came and reminded him that the building was closing at nine o'clock. He hurriedly made a few notes from a late-July issue of the *Huntsville Forester*, its yellowed pages bound together in a large black volume marked 1916–1917. Thomson's obituary reported that a painter, guide, and friend to some had drowned, alone, on Canoe Lake at age forty.

"Well, so what else is new," he mumbled, putting the bound volume aside, pulling his papers into a briefcase, and walking to the parking lot. "They got his age wrong. Thomson was thirty-nine. His mid-life crisis would not have officially begun until August 5, 1917."

The lights of the library darkened as he got to the car, opened the door, and hopped in. Kristian drove away, his canoe sticking far over the hood.

Thirty minutes later, he turned and continued up the long dirt driveway to Mary Alice's shop. The driveway turned across the front of the house. His headlights illuminated a small open shed out back, where Mary Alice usually kept her canoe resting atop two sawhorses. The canoe was gone. Kristian stopped.

Parked on the lawn in front of the porch was a battered black Ford pick-up with two aluminum canoes on an angle iron rack in the bed. The pick-up's lights blazed. Kristian stopped behind the truck, leaving the headlights on and the engine running. He got out and, before turning toward the porch, he heard a rustling beyond the shed, along with a muffled female cry and an angry male grumble. He made out a man, brandishing a white ash paddle in his left fist and a silver revolver in his right, heading down the path to the river.

"Shut up," a male voice snarled in the darkness.

"What the hell is going on?" Kristian asked himself. He found the front screen door on the porch smashed through, the door to the showroom hanging open, and a teakettle screaming on the stove. He turned off the gas. Alarmed, he turned around and set off down the path toward the river, where he had last seen Mary Alice.

A menacing black cover of clouds was moving overhead. A great storm was quickly approaching from the northeast, spreading out over the Oxtongue River. Kristian ran to get his canoe off his car and hoisted it onto his shoulders. He ran toward the river around Cedar Rapids. Kristian had taken the same path across two days earlier, but now a downpour obscured the narrow, rocky trail in forbidding black shadows.

Lightning flashed and a long, low rumbling rolled across the sky. Ahead, pushing out onto the river, was the man he had seen up by the shop. Mary Alice sat in the bow. Cedar Rapids, which she was about to head into along with a man pointing a revolver, was a dangerous rapid. Kristian knew they could easily come out of the swift water on their backs. He ran the portage. Arriving at the put-in, he saw a canoe well ahead, rocking in the waves and going downstream fast.

"Some good paddling," he thought.

Kristian hesitated, standing in the rain, canoe on his shoulders. He could feel that day's earlier paddle in his arms. Everything he knew said hang back, don't get involved, save yourself, and call the police. He had no place out here, in the stormy darkness on treacherous Oxtongue River, confronting a crazy man threatening a woman he had known for one afternoon and an evening. However, everything in him told him he had to do something, that he must answer the cry for help that he had deafened himself to seventeen months earlier. Mary Alice was out there, and he was here, safe on shore. God, he thought, the river was running fast. He had little faith in his ability to maneuver at night, in water growing higher and faster with the storm. Kristian watched as the canoe ahead swept out of sight. A flash of lightning lit the far shore. He could feel his shoulder and stomach muscles tense with anticipation. Kristian lifted the canoe off his shoulders and let it plunge into the river. He stepped in, positioned himself with his knees spread wide, unlashed his paddle, and pushed away from shore into the fast-moving water under a hard, steady rain that came in waves. He doubted that he could catch up before they reached Ragged Falls. The river flowed faster and stronger than when he paddled the same stretch the day before. He tried to reassure himself that he had studied it carefully. Mary Alice went over it with him and warned him about its treachery. If she could do it, so could he.

Kristian settled down, ferried across the current, and settled the canoe behind a boulder protruding through the rushing water. He steadied the canoe and made an eddy exit into the racing current. He then straightened the canoe and paddled hard downstream through the first of the two short swifts that guarded the *S* curve ahead of Hardwood Rapids, side-slipping around a huge boulder. The driving rain reminded him that he'd left his life jacket in the trunk of the car.

"Oh, God," he whispered.

Kristian had never paddled a whitewater river at night and never imagined doing so in a driving rainstorm. It was utter foolishness to attempt this on the twisting Oxtongue River. Wind and waves pushed the canoe back and forth, left and right. He knew he had to take the waves straight on. Kristian felt weakened as lightning flashed in one blinding bolt after another, peal after peal of deafening thunder boomed, and the winds howled fiercely. Cold rain stung his face like a thousand pinpricks. He worried about Mary Alice and never slowed. His arms ached. His left shoulder screamed. His fingers numbed in the driving, cold rain, and wind.

A lightning bolt reached into the river downstream, near shore. He lost his sight for a moment, and then he blinked, readjusting to the darkness. He paddled harder and faster. Water pooled beneath his feet and along his thighs as he kneeled low in the canoe. Lights far ahead cast halos and blurry images in the rain, which ran into his eyes and punished his face. Kristian worked the waves ahead, pulling through with a stroke up, over, down, ready for the next.

"Damn this storm," he cried out. "Goddamn!"

He closed his eyes briefly against the rain and prayed to himself as he struggled against the waves, stroking at a frantic pace. He could hardly feel his hands anymore. Another bolt of lightning flashed across the roiled water. The canoe crashed through a diagonally curling wave. Only a strong brace as he shot through kept the canoe upright. Water plunged over the left side, pulled at his paddle, and drenched him. Kristian struggled onward as roller waves pushed the canoe up and let it down, seeking weakness, awaiting the letdown.

He steadied to the center of the current, trying to orient himself against the skyline, sensing the speed and motion of the water and thinking back to the previous day's trip. He heard a cry ahead and saw a glimpse of Mary Alice's aluminum canoe flash in the lightning and then disappear in the darkness. He maneuvered through the second swift ahead of Hardwood Rapids.

"Big rolling waves ahead," he warned himself.

Lightning flashed again, and a deep peal of thunder rolled and tumbled down the river from the northeast. What he remembered running in low water from a day ago was of little use. The river was now running high, and this was a new trip altogether. It was wider and faster, plunging ahead as it swung left. He back-ferried river left, hugging the bank around a turn as the moon faded away again. He ferried over and eddied in behind a large rock in mid-river. He pulled up fast behind a large rock, the canoe bobbing violently underneath him. Another fierce glare lit up the river. Relax and ride with confidence, he told himself as he paddled forward and leaned out of the eddy back into the main current.

He spotted the first in a series of downstream V's, Hardwood Rapids, which he had first seen the day before from several vantage points along the shore. Only an expert could maneuver it, he had decided, walking around. He saw Mary Alice's canoe appear during another lightning flash and plunge away, leaving Hardwood Rapids. A furious blast of thunder roared down the river. Into the watery violence he continued.

Standing waves tossed the canoe as he back-ferried toward the right bank around a foaming souse hole. Kristian rode straight and true through a powerful set of curling waves. One blinding flash after another followed him down Hardwood Rapids, and the rain came again. Ahead he saw Mary Alice's canoe racing through a swift and down over what he remembered was Gravel Falls—not a straight down four-foot drop, but a narrow chute over a ledge followed by two more drops, one right after the other, as the river descended sharply to the left. The drops were spread across thirty yards, indistinct downstream V's followed by haystacks and big rollers. The second drop took a deceptively easy plunge into a souse hole half a canoe-length wide. If he dropped easily, the souse hole would swallow his canoe.

He paddled hard and fast, gaining speed with the river, going out and over the brink of High Falls. Only a deep forward brace held the stern as he pulled forward, tumbled left and right, and careened into an underwater rock, throwing the canoe sideways and down into a maelstrom of foaming water. Kristian put a firm offside paddle into the current, and it pulled the canoe over and back as the falls plunged down.

He paddled hard through Gravel Rapids, where he had made two practice runs that morning. Kristian had gained on Mary Alice considerably over the next two miles, before he heard Ragged Falls.

"Northway!"

It was her voice coming upstream. Kristian remembered what she had told him, and he understood the urgency in her cry. He heard the roar of cascading water ahead. Kristian struggled to get the canoe over to river left, preparing for the bend ahead. He passed the last marked safe portage exit, taking the north way she had earlier warned against.

The canoe bucked and twisted, and he put a hard brace on the left as he ferried around the sharp right bend and approached the other boat, four canoe lengths ahead. The bow paddler stood and dived over and into the water, swimming toward the left shore hard and fast. The canoe ahead, a lean black figure at the stern, was caught in the current in the center of the river and drove forward, careening on the back end, it bow rising up three feet, swinging back and forth wildly. A wild gunshot from the stern flashed and roared three times, as the canoe flayed and bobbed.

A figure appeared in the water ahead and to the right of Kristian's canoe, swimming straight toward him. The swimmer leaped and grabbed onto the bow of Kristian's canoe. He strained to see in the rain. It was her, Mary Alice.

"Get me out of here," she shouted. Booming thunderbolts drowned out her voice. He planted his paddle hard left and stroked forward with everything he had, pulling against her weight at the bow. Mary Alice leaned far over toward river left as Ragged Falls loomed ahead. He backstroked, pulling the canoe to the left, into smoother current. Mary Alice shouted at him again.

"Straight, then river left—hard!"

He heard and responded. Her arms clung tightly to the bow of the canoe. Her right leg flung up as the canoe rocked over a perfectly curling wave. In the faster water below, Kristian set his paddle straight on and pushed it forward, propelling the canoe even faster in a current that was still rising and pushing them along. Another blinding flash spread across the sky from behind them to ahead of them. Mary Alice flung her leg up as the canoe pulled hard to the right with her added weight. He leaned far over to his left and braced hard against the deep water. The next thing he knew, she was ahead of him, leaning back against the bow seat and loosening the spare paddle tied there. She shouted for him to steer river left again.

"Now!" she cried. "Hard left!"

Ahead, he knew, were a gunman and the brink of Ragged Falls. The low rumble grew more ominous by the second. At the sharp right bend above the falls, he saw the other canoe, bobbing and weaving in the center of the river, facing upstream, straight ahead. Lucky had found an eddy behind a submerged rock large enough to hold him steady as they approached.

Mary Alice made a crossbow stroke, bringing the two canoes and the submerged rock onto a collision course. Lightning crashed and flashed, piercing the stark blackness with brilliance. The other man's face and shoulders squared against Kristian, who followed Mary Alice's direction unswervingly, driving straight into the other canoe. Haskins held his paddle up in his left hand and the silver revolver in his right, pointing it at them. Kristian saw Lucky lean forward.

Then, a sudden, furious downpour and another flash of lightning blinded them all. Instantly, Mary Alice planted her paddle on the left side of the canoe and dug deeply forward. Feeling her movements, Kristian pried the stern. The canoe responded to their perfect strokes, the bow sliding around to the left of the rock as the stern charged forward in the current and rammed the right front end of Lucky's canoe, bringing Kristian and Lucky two feet apart. Looking surprised, Lucky froze as the bow of his canoe caught in the violent eddy line to his left and pin-wheeled out into the fast-flowing water churning downstream. He dropped both paddle and revolver into the racing river current, going for the gunwales with his hands to brace himself.

"Back ferry hard left," Mary Alice shouted, and Kristian responded, seeing the violent brink of Ragged Falls ten yards ahead on the right side of the river. Their canoe slid into the boulder garden eddy on river left, where the rushing back current swirled them and pushed their canoe roughly to shore. Lucky's bow lifted out of the water and headed straight for the log lodged squarely in the middle of the brink. Toppled back in the stern of his canoe, Lucky never saw what was coming as the canoe glanced right off the deadhead and plunged over the edge, picking up speed as the bow dropped, tipped over, and went down. Kristian heard a crash of aluminum as lightning flashed and thunder cracked. They held their canoe steady and sure around, safe for the moment in the churning eddy at the top of the last Ragged Falls portage, the stern pushed securely up against shore. Mary Alice had saved his life—and hers.

"Are you okay, Mary Alice?" he shouted.

"You didn't know anything about yourself, did you?" she responded, shouting over the roar of Ragged Falls. Mary Alice jumped out of the bow onto the muddy portage, positioning herself prone over the bow of the boat, her paddle spread across the gunwales in the event of a mishap.

"Now, get us home," she shouted again. "Be damn careful, Kristian. I want bacon and eggs for breakfast tomorrow, and don't you forget it."

He stepped ashore. She stood, pulling him over to shelter under the tall pine marked by a portage sign. She put her arms around him, leaned in, and looked up for a kiss. They held each other, shivering and wet, shoulder and abdominal muscles throbbing, hands quivering, fingers curled in remembered pain. Her lips pressed firmly to his, her hands feeling warm against his neck.

She leaned back and told him, "Next time, let's paddle an easier stretch of the Oxtongue."

Still shaking with fear, he lifted the canoe unsteadily to his shoulders and headed down the trail he had walked many times before in the daylight, but never in stormy darkness. Involuntary tremors shook his arms and hands. The portage was harrowing. Waiting at the path toward Route 60 below, Mary Alice said she thought she made out the shape of a body pressed grotesquely behind a canoe that was wrapped around a rock at the lower edge of the third pool below roaring Ragged Falls. Kristian barely noticed as stillness spread across the sky, from northwest to southeast, bringing a sky full of stars. The rain stopped, and quiet descended. A brief five-minute walk brought them out to the roadway. They saw automobile headlights heading toward them from both the east and west.

"Now," she said, "we go home."

"I go where you go."

32

Tom's Last Painting

Margaret Rose O'Gorman walked down to Canoe Lake at noontime on July 8, 1917 in a faint drizzle. She wore her chestnut-brown hair in long curls below her shoulders, tied with a wide ribbon at the back. Her long-sleeved cotton blouse with lacy cuffs was loosely tucked into a pale, yellow skirt, reaching halfway down her calves. A pair of equally pale yellow stockings covered the rest of her legs. She wore patent leather shoes with large buckles. She was becoming a woman, proud but cautious of her new femininity. Margaret Rose was a beautiful girl who had not yet learned to enjoy the eyes of men, younger or older, on her tall, full body.

Thomson was sitting on a smooth gray and pink boulder thirty yards from the lake, his sketch box in his lap. He turned to see her coming along the path. Thomson looked up, breathing in the humid air with his mouth. He turned to the young girl, who reminded him of another many years ago in Seattle, one whom he had loved and nearly forgotten.

"Come and watch," he called to Margaret Rose.

Thomson opened the box and removed a finished sketch, one of quiet lake water on a misty summer day. Trees in the background across the lake were topped by a pale shade of green, their leaves newly burst. Sun reflected off the lake in a noontime pose.

"Do you have a boyfriend, Margaret Rose? That Jack Wilkinson I've seen you running around with?"

"No, he's just my cousin, Mr. Thomson. Mother says I am too young to have a boyfriend."

"Oh, I think maybe it's happened before."

This young Rose is bright and full of promise, he thought, reaching for two crumbled tubes of paint. He wiped his brush with a rag. Onto his sketch box, he squeezed a tiny spot of gray and added a bubble of cobalt blue, mixing them with a practiced twist of his brush. Thomson looked up at Canoe Lake and Little Wapomeo Island.

"I want you to take this painting."

He turned back to the panel and manipulated the brush with easy virtuosity, hesitating in the middle of the stroke, turning it abruptly during the sweep, flattening and extending the width, contracting, and rolling the hair of the brush on its edge, without losing his rhythm. The brush caught enough of the underpainting to adhere and mark the pigment. With that quick sweep of his brush, he added a gray-green canoe to the scene, the bow rising over a small wave. The canoe's up-turned ends pointed downward. It was out on the water adrift. He handed it to her.

She recognized the painting. It was the same scene she had picked out at the Mowat Lodge, where he had put out all the last spring sketches. That night, Dr. MacCallum had come to dinner with him.

"Follow me," he said, jumping down and pointing to a clump of young birch saplings near the boulder he had just painted in his scene. He pointed out a paddle, fishing rod, and reel nearby.

"Please, take them, too."

Margaret Rose watched as Thomson hauled the seventeen-foot canoe up onto his shoulders, turned, and jogged down to the lake, leaving a dunnage bag out of sight on the ground among the white birch saplings for raccoons to haul away in the night.

Arms full, Margaret Rose followed.

Thomson dropped the canoe onto the gently lapping water and, before stepping in, reached into his right front pocket, and pulled out a silver coin.

"Here, Margaret Rose, it's the last nickel to my name."

She held out her left hand and clenched the silver nickel tightly as he got into the canoe and, kneeling, unlashed the portage paddle from its place across the gunwales. He stood and put his right foot over the side and pushed off.

Back at the cabin, in her room, Margaret put the new sketch, paddle, and fishing gear in the back of her closet. The nickel went into her pocket. She would spend it later that year, buying her mother a Christmas ornament in South River. At father's insistence, on the mantel to the left side of the wide stone fireplace was the Thomson painting of a canoe.

Nine days later, on July 17, 1917, standing with her mother, Margaret Rose listened pensively as Mr. Blecher read the funeral service. That afternoon, she passed the grievous hours alone in her room reading the Bible, remembering Tom Thomson as he paddled away. Margaret Rose happened upon a passage in Genesis 8:4, which described the Great Flood, from which Noah and those with him had survived, coming to rest in the ark on the mountain of Ararat on the seventeenth day of the seventh month.

Mr. Blecher ended the brief ceremony by saying, "We have entrusted our brother, Tom, to God's mercy, and we now commit his body to the ground. Earth to earth, ashes to ashes, dust to dust, in sure and certain hope of the resurrection to eternal life through our Lord Jesus Christ, who will transform our frail bodies that they may be conformed to His glorious body, who died, was buried, and rose again for us. To Him be glory for ever. Amen."

The gathering moved silently past the casket. Mr. and Mrs. Fraser went first, then Mark Robinson and his son, Jack. When her turn came, Margaret Rose, following her mother, kissed her right fingertips and touched the brass inscription, whispering, "Mr. Thomson, I pray that you come to rest here today."

33

Notebook: George Considers Tom's Drowning

The trip home to New Haven, Connecticut, gave George hours to go over the new information about his younger brother's death. The trip took take him to Toronto, across to Buffalo, south to New York City. George pulled a notebook out of his briefcase and began writing. He had not yet decided whether he would ever share his handwritten memorandum on Tom's death with anyone else. Certainly, he would not share it until the estate closed, and that could take years. George's father put brother-in-law Thomas J. Harkness, secretary-treasurer and manager of the Sydenham Mutual Fire Insurance Company, in charge of administering Tom's estate. George needed to leave Owen Sound, wanting to leave his brother's tragic story behind.

The bits of information that had come back to him following Tom's burial, from Bartlett and Fraser's telegrams and letters, confirmed what he already knew. Tom had drowned in forty feet of cold water in Canoe Lake, for the last twenty years a southbound lumber route following ice-out. The weather at Canoe Lake this previous spring had been unusually cold, according to Tom's letters and Mowat residents. If he had overturned the canoe and gone swimming in water less than 70°F (21°C), within a few minutes, he would have suffered fits of shivering and fumbling hands and legs. The cold water flowing across his body would have rendered him drowsy, incoherent, unconscious, and drowned in ten minutes. By swimming well ahead of the drifting overturned canoe, he would have confounded searchers as to what happened.

As his dying body sank to the bottom, his right forehead and ear struck submerged lumber, a fallen tree, or logging machinery. The head-down position of his corpse caused the injury to bleed, complicating later efforts to determine whether it occurred before or after the drowning. Therefore, George decided, the blow to his right temple and his bleeding right ear occurred after, not before, he plunged overboard.

At water temperatures below forty-five degrees at the bottom of the lake, decomposition would have taken many weeks or even months. The dead body's natural production of hydrogen and methane gasses would have slowed dramatically and contributed to the transformation of the fatty layers beneath his skin into a soap-like material. Over nine days, Tom's body would have bloated nearly beyond recognition and discolored to a pallid purple, rendering positive identification difficult and particularly distressing to personal acquaintances. From all he knew, those few persons at Canoe Lake who had seen the body had no doubt that it was that of his brother, Tom. George regretted that the steel casket had to be soldered shut before its return from Canoe Lake. The undertaker in Owen Sound had been told by none other than a senior vice president at the Canadian Pacific Railway office in Toronto that the railway would not transport an exhumed body in anything except a soldered steel casket.

"You have to understand," he explained, "since the war, we have transported thousands of bodies of young soldiers across Canada back to their loved ones. Our experience led to new military regulations, which we have now adopted for all transport of human remains. We put this safeguard into place for the protection of the body, our workers, and passengers. We can recommend an undertaker in Huntsville who is trained and experienced in the handling of steel transport caskets."

George knew he had failed to have the body identified. Reopening the steel casket at Leith was a task the local undertaker declined to perform. "I have neither the training nor the inclination to do so," was the curt reply. Therefore, George had to account for the possibility that the body in the casket buried at Leith might not have been his younger brother's. Nobody would ever know.

If Tom had surreptitiously slipped away from his own canoe into the missing Colson canoe, hidden away on the southeast shore of Little Wapomeo Island, and then moved it and his fishing and camping gear across the Gill Lake portage, he would have required yet a third canoe for the long trip across the park to the South River train station or elsewhere. If that is what happened, why did he leave behind in his canoe the maple syrup, jam, cooking equipment, and utensils?

Assuming the body pulled from the lake was not Tom's, George mulled over the possibility that his brother had, indeed, decided to move on, leaving everything behind, as he had done when leaving Owen Sound, Seattle, and Toronto. The trouble with this theory, George concluded, was that Tom was a passionate if troubled man who sought acknowledgement, not indifference, from others. If

Tom went off west, as he told the family in earlier letters he wished to do, why did he make his exit secretively? George thought it inconceivable that his younger brother, a well-known and popular painter of Canadian landscapes, his career as a professional artist secured, would toss it all aside by fleeing unannounced and unrecognized to the Canadian Rockies. And besides, if the body returned from Mowat was not his, Tom would have learned of the reported drowning and at least assured the family that he was still alive.

The evidence convinced him that Tom's disappearance was no accident. George dismissed the possibility of a canoeing or portaging mishap, particularly one that ended with his brother overturning his canoe and drowning in the middle of Canoe Lake, because the water was calm and Tom was experienced. In any accident scenario on the lake or along one of its few portages, his paddle and fishing pole should have remained, to be discovered by the search parties.

Nor was there evidence that suggested foul play. If Tom was killed, who was the killer? Nobody at Canoe Lake had the motive, method, and opportunity from noon to three o'clock on Sunday, July 8, 1917.

What deeply troubled George were the careful, subtle preparations evident in all of Tom's activities in the last weeks of spring, pointing to a single tragic answer to his brother's death: suicide. The calculus of his reasoning was as obvious to George as the fact that no one would ever know the truth for certain. What he did not know was why Tom would kill himself.

Suppose, George thought, Winnie Trainor and he had gotten engaged or she was pregnant by Tom, or both, and she confronted him before she left Algonquin Park to go back home to Huntsville for the summer lumber season. If they had been engaged or she was pregnant, however, why hadn't she immediately returned to Mowat upon learning of his disappearance? This possibility made no sense, George decided. Tom must have had a motive that neither the family nor anyone at Canoe Lake knew anything about.

As the train pulled into New York City's recently built Grand Central Station, George reached the end of his memorandum. He put the notebook in a file labeled simply "Tom Thomson." George waited one hour and forty-six minutes for the train to New Haven, spending a few moments wandering around the station's magnificent main hall with his wife before descending to the platform again. After settling into his seat for the last leg of the journey, he slept. In New Haven, he descended to the platform, offered a generous tip to the porter, and gestured for a taxi driver to take them home, where he sat in front of the fireplace for hours before reaching into his briefcase and pulling out the notebook and memorandum in order to commit it to memory. In the early morning, sighing deeply, he tossed it into the fire and sat back until it burned away.

A few months later, on January 2, 1918, George Thomson wrote a scathing letter to James E. H. MacDonald in Toronto, attacking Shannon Fraser as the source of news reports pointing to Tom's suicide. He said,

> At first I classified Fraser as an ignorant sort of fellow, but honest. In light, however, of what has occurred more recently in his dealings with Harkness and Dr. MacCallum, I have come to place not the slightest dependence in his word. I believe he has come near to manufacturing this evidence to suit his purpose, which was to show that Tom had committed suicide.

He accused Fraser of "fastening upon Tom's memory a stain that would be difficult if not impossible to wipe out." With these words, George rose as guardian of Thomson's reputation and the family, thinking, certainly with encouragement from Dr. MacCallum, that the Canadian spirit evoked by his brother's hundreds of remaining Algonquin panels and canvases would never develop in the public mind if it was thought the painter had drowned himself in Canoe Lake. George knew all of the circumstances of Tom's death as well as, if not more fully than, Shannon Fraser. Both Fraser and George, the prejudiced older brother, talked to all of the witnesses with any firsthand information about what happened. Tom lived in Fraser's Mowat Lodge throughout the last spring, bounding in and out, bringing back his last paintings on a daily basis until May 24, 1917, when they were displayed in the lodge dining room. Fraser's cook, Blanche Linton, supplied him with the fresh bread and raw ham for what all believed was a day trip out fishing. Robinson saw Tom and Fraser together at the Joe Lake Dam as the old friends they were hours before Tom safely set out on the lake never to be seen alive again. As a witness, Fraser's only shortcoming was the bad reputation ascribed to him in the weeks, months, and years since July 8, 1917, by George Thomson and Winnie Trainor, both of whom suffered from the denial, guilt, sadness, and anger that afflict the survivors of suicide.

George decided that Winnie Trainor needed to be put down, and that he was the only person who could do so with any authority. In the weeks following his death, she emerged with ambiguous threats, but never made any specific claim. Thus, she faded into a popular expectancy of later revelation. Winnie Trainor, however, was forbidden by overwhelming denial and guilt over his death from ever explaining her relationship with Tom. Therefore, it failed to surprise George that she never pressed her exceptional claim against the estate for all thirty-three of the family's panels in the last spring series and never explained her role in Thomson's life.

Winnie Trainor's correspondence with the family in August 1917 suggested not that she was pregnant, but rather harboring claims against the estate for Tom's paintings. In her letters to the family, she clumsily cast around for a settlement. She knew that the estate's ownership of the thirty-three panels recovered from her father's cottage was vulnerable, as they were a gift to her from Thomson. On Thomson's death, all of his other artwork would pass to his parents by intestacy law unless he had made a will.[1] Her peculiar, elusive correspondence persuaded George Thomson that she wanted the thirty-three panels returned to her. George decided that, pregnant or not, Winnie Trainor would never make a formal demand, and if she did, the family would argue that she had never accepted delivery of Tom's generous gift of his last spring sketches.

The two-pronged defense arose from George's conclusion that Winnie Trainor certainly was a dysfunctional person, barely capable of caring for herself. He knew that his sensitive, artistic younger brother recognized that and accepted her as a person needing his help rather than as a woman to marry who would bear his children. In a letter to Dr. MacCallum on December 23, 1917, George wrote, "His relations with the Trainor girl I don't consider to have much bearing upon the case. I don't consider that she would influence him greatly one way or the other."

The death of a loved one by suicide slashes into the deepest reaches of a survivor's heart, setting up a struggle with certain knowledge that their love was not enough to dissuade the other from following such a course. Even geographically or personally distant family members react to a loved one's suicide by doubting love or denying the suicide. George chose the latter. Winnie Trainor, however, doubted his love for her, and her guilt was overwhelming. Sensing this, George Thomson advised the family simply to ignore her. They brusquely turned her entreaties aside, driving bitter frustration into her heart. Winnie sought from them forgiveness, if not the acceptance she had got from Tom and never again found during the rest of her lonely life.

The second prong of the defense against Winnifred Trainor's claim to the last spring series was a lesson George had learned in the first semester of law school.

---

1.   Under the common law, the child of an unwed mother was a bastard with no right of inheritance from either its father or mother. Not until 1921 did Ontario adopt legislation that made bastard children legitimate, and even then only when the parents later married. Where marriage was not possible, social service agencies encouraged women to give up bastard children for adoption.

When is a gift a gift? When given, of course. When does that happen? Acceptance is the essence of a gift, which, in the common law of old England, inherited by Canada and the United States, means a gratuitous transfer of property. That requires delivery by the donor, intent to make a gift, and acceptance by the donee. Acceptance is the act by which one receives a thing with approbation or satisfaction. The act of making a gift is not complete until the person upon whom it has been conferred accepts. Thus, acceptance is the necessary link between the gift and the donee. If the donee is absent, she may be allowed time to accept the gift.

Tom delivered the thirty-three panels to Winnie Trainor's cabin in her absence. Therefore, George decided, she had never accepted them. However, George knew that acceptance of a valuable gift is presumed under the common law unless the donee affirmatively rejects. George concluded that Winnie Trainor's guilt over his death by suicide would obscure her thinking about the thirty-three panels, taken from her cabin by Mark Robinson, and that she might subconsciously think she rejected them, as he rejected life. George Thomson was right about how Winnie and the nation would view his death and her ownership of Tom's last spring artwork. The Canadian literature about Thomson's death has ever since rejected suggestions that this artistic genius was a flawed man who killed himself in Canoe Lake on July 8, 1917, and never recognized Winnie Trainor's rightful claim to these sketches.

Meanwhile, family and friends, devastated by rumors that Tom killed himself and worried, along with wily Dr. MacCallum, about the impact Tom's drowning would have on the market for his paintings, vehemently denied suicide against all contrary evidence. Dr. MacCallum subtly revealed his personal opinion about Tom's drowning in carefully measured words. Referring to the Tom's July 7 letter, Dr. MacCallum wrote to a colleague, "I suggest, as the lawyers say, that you draw some deductions from it as to the state of mind of the poor chap."

Dr. MacCallum was the most outstanding ophthalmologist in Ontario. His first position at the University of Toronto was as lecturer in pharmacology and therapeutics. He assisted the professor of gynecology. He did postgraduate ophthalmic study in London, England, before returning to work at the Toronto General Hospital and the Hospital for Sick Children. He was professor of ophthalmology at the University of Toronto from 1914 to 1929, published widely, and represented the university on the council of the College of Physicians and Surgeons of Ontario. His patronage of Tom Thomson and the Group of Seven painters, however, was, without a doubt, his major legacy.

Dr. MacCallum sought photographs of Tom from the family and wrote a brief article on Thomson published by *Canadian* magazine in March 1918. His brief tribute set the tone of all that has since been written about Thomson.

> Thomson painted not merely to paint, but because his nature compelled him to paint—because he had a message. The North Country enthralled him, body and soul. He began to paint that he might express the emotions the country inspired in him; all the moods and passions, all the somberness and all the glory of color, were so felt that they demanded from him pictorial expression. He never gave utterance in words to his feelings of the glories of nature. Words were not his instruments of expression—color was the only medium open to him. Of all Canadian artists he was, I believe, the greatest colorist. His aims were truthfulness and beauty—beauty of color, of feeling, and of emotion. Yet to him, his most beautiful sketches were only paint. He placed no value on them. All he wanted was more paint, so that he could paint others. He enjoyed appreciation of his work; criticism of his methods he welcomed, but its truthfulness was unassailable, for he had seen it. He never painted anything that he had not seen.

Dr. MacCallum early behind-the-scenes handiwork is revealed in a Toronto newspaper article reporting Thomson's death on July 18, 1917. Only he could have been the source of the *Globe and Mail* article, in which he envisioned the nation would view Tom Thomson's work.

> Critics look to him to carry forward the Canadian landscape painting far beyond anything at present realized. Wandering alone the best part of the year in Algonquin Park, inured to hardship and reputed the best guide, fisherman, and canoe man in the district, he lives with these wonderful seasons and they live by him. Here, again, is the decorative sense strongly developed and visible in every composition. There is no loss of character; the northland lies before you, whether it is a winding river fringed with gaunt black pines, or whether the green blocks of melting ice float on blue liberated waters of the lake.

Algonquin is a vast and splendid park of life and death where the Canadian spirit of rugged, individualistic, northern independence was given everlasting visual substance by a painter of stark landscapes on wooden roofing shingles and pieces of California orange crates. Canadian intellectual and writer Margaret Atwood summarized the nation's view of him, which she described in her 1995 book, *Strange Things: The Malevolent North in Canadian Literature*, during a series of lectures she gave at Oxford University in 1991. As many had before her, she garbled the facts. She wrote,

The painter Tom Thomson, known for his canvases of the North, was found floating facedown beside his canoe. He was an experienced woodsman, and was in the habit of going off for long trips, by himself, to paint. There was no indication of how he had come to drown. But everyone knew, or thought they did: the Spirit of the North had claimed him as her own. The death of Tom Thomson was treated as somehow legendary, somehow exemplary....Tom Thomson's death was found significant because it fitted in with the preconceived notions of what a death in the north ought to be.

His older brother's careful handling of Shannon Fraser and Winnifred Trainor shaped how his family and friends came to understand Tom Thomson's life and death at Canoe Lake. Thus, guided by Dr. MacCallum, he put down Shannon Fraser's rumors of suicide and shunned Winnie Trainor's claims against the estate. George Thomson molded how the wider family of Canada came to embrace artist, woodsman, and guide Tom Thomson, as brother, colleague, and discoverer of the nation's spirit.

34

Kristian Says Good-Bye to Howard Hancock

Mr. Hancock was surprised to see Kristian standing on the porch, a handsome woman by his side.

"Come on in."

"Good to see you again."

"Can I get you anything? Who is this lady? I think I remember her from somewhere. Face is familiar."

Mary Alice gave him her firm handshake.

"This is Mary Alice Gleason. We met a few days ago on my trip down the Oxtongue River. An extraordinary few days it's been for me and for her."

"You don't say. Come, come on in and we'll sit by the fireplace," Mr. Hancock replied, pushing open the screen door and taking Mary Alice by the arm. "You can tell me all about it."

Mr. Hancock showed Mary Alice to a chair, where she sat and told her side of the story, starting with Lucky Haskins.

"Of course, the snapshot in his shop," he interrupted.

She continued, describing how Haskins had broken into her cabin, armed with a silver revolver and demanding the deed to her property.

"He said, 'We're going over Ragged Falls together, Mary Alice, you and me—unless you give me the deed. So I told him, 'Get the hell out.'

"'We're taking your canoe,' he answered. "Now!' Then he wagged the gun at the front door, which he'd smashed."

She told the whole story of the race down the Oxtongue River to Ragged Falls, where Lucky went over, and how they had flagged down a motorist on Route 60, who called 911. Three highway patrolmen arrived. They took the two of them separately up to Ragged Falls Park, where, Mary and Kristian carefully walked up the muddy portage, telling their tale, looking for her canoe and Lucky's body.

There, in the third pool, crushed up against a smooth gray boulder, was a twisted arm that bobbed to the surface every few moments. One of the patrolmen, armed with a powerful flashlight, shouted to the others. They found two large sections of the canoe lodged among smaller boulders farther down Ragged Falls.

The highway patrol then drove them back to Mary Alice's cabin, Kristian's canoe strapped to a patrol car.

"I'd left my keys in the ignition," Kristian said. "The headlights were on and the engine was still running. We've been sleeping ever since. Came back to my campsite this afternoon over on Big Wapomeo and decided to stop to say good-bye."

"Well, darned if I didn't set this off myself," Hancock concluded, telling them what happened Sunday when he returned the garden tiller.

"Lucky sure was mad about something," Kristian said.

"No, he was nuts," added Mary Alice.

"He was probably drunk as a skunk, too," Hancock said. "He was in my group with Dr. Beckley a few years ago. The court ordered both of us to go once a week for twelve months."

Still tired, Kristian only half-listened. Mary Alice carried on with Mr. Hancock, who seemed as completely taken by her as he was. Mary Alice stood and asked where the bathroom was. Mr. Hancock pointed, and she strode away. They sat there, not knowing what else to say. Minutes later, Mary Alice took her seat in front of the fireplace once again. The fire had burned down, and the hearth was stocked with a supply of seasoned logs. It was late afternoon, and they needed to get going, but she gave in to the desire for warmth.

"Should I add a log?"

"Sure, go ahead."

Mary Alice picked a smaller piece from the brass carrier and pulled open the screen. She put the log across the remaining two and sat back, the poker in her left hand. She then yawned and stretched.

Kristian saw her right arm lift slowly and shoot up, pointing at a small painting on the mantel.

"Are these originals?" she gasped.

Kristian's eyes followed her upraised arm and hand, seeing where her index finger was pointing. His surprised eyes moved from the familiar panel on the left to a new one on the right side of the fireplace.

"Another Thomson?"

Mr. Hancock nodded.

Kristian stood and walked over.

"May I?"

"Yes."

He picked it up. Standing by his side, Mary Alice recognized the overturned gray-green canoe. He realized it more slowly. Kristian fell back into his easy chair as he held the panel between his outstretched fingers. He turned it over and saw writing on the back, embossed with a barely legible oval of blue with large yellow lettering reading "rity Flo." Across the bottom right, in carefully scripted black ink, someone had written, "Tom Thomson, 8 July 1917."

The new panel matched the one Kristian admired at the left side of the fireplace, leaning against the wall, also unframed. Kristian placed the new panel next to the first. They each depicted the same overturned gray-green canoe on the same lake in the same place under the same bright blue sky.

35

Leaving Algonquin Park

Kristian and Mary Alice returned to his Big Wapomeo Island campsite by the shore, where Rowe and Dickson had kept their all-night vigil over Thomson's body, keeping time by the trains passing Joe Lake and Canoe Lake Stations. Passenger trains ceased running through the park in the 1930s with the construction of Route 60. Salvagers removed the last railway tracks in 1959. So, Kristian and Mary Alice slept in Algonquin's timeless silence.

Across the lake to the north was Hayhurst Point. In the hours following Tom Thomson's burial, Dr. MacCallum determined to memorialize him, celebrating his life in Algonquin Park. He telegraphed his plan to Canoe Lake on July 19, 1917. Robinson's journal entry that evening read, "The Art [Association] purpose [sic] having a Memorial Exhibit of Mr. Tom Thomson's painting and place a memorial in the park near where he loved to work [and] sketch so well. Thus ends a career of unselfishness of a gentleman, a sportsman, artist, and friend of all."

Dr. MacCallum wasted no time. He owned many of Thomson's paintings and knew that his death would propel the market for them. He decided to finance the construction of a cairn at Canoe Lake befitting Thomson's death without knowing that his family had already moved the body to Leith. From Toronto, he arranged with James E. H. MacDonald to erect the memorial above a campsite Thomson used at Hayhurst Point. Details of the cairn's construction among the red pines high above the shore in September 1917 are lost to history but for a sole photograph taken by MacDonald for Dr. MacCallum, who wanted it to illustrate an article he planned to write about Thomson for *Canadian* magazine, a Sunday supplement to the *Globe and Mail*.

Thomson friends—John W. Beatty, Fraser, Rowe, and Scrim—carried six tons of fieldstone up to the site, where Beatty did all of the fitting and masonry. Fraser billed both the estate and Dr. MacCallum for the cement, the family having refused MacCallum's offer to pay all costs. MacDonald designed the heavy brass plate (engraved by Alexander and Cable in Toronto) that Beatty mounted on the cairn, facing west, overlooking the section of Canoe Lake where Dr. Howland found the artist's body. Dr. MacCallum paid MacDonald seventy dollars for the design work, train fare, film, and photo-developing expenses.

Little is known about what MacDonald and Beatty learned while they stayed at Canoe Lake. MacCallum arranged no memorial exhibit of his paintings that year or any other. No such exhibits are noted in Mark Robinson's journal or in any other Canoe Lake history. MacCallum had but one objective—to memorialize Thomson's love of Algonquin in a single photograph of the cairn. MacDonald and Beatty talked with Mowat residents over breakfast, lunch, and dinner at the lodge, paddled the lake, walked the portages, questioned Mr. and Mrs. Fraser, Robinson, the Blechers, Mr. Trainor, Dickson, Rowe, Plewman, train station hands, and any of the others who were there. Letters exchanged among Harkness, George, and Dr. MacCallum in the following months confirm that Beatty was convinced Thomson had committed suicide.

Harkness wrote to Dr. MacCallum on November 3, 1917,

> I cannot for the life of me understand how he, claiming to be a friend of Tom's, can so easily swallow all Fraser's bunk and knowing that Tom was one who had a high moral sense of duty to his fellow man, and he must know perfectly that he had nothing to run away from. I've thought the thing over from every viewpoint, and the more I think of it, the more fully I am convinced that Tom had no hand in taking his life. But it makes me feel sore to think Fraser, who claimed to be a friend of Tom, would make all these suggestions and Beatty ready to take them all in.

In response to a query for his opinion on the matter from Blodwen Davies, MacDonald said only, "I feel sure that it is best for me to associate myself with the silence of an old friend."

Kristian and Mary Alice, too, maintained a reverent silence as they packed and pushed off into the lake, heading for The Portage Store under a chilly morning sky, murmuring to each other once as a pair of loons came into the shallow bay with four youngsters, two riding on the female's back. Their paddling caused a bare ripple to float across the glass-smooth lake toward the shore. An hour later, Kristian and Mary Alice unloaded and hauled his things up to his car. He secured the canoe to its roof. Ten minutes later, he stood on the Portage Store dock looking across the lake, as Mary Alice filled his gas tank. She stood by him. Finally, he spoke.

"Here's a lucky nickel for you," he said, reaching into his wallet and digging out a small coin. She hesitated, gazing at the old Canadian five-cent piece.

"Daddy used to tell me not to take a plug nickel for a....Oh, I don't remember."

He put Papa's silver nickel into her palm and said, "I love you."

Mary Alice examined the small coin closely.

"1917!" she exclaimed. "That's when Thomson died. Maybe Tom Thomson carried this nickel in his pocket. You should keep it. Sure enough been good luck to you lately."

She handed the coin to him. He reared back and tossed the nickel far out into Canoe Lake. He handed her the keys and walked around to the passenger side of his car. She smiled, started the engine, and sped away from Canoe Lake heading west on Route 60.

Website Links to Tom Thomson Paintings

Tom Thomson's paintings are available for viewing at many excellent websites. Here are links to some of them:

Canadian Broadcasting Corporation, *The Jack Pine*, by Tom Thomson:
http://archives.cbc.ca/IDCC-1-68-754-4643/arts_entertainment/group_of_seven.

Cybermuse, Artist's Gallery:
http://cybermuse.gallery.ca/cybermuse/search/artist_work_e.jsp?iartistid=5427.

Group of Seven Gallery:
http://www.groupofsevenart.com/Thomson/Thomson_intro.html.

McMichael Canadian Art Collection, Kleinberg, Ontario:
http://www.mcmichael.com/web1/our_collection/thomson.shtml.

National Gallery of Canada:
http://www.gallery.ca/exhibitions/exhibitions/tom_thomson/index_e.html.

Tom Thomson Memorial Gallery, Owen Sound, Ontario:
http://www.tomthomson.org.

Bibliography

Addison, Ottelyn. *Tom Thomson: The Algonquin Years.* In collaboration with Elizabeth Harwood. Toronto, Ontario: McGraw-Hill Ryerson Limited, first paperback edition. 1975.

Andersen, Will R. *I Love You All the Time*, 1905 (Lyrics, sheet music, and audio recording on a 1904 Victor record label reproduced at http://www. hungrytigerpress.com/tigertunes/allthetime.shtml).

Art Gallery of Ontario/National Gallery of Canada. *Tom Thomson.* Edited by Dennis Reid. Vancouver, British Columbia: Douglas and McIntyre, 2002.

Atwood, Margaret. *Strange Things: The Malevolent North in Canadian Literature.* Oxford, England: Clarendon Press/Oxford University Press, 1995.

Betts, Jim. *Colours in the Storm.* Toronto, Ontario: Playwrights Canada Press, 1990.

Callan, Kevin. *A Paddler's Guide to Algonquin Park.* Erin, Ontario: Boston Mills Press, 2004.

Canadian Broadcasting Corporation. *The Mysterious Death of Tom Thomson* (featuring William T. Little) http://archives.cbc.ca/IDC-1-68-754-4631/ arts_entertainment/group_of_seven/clip7.

Clemson, Gaye I. *Algonquin Voices: Selected Stories of Canoe Lake Women.* Victoria, British Columbia: Trafford, 2002.

Davies, Blodwen. *A Study of Tom Thomson.* Toronto, Ontario: Discus Press, 1935.

—. *The Story of a Man Who Looked for Beauty and for Truth in the Wilderness.* Reprint edited by A. Y. Jackson. Vancouver, British Columbia: Mitchell Press, 1967.

—. Papers, archives, Trent University. Peterborough, Ontario.

Dickson, James. *A Nineteenth Century Algonquin Adventure*, Edited by Gary Long. Huntsville, Ontario, Fox Meadow Creations, 1997.

Edmison, Alex. Interviews Mark Robinson, typescript (October 1956) of a tape recording made at Canoe Lake, 1952. (Reproduced in part by Little, ibid., as *Mark Robinson Talks about Tom Thomson*, pp. 183–210.)

Friends of Algonquin Park. "Evolution of a Myth," *The Raven* 45, no. 2 (1 July 2004).

Garland, G. D., *Names of Algonquin: Stories behind the Lakes and Place Names of Algonquin Provincial Park*. Algonquin Park Technical Bulletin no. 10, Friends of Algonquin Park. Revised and reprinted. Whitney, Ontario, 1993.

Grace, Sherrill. *Inventing Tom Thomson: From Biographical Fictions to Fictional Autobiographies and Reproductions*. Montreal, Ontario: McGill-Queen's University Press, 2004.

Kates, Joanne. *Exploring Algonquin Park*. Vancouver, British Columbia: Douglas and McIntyre Ltd., second printing, 1983.

Lambert, Alice Elinor. *Women Are Like That*. New York, New York: Dell Publishing Company, 1936.

Little, Dr. Robert P. "Some Recollections of Tom Thomson and Canoe Lake," *Culture* 16, no. 2 (June 1955).

Little, William. *The Tom Thomson Mystery*. Toronto, Ontario: McGraw-Hill Ryerson Limited, 1970.

—. "The Mysterious Death of Tom Thomson." Interview on *Front Page Challenge*, CBC, 19 October 1970. http://archives.cbc.ca/IDC-1-68-754-4631/arts_entertainment/group_of_seven/clip7.

MacCallum, Dr. James M. Papers, library, and archives, National Gallery of Canada Library. Ottawa, Ontario.

—. "Tom Thomson: Painter of the North." *Canadian Magazine* 50 (March 1918), 375–85.

Machardy, Carolyn. "An Inquiry into the Success of Tom Thomson's *The West Wind.*" *University of Toronto Quarterly* 3, 1999. http://www.utpjournals.com/jour.ihtml?lp=product/utq/683/683_machardy.html

Mason, Bill. *Path of the Paddle: An Illustrated Guide to the Art of Canoeing.* Toronto, Ontario: Key Porter Books, 1984.

Mead, Robert Douglas. *The Canoer's Bible.* Garden City, New York: Doubleday and Company, 1976.

McGregor, Roy, *Canoe Lake.* Toronto, Ontario: McClelland and Stewart Ltd, trade paperback edition, 2002.

—. "The Legend: New Revelations on Tom Thomson's Art—and on His Mysterious Death," *Toronto Star, The Canadian* (15 October 1977).

—. *Shorelines.* Markham, Ontario: Penguin Books Canada, Ltd., 1985.

Moodie, Jim. "Unraveling the Mystery: On the (Cold) Trail of Canoeist Tom Thomson." *Paddler Magazine,* June 1999.

Murray, Joan. *Northern Lights: Masterpieces of Tom Thomson and the Group of Seven.* Toronto, Ontario: Key Porter Books, 1994.

—. *The Art of Tom Thomson.* Toronto, Ontario: Art Gallery of Ontario, 1971.

—. *The Best of Tom Thomson.* Edmonton, Alberta: Hurtig Publishing, Ltd., 1986.

—. *Tom Thomson: Design for a Canadian Hero.* Toronto, Ontario: Dundurn Press, 1998.

—. *Tom Thomson: The Last Spring.* Toronto, Ontario: Dundurn Press, 1994.

—. *Tom Thomson: Trees.* Toronto, Ontario: McArthur and Co., 1999.

Owen Sound Sun. Various newspaper reports 13–19 July 1917.

Pittaway, Ronald. Interview with Audrey Saunders at her home in Meaford, Ontario, on 28 November 1979. Algonquin Park Museum Archives.

—. Interview with Daphne Crombie on 14 January 1977. Algonquin Park Museum Archives.

Poling, Jim, Sr. *Tom Thomson: The Life and Mysterious Death of the Famous Canadian Painter*. Canmore, Alberta: Altitude Publishing Canada, Ltd., 2003.

Reid, Dennis. *Photographs by Tom Thomson*. Bulletin no. 16, National Gallery of Canada. Ottawa, Ontario, 1970.

Robinson, Mark. Papers, *1917 Journal,* Archives, Trent University. Peterborough, Ontario. (Used with permission of W. D. Addison.)

Sanders, Audrey. *Algonquin Story*. Department of Lands of Forests, Province of Ontario, 1947.

Shaw, S. Bernard. *Canoe Lake, Algonquin Park: Tom Thomson and Other Mysteries*. Burnstown, Ontario: General Store Publishing, 1996.

Smith, Jeffrey P. CNR Ontario Research (24 August 2004). http://cnr-in-ontario.com.

Smith, Mark Jameson, and Christine Kennedy. *The Adventure Map, Oxtongue River and Ragged Falls Provincial Park*. Uxbridge, Ontario: Chrismar Mapping Services, Inc., 2001.

Tait, George E. *Wake of the West Wind*. Toronto, Ontario: The Ryerson Press, 1952.

Town, Harold, and David P. Silcox *Tom Thomson: The Silence and the Storm*, third ed. Toronto, Ontario: McClelland and Stewart, Inc., 1989.

Globe and Mail. Various newspaper reports, 13–19 July 1917.

Transport Canada. *Survival in Cold Water*. TP 13822 E 2003-01. http://www.tc.gc.ca/marinesafety/TP/Tp13822/menu.htm.

Webb, Peter. "In Search of Tom Thomson" (2 December 2004). http://
www.bushwhacker.ca/thomson.html.

About the Author

Neil J. Lehto is a solo attorney in West Bloomfield, Michigan. He worked his way through Wayne State University as a reporter for a Detroit area newspaper, the *Daily Tribune*. Following his graduation in 1974 with a Bachelor of Arts degree in journalism, he received a Juris Doctor degree from the Detroit College of Law in 1978. Until 2003, he practiced law with a large suburban Detroit law firm. Since his first trip to Ontario's Algonquin Park thirty years ago, he has pursued the true story of Tom Thomson's 1917 drowning in Canoe Lake.

978-0-595-36132-8
0-595-36132-3